DISNEY DISCOURSE
Producing the Magic Kingdom

EDITED BY
ERIC SMOODIN

ROUTLEDGE
New York • London

Published in 1994 by

Routledge
29 West 35 Street
New York, NY 10001

Published in Great Britain by

Routledge
11 New Fetter Lane
London EC4P 4EE

3 3604 00088 1961

Library of Congress Cataloging-in-Publication Data

Disney discourse: Producing the magic kingdom / edited by Eric Smoodin.
   p. cm.
  Includes index.
  ISBN 0-415-90615-6 (hb) — ISBN 0-415-90616-4 (pb)
   1. Walt Disney Company. 2. Disney, Walt, 1901–1966—Criticism and
interpretation. 3. Popular culture. 4. Intercultural
comunication. I. Smoodin, Eric Loren.
PN1999.W27D57 1994
384′.8′0979494—dc20   93-32366
                                    CIP

British Library Cataloguing-in-Publication Data also available.

DISNEY DISCOURSE

AFI Film Readers
a series edited by
Edward Branigan and Charles Wolfe

Psychoanalysis and Cinema
E. Ann Kaplan, editor

Fabrications: Costume and the Female Body
Jane Gaines and Charlotte Herzog, editors

Sound Theory/Sound Practice
Rick Altman, editor

Film Theory Goes to the Movies
Jim Collins, Hilary Radner, and Ava Preacher Collins, editors

Theorizing Documentary
Michael Renov, editor

Black American Cinema
Manthia Diawara, editor

The American Film Institute
P.O. Box 27999
2021 North Western Avenue
Los Angeles, California 90027

Contents

For CJK

"Rest your head close to my heart . . ."

Acknowledgments

Many people assisted me in the preparation of this book. Mildred Smoodin, Roberta Smoodin, Steve Marvin, Arthur Kaplan, Doris Kaplan, Mitchell Kaplan, and Henry Flax provided all manner of familial support. I must also thank friends for their constant encouragement, sound advice, and good company; in particular Pamela Fox and Michael Ragussis, but also Mark Anderson, Fred Davidson, and Frank Tomasulo. At the very beginning of this project Lisa Bloom made a suggestion that greatly improved the final product, while Patricia Aufderheide, Huma Ibrahim, and Richard McCann, my colleagues at American University, were always willing to help me work out some of the problems of editing a manuscript. A special acknowledgment must go to those who contributed essays to this volume. All of them were a pleasure to work with, and it was a special pleasure for me to establish professional relationships with long-time friends such as Richard Neupert, Richard deCordova, and Jon Lewis, and personal relationships with scholars whose work I admired.

My editors, William Germano, Charles Wolfe, and Edward Branigan, were all extremely helpful and, most importantly, patient; in particular I would like to thank Edward for his early, enthusiastic support of this project. Kermit Moyer, the Chair of the Literature Department at American University, looked for and found important ways to help, and in the department office Dan Crawford always stopped whatever he was doing to give me a hand. The university's resident computer whizzes, Gloria J. Dinkins, Eric Peters, and Rebecca Davis, provided indispensable technological support.

Finally, a brief word on the history of *Disney Discourse*. This project took shape during a car ride to the Modern Language Association Conference in December 1990. Somewhere between Washington, D.C. and

Chicago, Caren Kaplan and I started talking about our next projects. It was Caren who suggested the idea of a book-length collection of essays about Disney, and convinced me that such a collection might be useful. Without Caren's brainstorming during that long ride, without her continuing help and encouragement, and without the example she has set as a writer and scholar, this book never would have gotten out of the garage.

Introduction: How to Read Walt Disney

Eric Smoodin

Annette Funicello captured the essence of Disney discourse in a 1991 television interview with John Tesh. She pointed out the place of honor that her mouse ears have in her home; under glass, a monument to her days as a Mouseketeer. But she also told Tesh that whenever a Mouseketeer lost a pair of ears, Disney took fifty dollars out of the kid's next paycheck. Thus, two different Disneys, and two different kinds of cultural currency. The first, with those mouse ears under glass, constructs Disney as a fit object of a middle-aged woman's nostalgia for the happiest period of her life. The second, signified by the punishing, penny-pinching Disney, shows that same woman's distaste for a former employer, one who made even his teenage meal ticket pay for minor transgressions against the corporation.[1]

At about the same time that Annette parlayed her fame as a Mouseketeer into a series of teen films, track athlete Tommie Smith emerged as her pop culture ideological opposite. It was Smith who, after winning a gold medal in the 1968 Mexico City Olympics, raised a black-gloved fist during the victory ceremony rendition of the "Star-Spangled Banner," thus portraying militancy to the middle-class masses watching the games on TV. More than twenty years later, however, Smith, like Annette, gave an interview to a syndicated television program specializing in constructing and commodifying nostalgia. Smith defended his actions on the victory stand, and did so while wearing a Disneyland T-shirt.

This, then, constituted material culture in its literal sense; the politics of what you wear. Smith eloquently explained the complex motivations for his 1968 actions, but his 1992 attire made his current political position difficult to read. Is there a difference between the younger Smith adding a black glove to his United States track uniform, and the elder statesman

1

justifying his actions while wearing the "uniform" of a multinational corporation? Was Smith aware of, and thereby subtly exploiting, the contradictions between his words and his attire? With the T-shirt, was he trying to make himself acceptable, after all these years, to a largely white audience? Had he simply and finally been co-opted by Disney, or was it only natural that Smith, a track coach being interviewed on the track, would of course be wearing a T-shirt, and just happened to be wearing this one?[2]

The issue may become even more blurred when we complicate Disney's own relationship with a variety of social and political movements. One of the recent character additions to Disney's theme parks has been Minnie Mouse as Carmen Miranda, with print and television advertising for Disney World and Euro Disney often emphasizing this oversized rodent with the tutti-frutti hat. Here the Disney company itself moves into nostalgia construction, this time evoking fond memories of United States imperialist and colonialist practices in South America. But in 1989 Disney's French products celebrated the "rabble" who were, at least mythologically, so instrumental in the revolution two hundred years before. Among the cheese segments in packages of La Vache Qui Rit, Disney placed cardboard cutouts of his characters dressed in revolutionary attire; my own shows a smiling Minnie in a getup reminiscent of Madame Defarge in *A Tale of Two Cities,* and the signification, at least at first glance, seems to negate the Minnie/Carmen equation.

The essays that follow seek to examine those contradictions, which Annette experienced so personally, and which different incarnations of Tommie Smith and Minnie Mouse apparently embody. More precisely, most of them take a look at the multiple discourses about Disney produced by the corporation and by those outside it, and generated by a variety of Disney products. Just a quick look at the history of the company and its famous founder shows how Disney has had its corporate finger in more sociocultural pies than perhaps any other twentieth century producer of mass entertainment. Moreover, and despite the received wisdom that Disney's politics were and remain simply conservative, a more detailed analysis shows how Disney is ideologically—and just like the various theme parks—all over the map.

Walt Disney himself projected a series of often contradictory public and private personae, and the incarnations have continued to multiply more than a quarter century after his death: individual artisan in the 1920s; technological and artistic pioneer in the 1930s; paragon of patriotism in the 1940s; benevolent educator/television host to the nation in the 1950s. Current scholarship and hagiography have added a more nuanced version, as well as one filtered through oversized Mickey Mouse ears. Thus, in just one example, Disney's vigorous and admirable defense of the Allied cause during World War II comes up against his determinedly antilabor position at his own studio, and leads to his contribution to the witch-hunts of Communists in the postwar period. But we also know that in spite of this, the FBI remained at least somewhat suspicious of Disney until his death, in part because of his attendance at a 1943 benefit sponsored by *The New Masses,* a communist newspaper, and his interest in visiting the Soviet Union. Here, then, Disney emerges as an unquestioned patriot, an archconservative, and a potential left-wing stooge.[3] Much of the current media discourse about Disney, however, seeks to simplify him in the extreme. As a result, television specials about Euro Disney (produced by the Disney studio) construct him as a utopian visionary seeking world peace through leisure activity. Even a highbrow effort like Max Apple's novel, *The Propheteers,* while seeking to critique "Disneyfication," creates not so much an Uncle Walt but rather a perpetual adolescent struggling against economic forces that make it harder for him to produce art.[4]

During his heyday in the 1930s, forties, and fifties Disney would typically be compared, in the popular media, to such "uniquely American" geniuses as George Gershwin and Irving Berlin. But without questioning this connection (and without examining how Gershwin and Berlin themselves have been mythologized), Disney might be better understood in relation to another type of American cultural icon, the systems builder. Disney has been responsible for a kind of Tennessee Valley Authority of leisure and entertainment. That is, like Thomas Edison and Henry Ford, while celebrated for individual artifacts, Disney was actually the master of vast "technological systems," to use Thomas Hughes's term. Those systems involved "far more than the so-called hardware, devices, machines, and processes," but also the "transportation, communication, and information networks that interconnect them," and the array of employees and regulations that make them run.[5] Like Samuel Insull, Frederick Taylor, and Ford once again, Disney imagined his systems as blueprints for a future based on efficiency, conservation, and communal living.

A number of the essays in this book examine those systems, systems that were local, national, and global. Richard Neupert, for instance, looks at the relationship between Disney and Technicolor, and the uses each made of the other in establishing a foothold in the motion picture industry during the 1930s; Douglas Gomery charts Disney corporate history and the company's gradual expansion into forms of entertainment other than cartoons; Lisa Cartwright and Brian Goldfarb analyze Disney's production of health films during the 1940s, and the interaction of cultural production, corporate interests, and foreign policy.

In doing so, these contributors pick up the slack in a line of scholarship that began in earnest in the early 1970s. In the late 1960s film critic Richard Schickel wrote *The Disney Version,* one of the first book-length, serious studies of the filmmaker/entrepreneur in a quarter century (Robert Feild's *The Art of Walt Disney* appeared in 1942).[6] But Schickel's work very much adopted fashionable auteurist and Freudian models, insisting on Disney the man (rather than Disney the corporation) as the prime creator of the cartoons, wristwatches, theme parks, and TV shows, and attempting to psychoanalyze Walt through those products.

Then, in 1971 in Chile, Ediciones Universitarias published Ariel Dorfman's and Armand Mattelart's *Para leer al Pato Donald,* a rejection of Schickel's simplified psychological model in favor of an ideological analysis placing Disney products within a context of United States cultural imperialism. Dorfman and Mattelart showed the trajectory of Disney comic books from the "metropolis" of the United States to the "satellites" of South American countries, and analyzed how the comics furthered the ends of Third World subordination. The book appeared in the United States in 1975 as *How to Read Donald Duck,* with an introduction by David Kunzle (which itself stands as a brilliant account of the links between cultural production and imperial policy), and with a new subtitle that clearly expressed the book's political project: "Imperialist Ideology in the Disney Comic."[7]

With the notable exception of Louis Marin's 1977 analysis of Disneyland as a "degenerate utopia," however, the ten years following the English-language version of *How to Read Donald Duck* saw few interesting additions to the canon of Disney scholarship.[8] This may have been in part because Disney seemed to fall through the cracks of the prevailing critical practices. Twenty years ago auteurist film criticism rejected him as a fit subject for study because he worked primarily as a film producer. Moreover animation, Disney's stock-in-trade, came to be seen as such a product of the assembly line and of an extreme division of labor that, despite the best efforts of a Richard Schickel, it defied the type of study in which auteurist critics specialized. During the 1970s and early 1980s the structuralist and semiotic projects of examining the feature-length film narrative also eliminated animation as a field of study. Feature-length cartoons were a relative oddity, while shorter cartoons were often unavailable for study and, arguably, developed their own fields of signs and mechanisms of spectator identification.

In the last ten years, however, film studies has become more and more aligned with a developing branch of cultural studies that examines networks of power, and that emphasizes the relation of the cinema to other disciplines and particularly to the social sciences. This has helped to create a new sense of Disney's importance, because of the manner in which his work in film and television is connected to other projects in urban planning, ecological politics, product merchandising, United States domestic and global policy formation, technological innovation, and constructions of national character.

In just the last few years, Susan Willis has written about modes of consumption at Disneyland, Steve Rugare about American nationalism at EPCOT Center (Disney's "Experimental Prototype Community of Tomorrow"), and Alexander Wilson about "the managed landscape" at Disney World (an issue reprised in his essay for this volume). Even a scholar, such as Steve Nelson, with more "traditional" aesthetic concerns, stresses the postmodern pastiche of middle-class experience at the Disney theme parks that provides a mix of the theatrical, the cinematic, and the interactive, all supplied by the modern technologies of amusement.[9]

This resurgence in scholarly interest in Disney over the past ten years has been matched, in just the last two or three years, by a new popular media interest in the entrepreneur and his empire. Between the early 1930s and his death in 1966, Disney received more coverage in newspapers and magazines than perhaps any other executive connected to the film industry (and, quite possibly, any other United States executive, period). Regardless of the source, from middlebrow to high—from *The Saturday Evening Post* to *The Saturday Review of Literature*—this coverage tended towards the celebratory. Recently, however, with the opening of Disneyland theme parks in Japan and France, and the twentieth anniversary celebration of Disney World in Florida, Disney has emerged as a fit subject for those op-ed page pundits who fancy themselves cultural critics and who generally have a right-wing political axe to grind.

Two examples from the *The Washington Post,* coming within three months of each other, demonstrate this 1990s-style Disney discourse. In January 1992 Charles Krauthammer rolled out the usual Disney theme park clichés—chronic friendliness and hypercleanliness—to engage in a kind of Japan bashing that warns that the barbarians have stormed the palace: ". . . efficiency has a price. The price—blandness, kitsch, mindless, commercialization—is also on view at Disney World, a triumph of discipline and simplification, a vision of Japan in America." In April 1992 George Will used the opening of Euro Disney to criticize unnamed, European, left-wing intellectuals who rail against cultural "homogenization." While unable to endorse the lowbrow, mass-market pleasures of the theme park, Will nevertheless endorsed the stabilizing effects of the Disney product on an unreliable continent. "For modern Europe," Will wrote, with its history of pogroms, national socialism, and Nuremberg rallies, "Mickey Mouse is a giant's step up."[10]

The four sections of this book reflect the early, celebratory Disney scholarship, and also interrogate it, and in addition seek to complicate the notions and uses of Disney discourse that currently make their way to the general public through the popular media. Such a project becomes important not simply to "recuperate" Disney, but rather to use both the entrepreneur and the corporation to analyze many of the tensions at work in global culture today. While European communism disintegrates and American-style capitalism seems ill-equipped to confront local let alone international problems, the Disney empire, complete with the world's fifth largest navy, flourishes.[11]

Accentuating the Positive

Part One, "A Disney Archaeology," serves as a sort of primer in Disney discourse, presenting a sample of popular journal essays from the salad days of the entrepreneur's relationship with the press—the immediate pre-World War II period—until his death in 1966. The choices here are, in one sense, random; an editor could choose literally from thousands of essays. But they are also absolutely representative, in that they chart the period's fascination with Disney's corporate efficiency and also his global responsibility. By 1940, the time of Paul Hollister's "Genius at Work" from *The Atlantic Monthly,* Disney had generally been recognized as a homegrown miracle, a farm boy who had revolutionized the motion picture business. Then, with the release of *Fantasia* that same year, Disney also came to be perceived as the consummate artist, the perfect combination of the corporate and the creative. Hollister's piece ignores the discontent at the Disney studio (which resulted in the bitter 1941 strike there), and establishes Disney himself as that Roman ideal—*primus inter pares*—first among equals; the genius who also works, the boss who insists that all of his workers call him by his first name.

The war witnessed a change in the perception of Disney, or more properly, an addition to that perception. As the studio head turned over more and more of his operations to the government, making training and domestic propaganda films, for instance, he became not only the Wizard of Burbank but an ambassador to the "civilized" world. Just as he had been completely at ease with the "common men" who worked at his studio, so too was he now comfortable rubbing elbows with Churchills and Roosevelts. In a series of articles in *The Saturday Review,* Walter Wanger, himself a film producer, lauded the Disney studio as a wartime "league of nations." Thus Disney had acquired a kind of global currency, one that would serve him well in the media during peacetime. In the late 1940s and fifties the popular journals shifted from an emphasis on Disney's position among the Allies to his position in world commerce, and celebrated the international scope of his products just as they had applauded the internationalism of his politics.

By the late 1950s, perhaps Disney's apotheosis as a national icon (he appeared in millions of homes each week on his television program), *National Geographic* could hail his global scope by discussing his "Magic Worlds." In the *Geographic* article Robert De Roos points out the important relationship between the magazine and Disney, whose artists and writers used the periodical for research purposes. In this mutual admiration society, we can see a particular kind of endorsement of a world constructed (at least for the consumption of a TV-watching, magazine-reading public) and commercially controlled by the United States. Disney's re-creation of various historical epochs and geographical regions in his theme parks, and his saturation of world markets with his various products, were hardly different from *National Geographic*'s monthly production of the world in the space of three hundred pages. Rather than standing for an overt ideological position, as in the 1940s when Disney clearly worked to advance the Allied cause, this new Disney (and the *Geographic,* too) indicate a commitment to the benefits of mass education, objective knowledge, and honest fun.

Disney at Home

Part Two, "National Production" analyzes Disney corporate practice in terms of business, aesthetics, and ideology (and the relationships between the three). Contemporary media representations of the Disney corporation have tried to deny precisely its corporateness. In 1992, for instance, a *Good Morning America* television broadcast about the twentieth anniversary of Disney World mentioned how, during the celebration at the theme park, "surprise followed surprise."[12] During this voice-over, however, the visual images showed characters from Disney cartoons, from the Muppets, and from the film *Pretty Woman* (chorus girls as Julia Roberts). Of course, this apparent diversity should come as no surprise at all; besides the original Disney cartoon characters, the company also controls the Muppets and produced *Pretty Woman.* So while the media tend to extol (even while depoliticizing) Disney's international empire, they downplay the company's far-reaching control over numerous domestic products.

Even as this domestic empire has expanded (more theme parks, a cable television station, "mature" motion pictures), it has also contracted. During the 1950s, Disney offered his Anaheim, California theme park to the FBI for surveillance purposes (the bureau, traditionally unwilling to link itself to any commercial enterprise, turned him down).[13] By the 1990s, the company still seemed interested in constructing surveillance as entertainment, but with a much more limited scope. In the last few years, Disney had advertised a Mickey Mouse doll with glow-in-the-dark eyes, an unnerving "Children of the Damned" look for a beloved icon. The television commercial shows a father looking in on his child, who is sleeping with the doll; the shining eyes make it easy to see the young boy, thereby assuring the father that his offspring rests easily. The advertisement's voice-over salutes Disney for producing "friends you can believe in," and, implicitly, for making useful toys, toys that keep the man of the family aware of everything that is going on in his house.

The essays in Part Two chart the development of this domestic Disney, and investigate some of the contradictions of Disney products, like that glowing doll that leads to absolute security on the one hand and invasions of privacy on the other. Disney has emerged in the last fifty years as a vigorous (and in many cases no doubt sincere) defender of American "family" values. But as Jon Lewis points out in his essay, the company has also become a no less vigorous defender of Disney property rights; and, in the case of the small-time day-care center that dared reproduce Disney characters in its advertising, even at the apparent expense of those family values. Douglas Gomery, in an overview of eight decades of Disney corporate practice, explains some of the conflicts between public perception and stock market portfolio. Disney-the-national-treasure remained a decidedly minor businessman for most of his career, really achieving financial success only a few years before his death.

Using Disney as a model, Part Two examines the fits and starts of corporate history, thereby complicating the most typical Disney discourse. In dealing with both micro and macro levels—the individual artifacts and the thirty-thousand-acre theme parks—the popular media usually construct Disney history, both that of the entrepreneur and the company, as following a strict evolutionary development, from simplicity to perfection. On CBS's *Grand Opening of Euro Disney* broadcast, for instance, a short clip shows Roy Disney, Jr. (a dead ringer for his Uncle Walt, even down to the well-trimmed moustache) in the small French village of Isigny-sur-Mer, saying, "This is a very sentimental place for me, because the roots of my family come right back here to this village. . . . It was over nine hundred years ago that Huw D'Isney and his son Robert lived here."[14] The triumph of the Disney corporation in bringing fully technologized theme park recreation to Europe marks, as well, the triumph of family history (or, at least, the triumph of the men in the family—Disney daughters and wives tend to be forgotten); Euro Disney is the return to the beginning, the full development of rural, pre-Medieval French roots.

Similarly, as a segment of ABC's *20/20* television program reported it, the fully computerized and Technicolored marvel of a Disney cartoon— in this case *Beauty and the Beast*—begins with the sharpening of a pencil.[15] Formulating a critique of this biological, evolutionary model, but without simply making economics an unproblematic final determinant, the essays in Part Two analyze the complex interaction of commercial concerns and cultural production. Richard Neupert, for instance, demonstrates that aesthetic "improvements," like Disney's pioneering use of sound and color, had less to do with the eventual perfection of the animated film than with the attempts of small companies to become big, the need for competing companies to differentiate their products, and the efforts of corporations controlling new technologies to control industry-wide production practices. An examination of Disney's corporate practice, therefore, helps explicate the network of power, competition, and cooperation that defined the Hollywood film industry during the heyday of the studio system, an industry frequently depicted as a single-minded monolith seeking inexorably to increase its power and improve its product.

Rather than examining national production, Alexander Wilson, in his essay in Part Two, analyzes the manner in which the Disney corporation produces nationalism. EPCOT in Florida virtually turns postmodernism against itself, or, at least, shows the potential for a deeply reactionary postmodernism. To its largely middle-class clientele, the park offers a pastiche of America and American history, in the process effectively neutering much of what it has collected and reprocessed: Woody Guthrie's songs, for instance, or Martin Luther King's speeches, or Susan B. Anthony's. In EPCOT the business of America, as well as the entertainment and education, is business (various corporations have sponsored showcases, with General Motors, as just one example, having "It's Fun to Be Free" as a theme song). Moreover, rather than signalling the end of history, the theme park exemplifies its collapse—all eras and figures exist simultaneously, reduced to funny anecdotes or sound bites about liberty—and, Wilson points out, thereby condemning us to "a recurrent and eternal present."

But the point of Part Two is not simply to take easy shots at Disney ideology, to show that, in fact, the entrepreneur and the corporation have been and always will be unproblematically "conservative." The theme parks in California and Florida, for instance, are far more complex than that. As all of the essays show in different ways, Disney himself was very much the inheritor of a post-Civil War tradition of the modern, a tradition that broke down national and global boundaries, stressing fluidity rather than difference. Standardized systems of keeping time, railroads across the country, wireless telegraphy, and the cinema, all "technologies of simultaneity" to use Stephen Kern's evocative phrase, produced, for better and worse, transnational systems of culture, commerce, education, and leisure.[16] Arguably, then, Disneyland marked the final triumph of the modern, a place where seemingly all history, all geography, and all forms of entertainment are instantly available. One of the marks of this shift to the modern, however, is the manner in which its greatest avatars mediate the tensions that it produces, and even caution against its coming. Thus Disney—the entrepreneur, the corporation, and all of the products—signified the homely values of family and country even while demonstrating the possibilities of the future, the inevitability of constant technological innovation, and the necessity for global rather than local interests and responsibility.

As the most persuasive salesman of his own products (through radio and television appearances, magazine interviews, and so on), Disney himself carried on and expanded the legacies of those who, in the nineteenth century, combined business with spectacle, men like Nikola Tesla who took their inventions on the road to amaze the masses and find wealthy patrons. Moreover Disneyland, that homage to the possibilities of the future, really functioned as a further development of the last century's gigantic public spectacles—the Chicago Columbian Exposition of 1893, for instance—or slightly smaller local affairs organized around holidays and special occasions, which Carolyn Marvin has analyzed so fully.[17] Largely generated by the invention of the light bulb, those spectacles celebrated the apparently endless possibilities of all sorts of new technologies, intending to invoke awe in more than one sense of the word; to create amazement, but also a fair degree of horror too.

Shortly after the opening of Disneyland, further advances in technology made such spectacles obsolete. Moon landings and Super Bowls were public events not because thousands of people gathered together to watch them, but because millions could view them in their own homes at the same time. In this scenario, rather than representing progress, Disneyland comes to be marked by a deep nostalgia for the kind of collectives that used to be formed by new technologies, by a longing for the communities of the last half of the previous century.

The Wonderful World of Disney

The essays in Part Three, "The Global Reach," analyze a kind of dual movement in Disney production, one that goes both forward and backward, creating a vision of an "American Century" of imperialist control and also a nostalgia for Western colonial hegemony. Of course, by the 1930s cartoons, the principal Disney product, had already gone global. Over the course of that decade and the next, however, other Disney products—the wristwatches, mugs, lamps, and so on—reached an increasingly international audience, an entrance into transnational capitalism for which Disney was duly rewarded. Besides all of the honorary diplomas and awards from "grateful" countries, Disney also received the overwhelming support of the United States popular media, and particularly print journalism.

During this period, Disney cartoons experienced peaks and valleys in terms of critical acceptance; in particular, the immediate postwar years through to the production of *Cinderella* (1950) and *Alice in Wonderland* (1951) marked a general decline for the cartoons among the movie reviewers. But one is hardpressed to find any criticism in the popular press of Disney's global commercial practices. In 1948, for instance, a few months after the studio's animated film *Melody Time* received generally unfavorable reviews, *Time* magazine celebrated the global scope of the Disney product. In an article called "The Mighty Mouse," Disney's main salesman defined his territory as stretching "from the Isthmus of Panama to Hudson Bay." Then, just in case the reader might wonder about Disney's grip on countries in different latitudes, the magazine added that "after Jan. 1 Disney's brother, Roy, will handle the rest of the world."[18]

Earlier in the decade, and at the behest of Nelson Rockefeller's Office of the Coordinator of Inter-American Affairs, Disney had become involved in selling not so much his own products, but North American "Good Neighborliness" in South America. As a sign of his status as an international icon of goodwill, Disney went on a 1941 government-sponsored tour of several South American countries; along with asserting friendship between North and South (and thereby trying to deflect the threat of fascist influence in such countries as Argentina), Disney was also surveying possibilities for establishing United States film-related industry in the area. In addition, the Office of the Coordinator had requested that Disney gather material for a series of propaganda films, some of which—shorts about health and hygiene, for instance—were designed for South American consumption, while others—the feature length *Saludos Amigos* and *The Three Caballeros*—were intended to "explain" South America to United States audiences.[19]

This Disney, a government emissary and agent of the Monroe Doctrine, is the one celebrated by Walter Wanger in the essays reprinted in Part One. And this is also the incarnation of the entrepreneur examined by several of the authors in Part Three. Julianne Burton-Carvajal, José Piedra, and Lisa Cartwright and Brian Goldfarb take a new look at Disney's South American projects in the context of United States foreign policy at mid-century, a policy aimed at bringing South America firmly and fully within the United States sphere of influence, and carried out largely through discourses of science and sexuality.

Donald Duck emerges here as a central figure, much more so than the increasingly (by the 1940s) benign and avuncular Mickey Mouse. In his 1940 *Atlantic Monthly* essay, reprinted in Part One, Paul Hollister wrote that "overnight the civilized world surrendered to Donald Duck" after his debut as a Disney character in 1934. Much of that appeal stemmed from the star's cartoon interaction with the "uncivilized" world, with both

Burton-Carvajal and Piedra concentrating on Disney's feature-length experiment in combining live action and animation, *The Three Caballeros,* in which Donald goes south of the border.

Like so much Disney discourse, the studio's South American projects demonstrate the apparent disjunction between entertainment on the one hand and international politics on the other. In fact, the success of the Disney South American undertaking may owe less to the individual films than to a kind of collective determination on the part of generations of film audiences to reject any link between ideology and animation in any Disney cartoons from any period. Julianne Burton-Carvajal addresses precisely this problem in her essay about *The Three Caballeros.* In all of its segments, the film provides "narratives of conquest in which the patriarchal unconscious and the imperial unconscious insidiously overlap." Of course many viewers, confronted with this analysis, would only shake their heads, doubting that any Disney film could be so politically charged.

Nevertheless, as Burton-Carvajal points out, *The Three Caballeros* functions perfectly as an allegory of First World colonialism, in large part because it is, primarily, a cartoon, and thus the kind of film that so many audiences believe to be beyond ideology. But animated films, functioning themselves as an "Other" within a production practice dominated by live-action films, serve as the ideal place to portray a cultural, ethnic Other. Moreover, South America becomes the ideal subject of this portrayal because of its history, in North America, of embodying the irrational, the exotic, the hyperreal; in other words, that in which the Hollywood cartoon has typically specialized.

Despite this ideal fit, movie critics disparaged *Caballeros* during its initial release, put off by the aesthetic implications of combining live action with animation, and by the sexual connotation of Donald Duck in pursuit of flesh-and-blood women. The complaints about mixing cartoons with real life seem ludicrous today; quite simply, *The Three Cabelleros* is an astonishing film to look at, more interesting, even, than *Fantasia.* But the sexual issue, taken from a moral level to a political one, retains its urgency. For example, in his essay, José Piedra discusses the United States' strategy from the 1940s and after of "political and sexual Pan–American 'unification,' " and charts the network linking the United Fruit Company, Carmen Miranda, Donald Duck, and the construction of a South America just waiting to be seduced by the cowboys from the North. For the State Department, Disney, and the primarily North American audiences watching *Saludos Amigos* and *The Three Caballeros,* imperial expansion and sexual penetration became one and the same thing, as long as the United States remained "on top."

Besides the feature films about the region, however, a significant aspect of the Disney project for Inter-American Affairs was a series of short, animated films about health care designed principally for Central and South American audiences. These cartoons shift the emphasis from seduction to sanitation, and as Lisa Cartwright and Brian Goldfarb point out, indicate the cooperation between cultural production, corporate interests, and government policy. While the feature films exalt the virtue of fluid boundaries (as long as the travellers were North Americans heading South), these health films, nostalgically invoking a world of strict divisions between countries, stress the importance of national borders, and the fear that disease might be transmitted through imported goods as well as through foreign workers and travellers. These Disney films show the discontents of the United States' wartime global commercial policy. José Piedra's essay examines a prurient Disney's representation of the ecstatic consummation of the relationship between Donald Duck and Chiquita Banana. Cartwright and Goldfarb's shows how Uncle Walt also threw some cold water on the lovers, insisting, for the sake of United States corporations and citizens, on transnational "safe sex."

These, then, were the contradictions of Disney in the 1940s; varying representations of nationalism, national interest, and international relations from films produced as part of the same government project (indeed, Disney/State Department ideology becomes even more interesting when we keep in mind that the health films were translated into English and shown to United States citizens living in rural areas—in other words, those people who inhabited a kind of domestic Third World, and who produced fears in an ever-urbanizing country similar to those generated by "unclean" Central and South Americans). But it is probably the international theme parks that most thoroughly display the studio- (and media-) generated Disney discourse about the importance of national borders and also their permeability, and about international influence and cultural self-assertion.

The popular media, often in cooperation with the Disney corporation, have frequently used both the foreign and domestic theme parks to assert the globality of the Disney product. In *Disney World: 20 Years of Magic: A Yearlong Birthday Party,* a magazine generated to advertise the Florida park and published by *Newsweek,* most of the articles use a system of global measurements to proclaim the park's accomplishment. One essay, appropriately called "Worlds of Wonder" (and invoking the "Magic Worlds" in the title of the 1963 *National Geographic* piece), marvels that if all of the tourists who have visited the park were to come at once, "that would make [Disney World] the 12th-largest country in the world, somewhere between Mexico and Italy, or a confederation of three smaller countries, each resembling Singapore or Switzerland, the tidiest countries on the globe."[20] The magazine adds that "for awhile," tourists can also "live in a country" where all countries and cultures come together, "where 'Lara's Theme' and 'Singin' in the Rain' and the theme from 'Lawrence of Arabia' come up from the speakers in the lawns."[21] Then, hungry from covering all of that musical territory, tourists can benefit from the five and a half million pounds of potatoes that Disney uses "each year just to make french fries . . . enough julienned potatoes to circle the world 2.5 times."[22] The magazine ends with a brief essay of appreciation by perhaps the only symbol of a globalized American popular culture that can rival Mickey Mouse; the Hollywood star who probably spends as much time outside the United States as in it, Bob Hope.

With the opening of theme parks in Japan and France, this kind of global discourse in relation to Disney has only intensified. On the *Grand Opening of Euro Disney* television program, hosts Don Johnson and Melanie Griffith talked about the international children's choirs at the opening, the stars from around the world representing various ethnic groups (Gloria Estefan, José Carreras, The Temptations), the African Tam Tam percussion group, and the French, German, and English influences on the Disney feature-length cartoons. Throughout, the program presented dubbed versions in various languages of familiar Disney movies, showing just how well those movies "travelled."

When more objective reports—those designed, at least nominally, as information rather than publicity—covered the opening of the French park, however, they concentrated on the problems of Disney globalism, and particularly on the exporting of American culture to France. On the local ABC evening news in Washington, D.C., a report on Euro Disney closed the program, after which the newscaster, weatherman, and sportscaster, in typical happy-talk fashion, joked among themselves; the newscaster said, "And apparently some other Europeans are upset about it. 'A Cultural Chernobyl,' is that what they're calling it?" After all the men laughed, he added, "Doesn't surprise me. The Japanese export cars, and we export Disney. Whatever works." The men laughed again as the program faded out. On the Fox network local news in Washington, a reporter said that "Although many are expected for the grand opening, some accuse Disney of American imperialism," and she added that many in France were "angry about the influx of American culture."

Whenever a newscaster uses the word "imperialism" it is worthy of note, particularly when it is applied to corporate or governmental actions originating in the United States. I can think of no similar description of American interests or policy decisions during the Gulf War, the last major international event before the opening of Euro Disney to capture the popular media's attention. That which seems apolitical—an amusement park—thus motivates at least something of a political discussion when it has been built by Disney. Certainly, that discussion is an uneasy one—

the newscaster's laughter is evidence of that—but it is a sign of Disney's continuing significance that the corporation's activities can produce a kind of discourse that United States media typically attempt to repress.

What I find particularly interesting about this politicized discourse is the manner in which it constructs the issue as a binary opposition—in the manner of George Will's column, noted above, the American corporation and the (pro-Disney) French masses versus left-wing (and anti-Disney) French intellectuals. In his essay about Tokyo Disneyland in Part Three, Mitsuhiro Yoshimoto analyzes this kind of interpretation of global Disney practices, one that he locates not only in the popular media but also in much modern criticism. Yoshimoto writes that "the most prevalent image of cultural imperialism is that of a hegemonic power, such as the United States, trying to indoctrinate and brainwash the population of the periphery." But while Yoshimoto points out that Tokyo Disneyland can be interpreted as a signifier of the subaltern mentality of the Japanese consumer, he also argues that the theme park functions primarily as a sign of Japanese nationalism rather than American colonial practice. Tokyo Disneyland, creating America "as a brand name . . . is only part of the system of differences which needs to be reproduced perpetually for the survival of the Japanese capitalist economy."

The same argument can be applied to Euro Disney, in order to complicate the debate between the defenders of corporate interests and the protectors of French cultural integrity. In his role as tour guide during the *Grand Opening of Euro Disney* program, Don Johnson tried to explain some of the differences between the various Disney theme parks. "Take Adventureland," he began. "Here at Euro Disney the jungles of Anaheim and Orlando have been replaced by the desert sands of Morocco." His cohost Melanie Griffith, however, reminded viewers that "all the Adventurelands do share some things in common. Things like mystery, intrigue, and pirates."

In other words, Euro Disney, even as it typifies the international scope of the Disney corporation, reproduces a particularly French colonialist fantasy, one in which North Africa, here signified by "Morocco," stands for adventure and for the exotic, and overflows with dangerous, uncivilized natives. Of course, this kind of orientalism has enjoyed a great currency in the United States; in movies alone, one need only consider *The Sheik, Morocco, Beau Geste, Algiers,* and *Raiders of the Lost Ark.* But it is also part of the genius, for want of a better term, of the Disney enterprise that, in producing particular forms of "adventure" and, more properly, "history" for particular audiences, the company does not simply inflict American mythology upon the unwitting masses. Rather, it creates a specifically nationalist fantasy, recalling a "glorious" era of one country's imperialist past. In a move towards truly global, or at least fully Westernized entertainment, however, that very fantasy certainly would not be lost on foreign audiences (American and German tourists, for example, can no doubt appreciate and partake in the ideology of Euro Disney Adventureland). As a result, the most effective critique of Euro Disney may not be to lament an international popular culture controlled by the United States (which, in any case, is nothing new). Rather, it would be to examine the construction of French racism and the nostalgic representation of a period of French colonial domination for the edification of a largely French audience.

This brings the issue of Disney discourse back to Minnie Mouse as Madame Defarge. As I noted above, and in an apparent departure from the corporation's typical politics, Disney, in conjunction with La Vache Qui Rit, distributed likenesses of his characters in revolutionary drag during the bicentennial year of 1989. But with the subsequent construction of Euro Disney, we can see this earlier promotion as an homage to another brand of French nationalism, with the characters, attached to cheese rather than to popular politics, signifying nebulous notions of *liberté, égalité,* and *fraternité*.

Around the time of the opening of Euro Disney, and on the eve of the proposed formation of the European Community, France found itself fraught with racial unrest and calls for immigration quotas (largely because of the presence of African "colonial" subjects not so conveniently contained within the borders of a Moroccan Adventureland); with an emerging far-right wing and the concomitant rise in anti-Semitism; and labor problems which a socialist government seemed unable to face (those truck drivers who tried to shut down the Mitterand-supported Euro Disney shortly after its opening). As a result, the Disney/cheese company bicentennial celebration, in addition to Euro/Disney, tried to construct unanimity and consensus through a call to unproblematic, national self-interest. France, through Disney, became the home of transcendental values of equality and justice, and, in the manner of the Disney company itself, the exporter of those values to primitive, unenlightened colonial subjects who, in Morocco-Adventureland, remain safely separated from the "true" French citizenry.

Interpreting Interpretation

Of course, this reading of Disney as the producer of French nationalism is not the only one possible. However much we demonstrate the manner in which Disney helped make the French Revolution safe for public consumption, the fact remains that Minnie as Madame Defarge can be read in a number of ways, including ways which, in the manner of the revolution itself, support vast and rapid social change. And it would not be completely out of character for Disney to produce something that could be said to encourage, if not a radical critique of capitalism, then at least a tentatively progressive questioning of the status quo. During the Depression, for instance, a number of Disney cartoons, which were designed for an audience made up of as many adults as children, clearly took pro-working-class or pro-labor stances (despite Disney's own opposition to the period's growing labor movement in Hollywood). In *Moving Day* (1938), for example, Mickey, Donald, and Goofy face the problems of eviction and finally gain their revenge on the sheriff who tries to throw them out of their house. Then, in 1940, in one of the more extraordinary of all Hollywood interpretations of work, *The Riveter* shows a completely disaffected Donald as a member of a construction crew; many in the audience at the time almost certainly viewed the film as a justification of the alienation that they themselves felt in the workplace. But at the same time, these cartoons might also be watched purely as escapist entertainment intended to remove many spectators from the grimness of everyday life, or, perhaps, to convince others of the infantilism of the poor (in both films, for instance, Donald throws his usual tantrums).

In cultural studies in general and film studies in particular, we are only beginning to understand these complexities of reception. My own work on *The New Spirit,* a Treasury Department-sponsored Disney cartoon from 1943 which seeks to explain sweeping changes in the tax code, shows how audience response to and interpretation of the film varied considerably according to such social categories as class and religious affiliation.[23] For more and more cultural critics and historians, the absolutely crucial question has become not "what do texts mean?" but rather, "who are these meanings available to?" and, related to this, "how does meaning vary from audience to audience?"

Because meaning is never monolithic, Part Four of this volume, "Reception," seeks to examine the various interpretations that the consuming public has made of Disney products and, as well, the manner in which the Disney company has attempted to quantify and control these interpretations. Of course, issues of reception have always circulated around popular culture in direct proportion to advances in the technologies that could produce and disseminate that culture on a wide scale (wireless telegraphy, for instance, or paperback books). With the development of the cinema in the late-nineteenth century, reformers immediately became concerned with the messages that audiences (and particularly children and immigrants) might collect from the movies, and with the sanitary conditions and moral atmosphere of those arcades that showed films. By the 1930s, the period of Disney's rise to prominence as a film producer, the concern about the cinema had moved beyond middle-class reform groups and extended into the social sciences.

During that era, the Payne Fund financed a series of studies of the effects of motion pictures upon children, and the "Middletown" project—an extended study of Muncie, Indiana—also appeared, measuring and quantifying all manner of behavior, with special attention given to leisure activity.[24] In addition, industry became interested in the science of consumer response, the better to sell products. This new corporate belief in analysis and quantification met its perfect partner in the father of modern polling techniques, George Gallup, who, for the firm Young and Rubicam, formed Madison's Avenue's first research department in 1932.[25] By the end of the 1930s, Hollywood had also recognized Gallup's potential, and hired the pollster to conduct audience surveys. *Time* magazine celebrated this marriage of entertainment and science with a 1941 article about Gallup called "Boy Meets Facts" in which readers learned that seventy percent of the audience for the Selznick film *Rebecca* was female, that advance publicity could significantly affect a film's performance at the box office, and that, because most Americans ate dinner before 6:30, double features beginning an hour later provided a theater with maximum revenue.[26]

Ever interested in technological advances, Walt Disney, more than most Hollywood producers, preached the gospel of Gallup's audience analysis. As Susan Ohmer has explained, beginning in the 1940s Disney used Gallup's findings before, during, and after film production.[27] If the theme parks built between the 1950s and the 1990s demonstrate Disney's belief in better living through science, then the films from just before this vast expansion into real estate show Disney's confidence not so much in using science to make better movies, but to make movies that would appeal to the widest possible audience.

Disney's belief in science was not absolute, however. Along with trying to shape his films to meet the public taste quantified by Gallup, he also tried to control possible audience response. Richard deCordova, in his essay, analyzes the manner in which Disney products—the cartoons and also the cartoon-related merchandise—in the 1920s and thirties constructed childhood so as to make it completely compatible with consumerism. Thus, children going to Disney movies would also, with or without the help of their parents, become the customers of department stores selling Disney products. Those same kids would become members of local Mickey Mouse clubs which were themselves tied to retail stores. Disney, then, sought no less than to influence virtually all kinds of childhood leisure activity, and, in fact, to make the purchase of Disney goods just one more kind of juvenile leisure pursuit.

In her essay, Moya Luckett examines the promotion history of one film, perhaps Disney's most famous—*Fantasia,* originally shown in 1940 but reissued (on film and later on video tape and laser disc) every few years since then. Through the advertising and distribution strategies for the film, Luckett shows the tension between Disney's acknowledgment of widely differentiated groups among the film audience (demonstrated by Gallup's research) and the belief—indeed, the economic imperative for a mass form of entertainment—that a single audience ultimately could be constructed. When Disney released the film in 1940 he suggested that different regions might arrange the segments differently, the better to appeal to regional tastes and habits. But he also tried to promote a general, nationwide response to *Fantasia,* insisting in the advertising campaign on the film as a special event and on its status as great art.

More and more, changes in the public's leisure trends and also in Disney production practice have led to an emphasis on creating and controlling audience response, or, more properly speaking, on concentrating on the largest possible audience group even while advertising its products as appealing to everyone. With the building of the theme parks, Disney did not simply send his products—the films, for instance—out to the public. Instead, the public came to him, to one location. As a result, with their Adventurelands, Tomorrowlands, and Fantasylands, the parks created the illusion of diversity, but also, at all times, catered to the audience with the time, money, and inclination to travel to such amusements; the white, middle-class family.

The national media, having adopted many of the methods pioneered by Disney, have been more than happy to place their stamp of approval on those practices. In the *20/20* special about *Beauty and the Beast,* for instance, the announcer intoned that the "acid test" was a preview of the film for three hundred kids and their parents, "recruited at random from shopping malls." Of course, Gallup himself may have wondered whether an authoritative random sample could ever be obtained from a mall, and, indeed, all of the people in the audience were white. On the *Good Morning America* celebration of Walt Disney World, an interviewer called upon two couples to testify to the park's appeal; a father and daughter who make a pilgrimage every year, and a husband and wife from England making their tenth visit. In the first case, then, Disney can scientifically select that "random" audience, and in the second, the company's product appears to have not only domestic but global appeal; in both examples, however, that appeal must be specifically familial (parents and children, husbands and wives) and universally white.

Luckett also points out, however, that corporations, even those as powerful as Disney's, can never fully control reception. In the case of *Fantasia,* and despite Disney's best efforts, critics varied widely in their assessment of the film, largely ignoring the company's pronouncements about art and quality. And in recent years, even though more and more people are "coming to" Disney (that is, attending the theme parks), the company itself is also distributing its products to more and more consumer outlets; specialty stores controlled by Disney, drugstores, video and laser disc stores, movie theatres, cable and network television, and so on. The public can also easily purchase or rent the most famous aspect of Disney production—the cartoons, now available on video—far more easily than ever before, and they can watch them at home. As a result, the company finds it impossible to regulate the viewing experience as it did in movie theatres, where Disney could influence, among other things, the selection of other films on the bill and the length of a film's run.

Because of this potential fractiousness, contemporary Disney discourse coming from the company itself highlights the universal experience of Disney goods more than ever before, seeks to placate more than ever, and stresses the theme parks—those places where the Disney product, and the public's interaction with it, can be carefully controlled. I do not mean to lament this development, to look back fondly on a golden age of Disney discourse when much of what was said about the company came from Walt himself. Gone are the openly political days of testifying before Congress, as Disney did in 1947, about the dangers of communist influence in Hollywood, and of singling out the threat posed by subversive Jews.[28] Today, of course, two Jewish men—Michael Eisner and Jeffrey Katzenberg—run Disney, and their own public utterances are as self-consciously apolitical as Walt's were, frequently, provocative. One example best demonstrates the new Disney inclusiveness, not so much a completely new discourse as a determination to stress global enjoyment above everything else, and in comparison to which all else pales. On the Washington, D.C. CBS local news segment covering the opening of Euro Disney, a reporter asked Eisner for his thoughts about the park's left-wing French critics. Truer perhaps to post-Cold War ideology than to Walt's memory, but stressing, in typical Disney fashion, the trinity of the palliative power of fun, the transcendent potential of family, and the child just trying to get out in all of us, Eisner had a simple answer. "The intellectual," he said, "and maybe even the Communist, when they bring their children to Euro Disney, will have a good time."

A Disney Archaeology

1

Genius at Work: Walt Disney*

Paul Hollister

I

The city bakes in an amber coastal plain, shut off from the world by a horseshoe of mountain to the north, east, and south, and by an ocean to the westward. The city is not Hamelin, in Brunswick, but Los Angeles, U.S.A., amid its litter of tributary towns. Two of them, side by side, are Hollywood and Burbank, and between the two, from the floor of the plain, crops up a mountain made of ultramarine and olive. They call the mountain "Lookout," but it might be the Koppelberg Hill itself. . . .

Walt Disney's new studio, a jewel on the Burbank flat, has no apparent communication with the mountain, which stands so far away that its long afternoon shadows do not temper the 112-degree August heat. But it is near enough so that Mr. Disney could, within five minutes, attain the apron of the ridge, pass by sorcery through the sealed green door, and see how his Productions are proceeding underground.

For he is the Pied Piper of our time, perhaps of all time. "I'm able," said Robert Browning's Piper,

> By means of a secret charm, to draw
> All creatures living beneath the sun,
> That creep or swim or fly or run,
> After me so as you never saw.

In his suave "modern" office Walt wears a pied ensemble consisting of a tasty pair of wine-colored flannel trousers, a loose jacket to match,

---

* *Atlantic Monthly*, December 1940, Vol. 166, No. 6, pp. 689–701.

an oarsman's shirt of cotton, and moccasins. His eyes are dark, his height is, say, five-ten, his weight one hundred and fifty. This Kansas City newsboy has been charming the children of all races and ages out of a melancholy world into a sanctuary-mountain fortified against all attack. But the Pied Piper of Burbank has only just begun.

His first studio was in a corner of a garage. His gleaming newest cost two million dollars, covers several hundred thousand square feet, is as severely gay as a World's Fair model, as immaculate as a hospital, and as functional as a research scientist's dream laboratory. Five years ago the little band of Disney faithful totaled two hundred souls; today the payroll shows eleven hundred. Until three years ago the studio had never made a long picture; today's schedule calls for three "features" and twenty-six "shorts" a year. That promises the final production of a serpent of celluloid nineteen hundred miles long, of which each linear foot will consist of sixteen "frames," or individual pictures. These individual frames will be photographed from a single color drawing on a sheet of translucent celluloid, or from two, three, four, or five such drawings superimposed upon each other, and held before a fixed and opaque watercolor drawing of the background of the scene. *Pinocchio,* for instance, required over half a million final drawings. And before each final single—or multiple—color drawing is ready for the camera it has been preceded by an incalculable number of preliminary sketches, moulding the characters, the situation, the action, the expression, to their final needle-focus of perfection.

Walt'll be thirty-nine this winter. He was born in Chicago, with Irish, Canadian, German, and American blood in his veins. When he was nine he had a paper route in Kansas City; when he was sixteen he had a train-butcher job. He studied photography in McKinley High in Chicago, and he had always liked to draw. That's all you need to know to understand the man's plot. To be sure, when he was turned down as too young to enlist, he got to France at the wheel of an ambulance, but when he came home he went to drawing again—catalogue illustrations, and free-lance commercial drawings, and finally cartooning for a company that made comical lantern slides. The problem of animating the action of the characters on successive slides absorbed him. He beguiled a group of cartoonists to collaborate with him in making films of fairy tales; the group sold the film to a New York company; the company went broke.

Armed with forty dollars, a suit, a sweater, and his drawing tools, Walt landed in Hollywood in August of 1923 to visit his brother Roy. Roy had a few more dollars of working capital, so the brothers, in a garage, made and photographed enough drawings to add up to a complete short film. Walt took it to the chief Los Angeles motion picture theatre for a trial projection. The house manager took some urging, but agreed to project it after-hours. Disney went into the theatre to watch a regular cartoon film on the bill. Instead, he suddenly saw his own baby projected on the screen. He leapt from his seat, scuttled down the aisle, and announced to the rather frightened audience that the film on the screen was his own. That was his first public showing of the Disney Production. Today that theatre manager is his vice president and sales manager, for Walt has a memory like an elephant, and the loyalty of adhesive plaster. Today the Idaho girl who answered an advertisement for an assistant in the garage is the first and only Mrs. Walt Disney, and the mother of his two daughters.

Cartooning or "comic-stripping" in the American manner is very simple. All you do is to think up a character and then put it through the paces of three or four scenes, in your mind, just as a playwright takes his character through three or four acts. Then you draw each scene in a simple pen-and-ink technique. If the action turns on words spoken by your character, you draw a balloon with its string near the speaker and letter the words into the balloon. If your character is a familiar animal, so much the better, for animals are droll ("they look so much like humans"), animals are anonymous, and therefore out of reach of controversial prejudices ("everybody loves animals"), and animals are highly animate. So Walt drew *Oswald the Rabbit*. The basic method of cartoon animation of which *Oswald* was a crude example is the basic method of the highly polished product of 1940. The *Oswald* saga was popular. Disney wanted to expand, kept trying to prove to his distributor that he needed more working capital. The distributor declined to put up the money. "If I cannot raise new money," reasoned Disney, "I'd better raise some new ideas." So he simply created *Mickey Mouse,* just as you would create Niagara Falls, the Tehachapi Mountains, the Panama Canal, or the Hope Diamond.

And then, as the silent screen titles used to say, came sound.

Overnight, when the first raw sound began to bark at you from your favorite movie screen, it became evident that you wouldn't long be interested in watching a silent mouse. *Plane Crazy* ("Mickey builds a plane, goes on an adventurous flight") was on release to the theatres; the little one-mouse-power factory was readying *Gallopin' Gaucho* ("Take-off on Doug Fairbanks. Mickey rescues Minnie from Pete in Spanish locale"); a third film, *Steamboat Willie,* as mute as the other two, was ready to go—when sound "arrived." *Steamboat Willie* was yanked back into the plant, its story torn apart, new sequences and new "gags" were drawn in to show musical instruments, actual music to fit the instruments was recorded and patched into the film by a strange new device called a "sound track"—and *Steamboat Willie,* delivered to the exhibitors on July 29, 1928, served notice that Walt thenceforth aimed to please not only the eye but the ear.

Today, after twelve years, this young man, who shyly professes his

ignorance of classical music, has just made a two-and-one-half-hour picture, the body of which is a full-rigged classical orchestral concert by
Leopold Stokowski and the Philadelphia Symphony, and the *decor* of
which is a pictorial fantasy on the screen contrived to interpret, animate,
enrich, expand, and vitalize the music as music has never before come
to life. It is called *Fantasia,* and it is a revolution. It projects Creation,
for instance, with a little help from Stravinsky. Up round Disney's place
it is only a stone's throw from *Steamboat Willie* to Leopold Stokowski,
Deams Taylor, Ludwig van Beethoven, Johann Sebastian Bach, and Creation. Mickey's first sound voice in *Steamboat Willie* was Walt Disney's
voice, and so it is as Mickey plays the Sorcerer's Apprentice in *Fantasia,*
and so it has always been and, please God, may always be.

II

It would help solve international problems if you were to understand
the process of making a modern animated cartoon.

Having decided upon a story to tell, you talk about it with your associates. If you cannot kindle them all with enthusiasm for its graphic possibilities, you choose only those who seem to share your hope. Luckily these
people can draw, and in the course of infinite experiment on paper and
by voice they evolve a great many "sequences" of interesting pictorial
action, and they show them to you, and first thing you know you see
before you tacked on the wall a series of sketches of the dramatic high
spots of the story. If it is a pretty long story, too cumbersome for a single
group of artists to digest, you choose four or five men as a "story crew"
and give them the first section of the story to sketch in further detail; to
another crew you assign the second section. You have thus set twenty
or twenty-five seasoned artists off prospecting along a single romantic
trail. Each of your four or five crews, or scouting parties, keeps running
to you at the head of the file to show you what new treasure it has
unearthed. Each of the new sketches you tack in its proper place on a
very long wall, and presently all the key pictures of the action of the
story are in place before you, the characters are taking on the form
of distinct personalities, and the picture has quietly gone into actual
production.

Article I of the Disney constitution stipulates that every possible element
of a picture shall be not a mere pictorial representation of the character
or an element of scenery, but an individual, with clearly defined characteristics. Disney lieutenants have grown gray in the service repeating that
Mickey is "*not* a mouse, but a *person*." So your story crew will psychoanalyze each character, and from each man's suggestion will evolve on paper
a character with defined proportions and mannerisms. Before you set

about drawing your semi-final story, therefore, you turn your characters over to your Model Department, where they not only make accurate portraits of the characters on paper, as a guide for the animators, but even model the characters in plaster so that they may incite the artists to the feeling of vitality that only a three-dimensional statue can give. You now understand why the shelves, the top of the grand piano in Walt's office, the top of the master's desk, and the window ledges hold a ceramic pageant of colored statuettes of kaffir warriors, pygmy pickaninnies, fauns; a noble portrait bust of Neptune; a ballet figure in which the coryphées are not human beings, but hippopotammi, ostriches, and crocodiles slightly under the influence of Degas and Helen Hokinson. You now understand why the files of the Model Department are packed high with photostats of sketch sheets each containing dozens of character notes on each personage in each picture: one such here before me outlines the personality of a baby rabbit, M-9-B, *Snow White*—a character of the utmost triviality in the action of that extravaganza—and on this sheet are forty-three sketches of that single, obscure rabbit. With the help of the Disney Model Department a left-handed plumber could draw the Durbar and make it human.

If it is to be a picture to run ten minutes on the screen, you know that you will ultimately have to show the audience 14,400 pictures. If it is a picture to run one hundred minutes, as a feature picture often does, you need only make 144,000 final drawings.

Remember that (thanks to sound) your characters may talk, laugh, sing, sigh, grunt, whinny, and quack; that the trains you draw may rattle and howl and puff and click, that the teakettle on the hob may whistle. For as you can draw with paint and brush, so you can paint with sound. And remember, too, that just as most music stimulates eye responses in most human beings, so most pictures are enriched in the seeing by complementary sounds.

So first you make your music. Just compose it to the precise length you want your picture to play, and, on the staff paper you give your musicians to write on, paste the key sketches of your story, at the minute-and-second points at which they should occur. Your musicians will then write the notes. You now have your orchestra rehearse it, to make sure that it really illustrates the picture-story your drawings will presently tell, and when the score is finally shipshape you bid the musicians blow their best for the final and imperishable recording of the music on the margin of a ribbon of film—a recording so narrow that to the naked eye the sound track looks like no more than a ruling made with a post-office pen on the wrong kind of paper—a shaggy line not more than one eighth of an inch wide at its loudest.

Since the characters in the story may talk and sing, and since the devices you draw may have characteristic noises, you bid appropriate voices speak lines, or sing, or talk animal-talk, before microphones. You have a secret society of sound-effect men who can make a thunderstorm sound, not as a thunderstorm does on a microphone, but as a Thunderstorm With Personality *should* sound. They will work all afternoon for a proper recording of the word "Hello." They won't teli you or anyone else how they achieve their sound effects; they are jealous as panthers. They will spend several hundred dollars to construct a three-foot metal fan operated by electricity so that a singer may chirp a ballad into a glass lamp chimney and thence into the whirling fan, in order that his song may be recorded with a certain querulous flutter. They will record all manner of synthetic sounds for you, and by replaying the music track on one phonograph, and the sound-effects track on another, both at once, and by fiddling with dials controlling each, you can blend the music and the talk so that each helps the other and makes a final master sound track.

Now some more drawings.

The first drawings will be made with black pencils on white paper. Our preliminary key sketch on the wall says that Mickey is wearing a centurion's helmet. Minnie, a scarf thrown over her shoulder as a Roman maiden, appears before him. He takes off his helmet. It must be a courtly gesture. On the screen it should use, say, the whole of ten seconds. You ought to know that you will need 240 drawings to get Mickey's helmet off his head and into the crook of his arm, in the approved polite-centurion-with-his-helmet-off attitude.

So one of your lieutenants, known as a head animator, sets out to make the 240 drawings. He makes first, on a sheet of translucent paper, Drawing No. 1 (Mickey with helmet on head). Over Drawing No. 1 he places a fresh sheet of paper, so No. 1 drawing will show through the sheet. He then draws Mickey with helmet in crook of elbow—the final drawing of the sequence, which is therefore Drawing No. 240.

Next, he draws the action logical at what we may call the "half mile," then the "quarter mile"; then he draws the "three-quarter-post" action. He assigns each fractional series (1 to 60, 61 to 120, 121 to 180, and so on) to one of four assistants, and from his own start-and-finish guide drawings it is a simple matter for each assistant to produce his own series of final drawings. The 240 sketches are then assembled in sequence, given to the camera department, photographed in black-and-white only, one exposure to each drawing, to make a negative film ten seconds long.

If your name is Walt Disney, the animator team who have made this sequence will call your secretary, tell her they have something to show you. She says, "I'll send him in." She does. The animator threads his ten-second film into a miniature movie projector. You say, "Let's see it," and the 240 drawings, white on black now, and sketchy as can be, appear as motion picture action on a small ground glass panel.

If the assignment has been carried out with *élan,* the rest of the task is merely to do the 240 drawings all over again, in exquisite India-ink penmanship. These final black-and-white drawings will be sent to the inking division. There each will be copied by simple tracing, on a sheet of transparent and colorless celluloid. When the 240 drawings of this ten-second bit have been inspected for microscopic flaws, and passed, they will proceed to the coloring division, where young women of steady hand will apply water colors to the areas on the celluloid.

The pigments are made in the Disney laboratory. They are issued to the painters in numbered and sealed and inspected china jars, each containing just enough paint to cover the specific task—not for parsimony so much as to ensure uniformity and permanence of color tone. The completion of the 240 "cels" in color indicate that you're not far from home with your picture.

But if the action has not been well drawn, or (which is more likely) if new ideas have darted in to make the action more effective as entertainment, back goes the assignment to the animators for resketching. If they go stale on it, the episode may go to a new animator group fresh to the problem. A story can go through miraculously from start to finish in a few weeks, or, which is more likely, it can be postponed for months and years while it is being reshaped. But not one of the two-hundred-odd films put into production and promised has ever been abandoned.

III

"Story conferences" obviously take place throughout the production of a Disney film, from the first consideration of the narrative to the final cels. Let's eavesdrop a random story meeting which took place on Wednesday, December 14, 1938, from 2 to 4:30 p.m. in Music Room No. 1. The stenographic minutes record that there were present Walt, Ben, Ted, Bill, Paul, Webb, Woolie, Dick, Joe, and Steno. (Steno signs the minutes on page 8 merely "irene.")

The subject is Sequence 10 of *Pinocchio.* On the first board, third row, is pinned a sketch, which is the focus of the discussion.

> WALT: We can get a funny action on that big one—the Japanese spider crab. All his legs don't work the same. Those legs all ought to be working like a piston in an automobile. One is up and the other is down. But it's got rhythm to it. Not too mechanical. It should be a cycle. The minute you see it, it's funny.

JOE: I'd like to see the processing start right off. The anemone should start with a small shot at the feet and come right back.

WALT: We should have that first thing, and then a close-up of Pinocchio walking. Cut back; they all follow. Suggest them following, but don't show them gathered in the scene. Show them start to gather. He goes through more and more fish. In the close-up he goes by their eyes and they follow. Then cut to a larger field and you see all these fish—then you've got the laugh. . . . I think it's all right.

JOE: I wish it was the feet and the rock. I would like to see a continuity of business of him being smart with the lobster and just complete the ideal of the rock and the Cricket.

WALT: The part where he is riding the sea horses is a spot I don't like. It gets a little rowdy. I feel that they have lost their purpose. Cut to Pinocchio; he begins to float up; the Cricket is trying to push the sea horses off him. Leave the Cricket down there pushing the sea horses. . . . You shouldn't show the fish until the Cricket pulls loose. It's a surprise. You know how a fish goes along: here comes something and he just opens his mouth and swallows it. Maybe the grill would open up there, and the cricket comes swimming out. But he forgot his hat inside, so he puts the cane in there and swims out to beat hell. The Cricket would have to make some remark as he swam away from the fish. It would have to be a quick thing.

TED: The thought is, "If it isn't one thing, it's another."

That is how pictures are thought out before they are animated, and while they are being animated. How they ever reach the stage of approval for final drawing and coloring is the mystery of Burbank and the despair of Disney's competitors, and the reason why Disney pictures draw audiences into theatres whether china dishes are being given away or not.

After the cels are colored, special-effects division seizes them and introduces shadows, and modelings, and predetermined devices altogether too complex to explain here, so that the finished drawing may contain its maximum of depth and harmony. Remember that the action of the character on this cel may be played, in the final picture, against a second character, or group of characters, and that while you are making these 240 pictures of Mickey doffing his casque another animator team was making 240 more cels showing Minnie bowing graciously to Mickey. A final "scene," one twenty-fourth of a second long, may consist, as it reaches the camera, of a "setup" of as many as five or six cels superimposed in a "cel setup" upon a fixed background.

So your final ten-second series of cels may really total from 240 to 1200. They will go to your particular cameraman in the Holy of Holies—

the dust-proof, spy-proof, visitor-proof building which is an orderly cata-comb of photographic dens, each the lair of a multiplane camera and its operator. Each scene will be "shot" as a single frame of the endless serpent of Technicolor film which winds out of the Burbank Labyrinth and round and round the earth. But before it issues, remember, it must have a final, wiggly pen-ruling traced along its margin—so the sound track is there recorded, to seal the perfectly timed triple alliance between Music, Sound, and Picture.

Picture sequences are elastic: you can make as many drawings or as few as you like to depict a given scene, but you cannot squeeze or stretch a recorded sound track. That is why you completed the sound first and drew the pictures later to fit the sound. To be sure, you had to have a clear conception at the start of precisely what music would best fit your story, but if you are Walt Disney, or one of his musical geniuses, that wasn't really a problem. Walt has no musical training and perfect musical appreciation. His musical director is a prodigy of musical expertness, and his ear goes to an error in recording as unerringly as a wet spaniel puppy goes to a light and costly Aubusson rug.

IV

The only extant record of the pictures Walt has made since *Steamboat Willie* lies here on the desk, and shows that over two hundred shorts and two long features have spun down the twelve years. Let's transcribe from that record a random outline of the plots of the early shorts, for in them you will see a strain of what makes Disney pictures:

> A battle between Mickey and his mice gang [*sic*] and a bunch of cats
> Duck revue. Pig sings opera and Mickey sings and dances on piano
> Mickey as a train engineer
> Mickey plays organ to skeleton's dance
> Mickey at beach—saves Minnie from drowning
> Auto gags—insects and animals steal picnic lunch
> Covered-wagon type of story—Western locale
> Mickey as taxi driver
> Mickey goes fishing with Pluto
> Spring-cleaning—gags with Pluto and lawn mower
> Hunting—Mickey flying with ducks
> Burlesque on athletic events. Bicycle race
> Explorer—Mickey with the cannibals—musical ending
> Mickey operates steam shovel. Minnie sells box lunches. Chase through steel building. Pete in funny riveter gag

Mickey as cellist—sells Pluto to raise money for poor family—
Christmas

And so on. Chivalry, the chase, a fool dog; gentle, keen, amiable satire
of current tastes, of new books, new pictures, new inventions; sympathetic
refraction of the minor ills that beset us all; heroism, an unwavering
confidence in the ability of machinery to do anything at any time, right
or wrong, which probably would be called gadgetry—these are disclosed
by the record as a few of the blocks on which the Disney legend grew
at the rate of sixteen patient pictures a foot, 5280 feet to the mile. And
under it all you hear the roll of a surf of laughter—the laughter of little
children and very old men and women, the cleansing, tearful, roaring
belly laugh that remains one of civilization's last claims on immortality.

The growth of the Disney project was pretty helter-skelter. From time
to time actors who sing or who make other noises appear for an audition
at the plant by the Koppelberg Hill. Years ago a Chautauqua ventriloquist,
imitating animals in the playgrounds of public schools on behalf of a
local milk company, came to the studio to offer his services. One of his
exclusive specialties, performed by pursing his cheek, and by talking
very fast in his throat as if he had a larynx full of hot golf balls, was an
imitation of a little girl reciting "Mary Had a Little Lamb." Disney
listened, mildly interested, and remarked, "Sounds like a damn duck."
A year later, in need of a new character who might serve as salty foil to
the gallantry of Mickey, Walt conceived the notion of introducing a hard-
boiled, self-reliant, short-tempered and unquenchable duck into a picture
called *The Wise Little Hen*. "Where's that guy that did 'Mary's Little
Lamb' like a duck last year?" he asked. The ventriloquist's name popped
out of the casting file, and overnight the civilized world surrendered to
Donald Duck. Walt forgets nothing except the unimportant, irrelevant,
and unpleasant. Ruthless self-criticism, manic ingenuity, and precisionism
are the assets no other animated film team has been able to match. It is
trite but true that each new film represented new and hard-earned technical
victories and was the best the camp could make, but it was admittedly
only a step to the next picture, which would be better—"or else."

As color multiplied graphic opportunities, so it multiplied problems.
Every black-and-white sketch is susceptible of a thousand, ten thousand,
interpretations in color. When Mickey's familiar short pants first appeared
in color, *what color* should they appear in? Of such grave issues are
major crises born in Burbank, for in pictures, as in life, it is dangerous
to swap trousers in the middle of a reputation.

Wholly aside from the solemn dictum of publicity policy which declares
that "there is no one in the company except Walt," there are, as a matter
of workaday fact, no surnames on the lot. The day after Deems Taylor

started work on *Fantasia* in an office not far from Walt's Corridor, he wanted to consult Walt about several little matters. "This," said he timidly to the operator when he picked up the telephone, "is Mr. Taylor. Could I speak to Mr. Disney's secretary, please?" "I'll call you right back, Deems," said the operator; "her line is busy now." Walt's secretary presently told him that Walt was tied up, and asked what he wanted. Oh, said Mr. Taylor, he would like to catch a moment of Mr. Disney's time when he was free. "Okay," she replied; "the minute he comes back I'll send him in." An hour later Walt came into the Taylor den, eased himself on to a corner of the Taylor desk, and said, "Well, Deems. How's it going? Want me?"

Leopold Stokowski held out for a while, but became "Stokie" to one and all. He even signed his photographs "Stoki." " 'Stokie' *would* have to leave that "*e*" off," said Vern. (Vern hires the 650 artists.)

The telephone rings in the immaculate sweatbox where a film is being run. Janet answers: "Oh, yeah—Herb. I'm in 1-B-9. Say, could you find out where Lorette is? . . . Lorette, is Al going to be free about 4:40? Swell, thanks a lot." A voice from the wall cracks over a speaker: "Say, Janet, what account do we charge this projection to?" "Oh, publicity, I guess, Eddie—thanks." "Thanks very much," says Eddie.

At the office door of each of the inmates is a small card prettily lettered with the names of the occupants. One cubicle contains a certain two who have been a happy and facile working team for a long time. The card says:

Carl Smith
vs.
Bob Johnson

Another office is the fortress of five young artists. The card outside reads:

Errol Waltzinger
Errol Shanahan
Errol Priest
Errol Fletsch
Errol Perkins

On a desk in another office, in the manner of a Big Executive, is a name in 84-point type; instead of being on a detached fixture, this name is cut from a newspaper, and is pasted on the edge of the desk. The name is HEDY LAMARR, but the LAMARR is blue-pencilled out. On the studio door of a talented Japanese artist whose name is Gyo is lettered: steGYOsaurus.

The waitresses in the cafeterias (of which there are roughly five on the premises) wear agreeable and washable uniforms like every other wait-ress's uniform except that on their left collar tabs are embroidered their given names. You may eat today with the ministrations of Margaret, but tomorrow, like as not, you will be attended by Lucille, Marie, or (so help me) Hebe.

Gertrude Stein has pointed out that familiarity, far from breeding con-tempt, usually breeds the opposite. Every so often Disney gets tough. When he found out that an undue number of people were arriving too late in the forenoon, and leaving too early, he issued an Ultimatum. With no regard for multigraphing costs he circulated a Sermon on Tardiness. He pointed out its devitalizing effects. He put himself, as he cannot help doing, into the boots of the ten o'clock scholars, and dramatized the reasons why they had probably been late. He whipped himself up to a first-rate pitch of stern plausibility, approached his grim climax, and rammed home his point by stating, "Those who can't find time to do your errands before or after work, why not ask your wife to do them?" Dreadful punitive measures were implied if Matters were not Corrected. Such drastic measures would probably have taken the form of, say, closing the men's clubroom, free massage parlor, and squash court for a half day.

Punitive measures are not often necessary. One group of animators, envying a brother who was making an early sneak in the afternoon, crossed the wiring of his motorcar so that when he turned on the ignition a series of smart internal explosions, borrowed from the sound-effects department, would ensue, and clouds of black smoke would utter from the louvers. When he slid away from his drawing table about four that afternoon and climbed into his car, a noble bombardment drew every Disney employee on that side of the plant to the windows, cheering. He stayed long after five-thirty trying to find out what was wrong with the car, and he came in at eight-thirty next morning. It was recently found necessary to turn out certain lights in the evening, and stop cafeteria service, in order to persuade certain of the brethren to go home from work.

Since celluloid film will burn, and though the new plant is fireproof, the chief engineer recently took it upon himself to lecture a group of staff heads on fire protection. One artist, chided because he had not been at the meeting, scoffed at his dutiful colleagues. "*I* should take," he said, "a boy-scout lecture on not rubbing sticks together." "Wait a minute," said one who had been present. "Wait—a—*minute*. Twenty bucks a month extra, just for doing fire-alert inspection twice a day. Is that so hard to take, twenty bucks, now?" "Whaddye mean, twenty bucks? Twenty bucks for what?" "Listen—for just stepping outside your office twice a day into the main corridor, and looking both ways, for fire—

see? And if there is a fire you report it, and if there is no fire you go back. Not so hard to take, for twenty bucks extra." The absentee agreed that twenty bucks was not hay. "But you got to have the examination, that's all," went on his adviser. "You just go down to the main Burbank fire station, and the firemen give you the exam, and you pay five bucks for your certificate, and then you're in."

Down to the main fire station went the applicant. The city firemen, apprised by telephone of their opportunity, stripped him, put a helmet on his head, a gas mask on his face, and boots on his nakedness, slid him many times down the brass pole. They thumped and measured him, blew smoke in his face, probed his heredity, borrowed his cigarettes, congratulated him, accepted his five dollars, and gave him a certificate. He came back to the Castle Disney proud as a crusader with a paynim scalp. The boys welcomed him to their brotherhood, and after a while they told him all, and paid him back his five dollars. The fire risk is negligible today, but the fire consciousness is pretty well developed.

Here is probably the only factory on earth where practical jokes are a part of the production line. It is inevitable that several hundred men whose lifework it is to produce humorous catastrophes in picture should try a few out on each other.

V

The Disney library contains all the durable children's stories ever told. It also contains five hundred joke books and bound files of the notable humorous publications. It contains a battery of steel filing cabinets which hold a million and a half typed and classified jokes, each legally ascribed to the source from which it was set down. There are 124 classifications of such jokes, and each has from five to twenty subclassifications. A locked case protects first editions of Joe Miller, Alice, and the other important greats in the area of activity of Walt and His Friends. Along one wall is a steel file of sixteen solid cabinets of cartoon jokes, labeled "Inventions, Mountains, Costume, Mummies, Tunnels, Panthers, Astronomy, Liar, Household, Moderne, Local, Military, Party, Climate, Crime, Organizations, People, Radio, Real Estate, Scandal, Science, Sports, Fish Holidays, Art, Birth, Anatomy, Appearance, Baby, Ailments, and Dumb Dames." The library also boasts complete scrapbooks of the original key sketches and plots of all Disney pictures, and a lavish collection of old Sears, Roebuck catalogues.

Under the influence of such a source of inspiration, a man can never be sure, in a certain studio, that when he goes for a drink of water in the morning that he will not find a school of pretty goldfish swimming about in the cooler. Word came to Walt one day that the boys in 4-B-16 had been developing a new character that they'd like to have him see. "Swell," said Walt. "I'll come right down." They had gone to great pains, they said, to work up this unusual character, and to photograph a sequence of unusual animation for it. "Fine," said Walt. "That's the stuff. Could a fellow have a peek?" They turned the sketch film on the screen, and the new character they had worked up for Walt proved to be his old friend Popeye the Sailor—perhaps the most popular animated character not made by Disney at all—and incidentally a character Walt loves.

Where do these people come from? They are not graduates of schools of business administration, or of advanced courses in motion picture production. Some of the older heads are alumni of other animated-cartoon companies. The average age on the lot is not more than twenty-six or twenty-seven. Joe (and that is not his name) whom you might describe as chief technical engineer and who is festooned with academy awards for engineering triumphs, never had any technical training and never got beyond high school. The chief of the staff of guides is a youth just out of UCLA who did a good deal of writing and acting in college, and who knows he got "a great break to get in here," where there is no market for actors on the hoof. The 650 artists, who are the backbone of the establishment (if you don't let the sound-effect men hear you, or the musicians, the photographers, chemists, engineers, story department, traffic, color mixers, or air conditioners), come from wherever artists come from: from the art schools, from free-lancing, from the pages of magazines and books, from advertising agencies and commercial art agencies, and from half a dozen other nations as well as most of the States.

On the floor of a lumber room Gyo points to a pile of sketches and wants to know whether you saw Kay Neilson's atmosphere drawings; on the wall is a Tenngren color sketch for the interior of the Dwarfs' house in *Snow White*. The preserve is knee-deep in masterpieces. Disney goes after top men in their specialties: he'll be after Picasso, Grant Wood, and Ung any day now. One of the best volunteer "gag" men is Alois, the Swiss gardener, who gives special coddling to the petunias under the open windows of the story department, for there he can eavesdrop, and into the problem of the story men he can inject a suggestion for a "twist," an "angle," or a gag suitable for special reward. He has won many such. His petunias are lush and brilliant, and those under the windows of the story department are the best. Two messenger boys thought up a Pluto short, and Walt put it into production.

To choose the 650 Disney artists, to regiment them without freezing their graphic muscles, to condition them in the shalls and shall-nots of the local rendering, to inspire them and above all to make them grow, is probably the nicest responsibility in the whole show. "Ducks I don't like, I do not," says Emil, a grade-A animator. "Ducks I got no patience with." The fact is that this man can draw a magnificent duck. But Emil likes, he says, "to futz around with big characters," so it is Emil who created *Stromboli,* and *The Giant;* it is Emil who created for *Fantasia* a devil who will scare the whey out of you; it is Emil who created in *Pinocchio* the Whale to end whales. There are Duck Men and Mouse Men. Top Duck Men or Mouse Men wouldn't "feel" Emil's characters.

Some artists have innate (probably optical) preferences for small, tidy, tight characters, like beetles and chipmunks. Some run to decorative miniatures. Some prefer long, limp, loose contrivances like Pluto. To discover in each artist the caprice he best likes to draw, then to harness that specialty, is just one more example of Walt's determination to use the best available person for every task, even if he has to make that person the best. One man likes pretty girls, reels them off by the mile, and gets miles of them to reel off; another thinks they're stupid. An artist especially expert in facial contortions wails: "They always give me the Inner Struggles to do." Another specializes in milkweed-down fairies.

Newcomers are put to school to learn the types of drawing, both as to *Geist* and as to specific applications of lines and colors, which will evolve into the final celluloid. There are free night drawing classes for all who want to enroll, under competent instruction. New work by representative "academic" painters and draftsmen of other sorts marches through the gallery in a constant series of well-attended exhibitions. At noon hour, in the theatre on the lot, a special program of motion pictures runs for thirty minutes. It may be a recent release from a live-action studio, an unusual sequence of exploration pictures of the private life of the Kodiak bear, the Florida alligator, the South African dik-dik, or the training of the Arabian saddle horse; it may be a good corny comedy from the full-life studios over the Koppelberg Hill, or a newsreel of skiing or surf-riding or the explosion of an atom; it is chosen because it is relevant somewhere to what the studio is currently producing.

Your correspondent walks on eggs for fear of accenting one division at the expense of another. It has been made clear that the graphic artist and his business of producing drawings for photography are the function without which there would be no Disney Productions. And yet one of the soberest analysts on the lot, who by virtue of his traffic-control job might be called Head Dispatcher, says that the supreme value of the Disney enterprise lies in the story department, and the supreme value in the story department is a man named Walt Disney. The story department, of course, consists not only of men of words, but of men who can translate words into picture action—artists who can tell stories as well as storytellers who can draw. For these men, battalioned into their four "units," exist the service departments:

(1) the division which "inks and paints";

(2) the division which adds "special effects" to the pictures;

(3) the division which takes the photographs of the final drawings;

(4) the division which develops and prints and cuts the film;

(5) the division which provides the sound, both musical and otherwise; and

(6) the housekeeping divisions which provide clear air (no air is used twice, on Walt's order), empty wastebaskets, and look out for fire in corridors.

Somebody has made a successful effort not to festoon the place with the lambrequins and trappings of business pomposity. Walt is the president. Roy is the executive vice president. The rest of the official titles you can put in Mickey's eye. "We've made a real effort to cut every possible bit of red tape," says the head of the red-tape division. The Chief Red-Tapir keeps lucid and intimate charts of the status of production of each picture. His charts show the number of film feet which the people and their methods, machines, and chemicals are able and expected to produce, and the performance against those quotas, and cousin charts sum up the hopes and deeds of the service divisions. But the Troupe Disney as a whole regards Herb's charts as the funniest pictorial treasure in the gallery—perhaps because they are so eloquent with no animation. Herb himself is a little shy about them.

VI

Walt is the spark plug of production. No story starts toward a picture until Walt has bought it or invented it, shaped it, tried it out, and given it a push. The General Production unit is therefore responsible to Walt for getting the picture made. The utmost responsibility for efficient use of the myriad special talents thus rests upon the central casting bureau, which assigns men, squads and companies of men, to the given task which forms a fraction of the whole picture. Through the production pattern of every picture Walt threads in and out like a guiding outline. Having done single-handed, at one time or another, nearly everything that is being done in the studio, and having designed every functional fraction of the plant, Walt knifes into the most minute step of the most microscopic element in an effort to help, help, help. "He knows every detail of every process in the place," they say. "Don't look to me for the answers," he warns; "all I want you to use me for is approval."

To the unending daily encounters with his people he brings not only the stimulus of working with a likable enthusiast, but uncanny accuracy. "He can top a gag like nobody else," says one, topping a gag being a certain divine ability to twist and sharpen a point so that its direction and timing pierce the human heart. Strangely, having The Boss bust in doesn't make for shoddy politics. "We have our apple polishers," says never-mind-who, "but with Walt and Roy there is no politics net." When a boy or girl who just hasn't made the grade is recommended to Walt for dismissal, Walt is more than likely to maintain that the suspect hasn't been used right; often his recommendation for different work for the suspect proves successful, salvages a job. "That son of a gun can see good in a person when ninety percent of the rest of the people can't."

When Walt laughs, he laughs inside; he doesn't buckle walls, as Benchley (the Reluctant Dragon Benchley) does. In a rebuke Walt leaves no doubt: "You just don't get the *angle*," he declares. His scoldings are often loud and clear, and then he is contrite and says, "I was just excited. When I am excited, I get loud. Getting loud when I am excited is just my nature. I just can't help it." "We have never found Walt's judgment lacking," his playmates say; "wouldn't we be foolish not to use it all we can?" "The only employee that's against Walt is the electric elevator," they say. The staff voted not to unionize.

Among the other reasons why people like to work for Disney is money. The average pay is higher than the average in any other Hollywood studio. (We are now talking studios, and not star salaries.) It is a reasonable guess that none but the extreme peaks at the top of the enterprise draw more than three hundred dollars a week, and a certainty that the least-paid draw more than is paid for like work elsewhere. The employment mortality rate is strikingly low. Disney needs to spend no nights lying awake worrying about star salaries, for Disney's stars are in his head, and in his eyes, and in the eyes and minds of eleven hundred people on the lot, and that saves him a lot of time to dream about new stars at night. Most of the profit the company has made has gone back into the business. The one and a half million dollars borrowed to make *Snow White* was repaid within three months after *Snow White* reached the screen.

But of the elements that make for personal economic security, and relating to money, three systems sustain a high tempo of ambition and provide its outlets. One is a system of rewards for suggestions, which may range all the way from a routine matter of conveying paper from one side of the desk to the other (the basis of all American office organization) to a suggestion for a new method of changing a typewriter ribbon under water, suitable for animation. The suggestion system holds open house every working day. And it pays off.

The second system bases on the principle of bonuses customarily paid to contractors who complete their work, above standard, under the allotted time. Production units who make a picture better and faster for less than the budget share in the savings they make.

The third system is the familiar "periodic salary review" common to enlightened business, except that in the Disney plant it is not periodic but constant: the man set to each task is recorded for his excellence in quality, quantity, and "savvy," and his status is automatically improved. "There are more jobs to be done perfectly here than there are people to do 'em perfectly, so when they do 'em perfectly they get more dough." It works.

"Why do people work here? And that means you," your correspondent said to a responsible individual in the scheme. He tousled his hair, scowled hard into his coke to aid thinking, and answered: "You know, you and I have seen some outfits that *had* it. They had *something*. The thing here is like that—you know, you can't help feeling that you're going to grab that goddam Holy Grail. That sounds terrible. I just can't express it exactly."

"Where are you going to be ten years from now?" was asked of Walt. "Going along, I guess," he replied. "Doing the same sort of thing, only I hope it won't be—and I know it will be better." Pause. "Or else," he added.

"What are you doing about the war?" was asked of a story man. "Trying to do our daily job as well as we can," he said.

> When the foreign market was cut off we stepped up production for the countries that haven't gone crazy. If the government comes along and asks us to make propaganda films, okay, we'll make propaganda films. Glad to. So far there's only one man from Washington been out here, but he was from the Army, and he wanted to see something about the cameras, or something. . . . Look, Gyo, the more I think about that question of whether the music strip for the *Fantasia* book can run across each two pages in a tint block or a half-tone screen, the less I like the screen idea. Let's see if we can't. . . .

Let's see if we can't. . . .
Let's see if we can't build a skyscraper of vitamins. Let's see if we can't have a dogfight of butterflies in the interest of peace on earth. Let's have a conference of cattails and platypuses and bright new false teeth. Let's get into an oyster and be a pearl, to dominate the diadem of the beautiful and tender Princess Caroline Elizabeth, who wears a hibiscus over one ear, and who is rescued by a prince named Gus, who is a centaur—a zebra centaur, and none of your black-and-white zebras, but an orange-and-black Princeton-Freshman zebra. Let's go play badminton in a seven-billion-dollar sound recording chamber. Let's, by all means, have a rescue—and a chase. Let's have a chase in which Stokowski chases Koussevitzky, who chases Barbirolli, who chases President Angell, who chases Einstein, who chases Mickey Mouse. Let's have a rescue in which Donald sues the Secretary of the Interior for infringement of

personality (Walt will kill this because it is too topical to be clear in Peru, and too political to be decent). Let's see if we can't turn music and science and sculpture and painting and writing upside down and shake them out and reassemble the pieces in a fashion which might make people sit still for ten minutes and giggle and weep, instead of bombing schools. If we could only get enough people to do that, multiplied by ten minutes, just think what Herb could do with his charts! The whole thing is simply a matter of production. The new plant can take it.

Let's see if we can't. . . .

2

Film Phenomena*

Walter Wanger

Hollywood is as busy as a league of nations. In the Disney Studio, the one and only Walt is carrying on with the Army, the Navy, the Department of Agriculture, the Office of Coordinator of Inter-American Affairs, the Canadian Government, etc. After all the abuse the industry has been enjoying these many years, it is nice to see the gold braid and to receive long-distance calls from Washington asking to please dream up something. And what effective dreams—the kind Lewis Mumford must have been referring to when he said: "Only the dreamers are practical men."

In the commissary at Disney's, you see sitting quietly at one table an American Naval Officer who has just returned from experiences on two carriers—now lost. But his squadrom shot down seventy Nips before the sinkings. He is an expert on naval aviation tactics and gunnery. He is working with Disney to rush through Priority Double Triple AAA films that will show our Navy fliers how to get better results. At another table is a British officer, sent here by the English Government to assist in the preparation of what should be a Disney *chef d'oeuvre—The Gremlins*. Could there be a better case to prove the difference between the Democracies and the Axis than to know that our side, in the midst of battle, can spare an officer to help glorify the Gremlins and that the British want to protect their fantasy by military assistance.*

The *Story of Corn* by Disney is another colossal achievement prepared by the experts of the Department of Agriculture. *Saludos Amigos,* the

---

* *Saturday Review of Literature*, February 6, 1943, p. 19
* Editor's note: During the war, the RAF jokingly blamed Gremlins for technical glitches. Disney's project, based on Roald Dahl's short stories, was finally abandoned. See Charles Solomon, *Enchanted Drawings: The History of Animation* (New York: Alfred A. Knopf, 1989), p. 127.

result of the Disney-Rockefeller expedition to Latin America last year, is now a wonder picture already in release among our sister Republics. Watch for it. It is really something!

Major Seversky is also in evidence on the Disney lot. He is assisting in the filming of *Victory Through Air Power,* which Disney is bringing to the screen. Little sensations like *Education for Death* and *The Fuehrer's Face* are ready for release as well. All of this and a great deal more is coming from the modernistic pastel-colored fairyland plant where thousands are creating and delivering in the interest of the new education of the free world. At this writing Disney and his staff are visiting Mexico. Guess what's coming next!

3

Mickey Icarus, 1943:
Fusing Ideas with the Art of the
Animated Cartoon*

Walter Wanger

Every once in a while a motion picture flashes across the horizon to
prove our industry an instrumentality of human enlightenment. When
such a picture is combined with the gamut of entertainment, we have a
box office success. Unless we have a picture which appeals to the greatest
volume of our people, we frequently lose the purpose for which the
production was designed.

This is true regardless of the fact that we like to place art above financial
returns.

Yet it is the number of admission tickets sold which ultimately determines the greatness of a film, for in the motion picture we have the
foremost of the three great mediums of communication—press and radio
are the others—and our aim can be defeated unless we reach and appeal
to the masses with our product.

I know that when Walt Disney decided to make the screen version of
Major Alexander P. de Seversky's best selling and controversial book,
Victory Through Air Power, he was motivated not by the promise of
financial reward but by a sincere desire to place before our people a theory
which he believed as firmly as the author. He knew that we are the most
air-minded people in the world, because after all the aeroplane is an
American creation, developed to its highest stage by American brains
and American brawn. Nevertheless, he understood that too few were
cognizant of the role that true air power must and will play in the wiping
out of our enemies. He felt, as Seversky did, that hundreds of thousands
of lives of Americans and Allied boys could be saved by the proper use
of air power. Furthermore, the making of such a picture was a challenge

* *Saturday Review of Literature*, September 4, 1943, pp. 18–19.

to his medium—a medium which I feel is the only one that could bring to the screen the powerful theme of *Victory Through Air Power*.

The real challenge, however, was not to his medium but came from minds chained to the ground and to the seven seas, who saw our enemies develop air power to the point where it blotted out cities and sent powerful battleships to the bottom of the ocean, yet who stuck to their own hidebound theories, which never comprehended the striking force of the aeroplane.

They were the minds who broke the heart but never the spirit of General Billy Mitchell. To them Homer Lea, the little hunchback military prophet who thirty-five years ago warned of Japan's perfidy and power, was just a crank.

> To free a nation from error is to enlighten the individual, and only to the degree that the individual will be receptive of truth can a nation be free from that vanity which ends with national ruin.

Lea said that in 1909, and in 1943, despite many obstacles, Disney in *Victory Through Air Power* has attempted to bring the truth of our military situation to our people in such a form that all can comprehend it.

You do not have to agree fully with Seversky to appreciate there is soundness in his logic. Millions read his book, and many disagreed with it. Disney has employed the magic of his art to put in picture form the main ideas advanced by Seversky, who from his record has a perfect right to speak as an authority. He has done this with simplicity, yet with such comprehensiveness that a nine-year-old can understand the whole outlook of the worldwide conflict.

He has resorted to new devices, and yes, without Mickey Mouse or Donald Duck, to hold the interest of an audience.

He has opened up an entirely new horizon for the future of the motion picture as a medium of enlightenment. People today are craving information. They want to know what is going on. They yearn to have a share in the direction of things. They are speaking to Washington and their voices have been heard, as Washington well knows.

They have, however, implicit faith in the men who are leading our military forces, yet they want to know that they are using every device to bring about a quick cessation of hostilities and with the minimum shedding of blood.

Victory Through Air Power vividly portrays such a device. It is a plea—like the book—for long-range air power. It calls, without kid gloves, for the creation of a separate air command, for an air force not chained to tradition and independent of long sea lines of communication.

It's a cry and a challenge for Americans to build planes that will fly from continental America directly over the heart of its main targets and loosen the tentacles of the beasts by hitting right at their hearts.

Even while *Victory Through Air Power* was in the making, such scenes as the blowing up of the Rhine Valley dams—which were filmed eight months before—were being enacted. We saw Pantelleria fall, strictly from the power of air blows. We have seen the landing of hundreds of thousands of our troops in Sicily largely because we controlled the air.

It is already prophecy coming true.

Disney has been close to this war. More than ninety percent of the facilities of his studio has been devoted—since Pearl Harbor—to the making of films for our armed services and other governmental agencies. These are pictures for the most part which never will be seen by civilian audiences. They are making pictures there which in many instances have helped cut down the training period of our boys as much as forty-five percent. These are of incalculable value in bringing through sight-and-sound fighter tactics, for instance, in which aviators who have been through the mill tell their stories to fledglings.

I have made many trips to the Disney studio since the beginning of war. If every American could visit the studio, he would have a new admiration for his country. There is nothing comparable to it in all the world. More experts, scientists, and technicians operate under Disney's roofs than in any other one organization in the universe. Out of that amazing studio come films on meteorology, on countless forms of technical instruction, on the prevention of malaria, in fact on every subject that might be, and is, useful in time of war.

All such pictures come first at Disney's. Everything is pushed aside when the Government wants a job done in a hurry. I am amazed that such an important contribution to the war effort—and it is that, even though it is an entertainment venture—as *Victory Through Air Power* could have been made there. It was a year in the filming. Seversky, who appears in the picture expounding his theories, spent more than eight months working with Disney. It was like keeping the front page of a newspaper fresh in news. New developments were incorporated from time to time, so that the picture is still front page news. Literally, millions of drawings were made, and probably 125,000 were used in the completed version.

We know that people want to be informed today, and information means education. Today, through the film, education can be carried to the entire world—to the remotest village—and a medium like Disney's which every day is turning out pictures in three and four languages—and has made them in as many as ten—is a logical means of carrying out such a mission.

It's only a short cry to the day Mickey Mouse first crept into the lives

of countless of millions the world over. Fifteen years, to be exact, I have
followed closely the Disney career. *Snow White, Fantasia, Bambi,* all
have led to the development of what Walt likes to refer to as a "medium."
Yet that medium is Disney. He enjoys tackling the provocative, and
overcoming handicaps. Twenty-seven percent of his trained personnel are
in the armed forces, yet there is ten times as much film coming out of
the studio each month now as was produced eighteen months ago. In one
month in 1943, the studio equalled the output of 1941.

Disney is doing a tremendous job. He has a youthful organization
which is tempered by the mature judgment of men who know what war
is all about. They saw the last one. There is instilled in all a desire to
get the war over—by making their own contribution as thorough as
possible.

I think this enthusiasm reflected from Walt down accounts for the
spontaneity, the vigor, the engrossing nature of *Victory Through Air
Power.*

4

The Magic Worlds of Walt Disney*

Robert De Roos

One autumn evening in 1928, a new actor appeared at the Colony Theatre in New York in a movie called *Steamboat Willie*, the first cartoon ever produced with sound.

He had ears bigger than Clark Gable's, legs like rubber hose, a grin wider than Joe E. Brown's, and a heart of gold. His name was Mickey Mouse.

Beginning that night, Mickey and his creator, Walt Disney, grabbed the world's funny bone and have never lost their grip.

The *New York Times* praised the new film as "ingenious."

"A wow!" cried the *Weekly Film Review*.

Thus was born history's most influential mouse. Mickey led the way in the development of animation as a new art, to the exploration of the world of animals and faraway people and of their adventures and geography.

Mickey Mouse has skipped from triumph to triumph—always preceded by three words in big letters: WALT DISNEY PRESENTS.

Mickey is featured in comic strips and books in fifteen languages, became the star of television's Mickey Mouse Club, and, finally, founded a magic kingdom called Disneyland.

He is Topolino in Italy, Mik-kii Ma-u-su in Japan, Ratón Mickey in Mexico, Mickey Maus in Germany, Mikki Hiiri in Finland, and just plain Mickey in scores of other lands. He is known around the world—always with approbation and love.

Mickey, a versatile fellow, has been everything from farmer and magician to great lover and fire chief. He has directed planets and comets in

* *National Geographic*, August 1963, pp. 159–207.

their courses. He has defied time, space, and gravity. But, though bound to win, he has always fought the clean fight.

True to character, "Mickey Mouse" was the designation in World War II for diagrams of convoy movements toward Normandy's D-day beaches, and Mickey rode into battles as the insigne on hundreds of ships and planes.

When King Bhumiphol of Thailand presented Walt Disney with a medal, he said quietly for Walt's ear alone: "This is an honor from my government, but more than that, it comes from me. I grew up on your cartoons."

Franklin Roosevelt demanded Mickey in the White House. Dowager Queen Mary of Britain liked to find Mickey on the bill whenever she went to the movies.

It can be said that Walter Elias Disney, the man, and Mickey, the mouse, have made a lasting impact on mankind.

Seven Hundred Awards From Around the World

Last fall, in Walt Disney's outer office at the studio in Burbank, California, I got a glimpse into the dimensions of this durable pair, thirty-five years after the mouse clicked in the fertile Disney mind.

In cases ranged along the walls, on shelves and tables, are some of the more than seven hundred awards the Disney organization has received. There are dozens of medals, citations, and plaques from appreciative governments attesting the international amity created by Disney's make-believe characters—Mickey, Donald, Goofy the dog, and all the others.

Walt once sent a proud director home with a newly won Oscar. "How did the family like it?" he asked next day.

"The kids weighed it first thing," the director said. "You might like to know an Oscar weighs six pounds, twelve ounces on our bathroom scale."

The awards from the film industry mean most to Walt. But he is proud that conservation groups have also recognized his interest in protecting wildlife. He is proudest, perhaps, of the Audubon Society Medal awarded in 1955.

Walt's office has become so crowded that recently four cabinets of awards were placed in the studio commissary. Some of the employees promptly nicknamed the commissary "the awards room."

Disney Films Used in Teaching

Although Walt constantly denies he is an educator, his nature films, which he calls True-Life Adventures, have received accolades from educators. Films like *Seal Island, In Beaver Valley,* and *The Living Desert* were pioneering achievements. Walt's early edict for them and all the True-Life Adventure pictures was to get the complete natural history of the animals with no sign of humans: no fences, car tracks, buildings, or telephone poles. This concept, plus the intimacy, the extreme close-up view of the animal, completely won the public.

The True-Life Adventures; films of the nomadic Blue Men of Morocco, Japanese fishermen, Siam, the Alaskan Eskimo, and Switzerland; Donald Duck's adventures in Mathmagic Land; the man-in-space series, with technical advice by Wernher von Braun; Disney safety films, and many others are a solid part of the curriculum for thousands of school children, not only in the US but abroad—including countries under communist control.

I first saw Walt Disney sitting at a low coffee table, wearing his usual working garb: a short-sleeved sport shirt with a woolen tie, slacks, and a sleeveless alpaca sweater.

An aerial photograph of Disneyland dominated one wall. There were photographs of his family, including his five grandchildren; the Disney coat of arms; his first Academy Award.

"That first Oscar was a special award for the creation of Mickey Mouse," he said. "The other Academy Awards belong to our group, a tribute to our combined effort. The whole thing here is the organization. And the big problem was putting the organization together.

"Look at Disneyland," he went on, waving toward the aerial photograph. "That was started because we had the talent to start it, the talents of the organization."

"What's your role?" I asked.

> You know, I was stumped one day when a little boy asked, "Do you draw Mickey Mouse?" I had to admit I do not draw any more. "Then you think up all the jokes and ideas?" "No," I said, "I don't do that." Finally, he looked at me and said, "Mr. Disney, just what do you do?"
>
> "Well," I said, "sometimes I think of myself as a little bee. I go from one area of the studio to another and gather pollen and sort of stimulate everybody." I guess that's the job I do. I certainly don't consider myself a businessman, and I never did believe I was worth anything as an artist.

Until a few years ago, Walt was president of the company, Walt Disney Productions. He resigned and was made board chairman. His older brother Roy became president. Then Walt, tired of signing things, resigned as chairman too.

Walt laughed at the memory.

> Now my only title is executive producer. I'm the boss of everything
> that's produced here. I work on story ideas and gags; I work on every
> script, writing dialogue and planning scenes. When the story is set,
> I turn it over to the boys, and they make it.
> We film twenty-five new stories for television and six feature-length
> pictures a year—and, of course, we think up ideas for the park,
> Disneyland. The corporation gets its vitality from what we create.

The corporation exhibits considerable vitality: In 1962 this magic world
showed a gross income of $74,059,000—more than twenty million dollars
from Disneyland alone—and a net of $5,263,000.

The Secret Life of Mickey Mouse

All this vitality stems from a mouse that was conceived in desperation,
gestated in secrecy, and almost died at birth.

In the fall of 1927, Walt Disney returned to Hollywood from New
York without a staff and without a star. He had gone east to negotiate a
new contract for his series *Oswald the Rabbit*. His distributor refused to
meet his price and threatened to lure his whole organization away.

"I've already signed all your animators," the distributor told Walt.

Walt and Lillian Disney, his bride of two years, had a doleful trip
across the continent. Walt needed a whole staff of animators. He also
needed a new character—fast.

The idea for Mickey Mouse was born on the train. "I've got it," Walt
told Lilly. "I'll do a series about a mouse. I'm going to call him Mortimer
Mouse."

Lilly Disney frowned. "I like the idea, but Mortimer sounds too digni-
fied for a mouse."

Walt thought a few minutes. "All right, we'll call him Mickey Mouse.
Mickey has a good, friendly sound."

In Hollywood, Walt and Roy Disney and chief animator Ub Iwerks,
now director of technical research, began work on Mickey. The defecting
animators were still at the studio finishing the *Oswald* contract, and Walt
did not want them to know he was starting a new series. So Ub Iwerks
was sequestered in a locked office, and there in four hectic weeks, he
animated an entire Mickey Mouse cartoon.

That first Mickey was entitled *Plane Crazy,* a bit of nonsense inspired
by the Lindbergh flight. To get the drawings inked and painted on celluloid
for the camera, Walt set up tables in his garage at home. There, Lillian

Disney, her sister, and Roy's wife Edna did the job. A cameraman returned to the studio at night to put the pictures on film.

When Walt took the movie to New York, distributors were not interested. They were also not interested in a second Mickey, produced while Walt was traveling.

Mickey Saved by Plinks and Toots

Mickey was close to death. But he was literally saved by the bell—bells, whistles, plinks, and toots. Sound had made its first real impact on motion pictures with the release of *The Jazz Singer* in the fall of 1927. Walt decided to try it.

He and Iwerks rigged a homemade radio with a microphone. They put up a white sheet as a screen and, with two helpers, stood at the mike behind it with noisemakers, a mouth organ, and a xylophone. For six hours, Roy projected a short bit of animation from *Steamboat Willie,* the third Mickey film. The sound makers watched the image and whanged away. It was ragged, but it convinced them that sound was for cartoons.

Walt hurried to New York with the film, and there *Steamboat Willie* was completed with sound. And it was ingenious and funny sound which transcended the mere novelty of actors singing or mouthing lines.

Sound was added to the first two Mickeys. Suddenly and dramatically, everybody wanted the talking mouse.

Walt and the mouse have come a long way since. Nothing about Walt Disney's background easily explains his success, though he began to draw at an early age.

His father, Elias Disney, was a carpenter in Chicago when Walter Elias Disney was born there in December of 1901. When Walt was four, the family—there were three older brothers and a younger sister—moved to Marceline, Missouri. Walt still recalls the horsecar ride to the railroad station.

At Marceline, one of Walt's first chores was to herd the pigs on the family farm. The Disneys were forced to sell the farm, and in 1910 moved to Kansas City, Missouri. There Walt's father bought a paper route with eight hundred customers. Roy and Walt were delivery boys. They started work at 4:30 in the morning and made their rounds on foot.

The family moved back to Chicago in 1917. Walt went to high school, attended the Academy of Fine Arts, and took correspondence courses in cartooning. He also worked at the post office sorting mail and delivering letters.

"As long as I can remember, Walt has been working," Roy Disney told me. "He worked in the daytime and he worked at night. Walt didn't play much as a boy. He still can't catch a ball with any certainty."

When Walt was sixteen, he joined an American Red Cross unit as an ambulance driver, but he did not get overseas until after the Armistice. He had eleven months in France, then went to Kansas City and set up as a commercial artist. He finally landed with the Kansas City Film Ad Company in 1920, preparing animated commercials for silent-movie houses.

Walt recalls those days. "The pull toward Hollywood became strong. Animation was big there, and if I couldn't be successful at that, I wanted to be a director or a writer."

In 1923 he went off to Hollywood with forty dollars in hand, and for two months tried to hitch on at the studios. His forty dollars disappeared.

"Before I knew it, I had my animation board out," Walt recalls. He finally got an offer for twelve cartoons—*Alice in Cartoonland*—at fifteen hundred dollars each.

"I talked my big brother Roy into going in with me," Walt told me. "I couldn't get a job, so I went into business for myself."

Business was good. *Alice* was followed by the successful *Oswald the Rabbit* series. Then came Mickey.

"The mouse gave us an opportunity to improve the cartoon medium," Walt says. Experiment and expansion began in 1929 with the first *Silly Symphony,* in which music played a key role.

Walt worked at the studio all day and every night. Only in recent years has he mastered the compulsion to work *all* the time. "I still take scripts home," he told me, "but I don't read them at night. It's a temptation to peek, but I wait until morning. I used to read at night and then worry until morning. I used to be tied up all night, but no more."

Donald Duck Becomes a Star

Walt's next enthusiasm was Technicolor's new three-color process for film. A *Silly Symphony, Flowers and Trees,* was already fully photographed in black and white. Walt decided to remake it in Technicolor. It was a gamble, since Technicolor was extraordinarily expensive.

The picture was made in color and caused a revolution in the animated-cartoon industry. In 1932 it became the first cartoon to win an Oscar. Some of Walt's funniest pictures were *Silly Symphonies*—notably *The Three Little Pigs* and *The Tortoise and the Hare.*

In 1934 Donald Duck made his first sputtering appearance in *The Wise Little Hen.* That egregious fellow became an immediate hit—and now has surpassed Mickey as the star of the stable.

"We're restricted with the mouse," Walt told me. "He's become a little idol. The duck can blow his top and commit mayhem, but if I do anything like that with the mouse, I get letters from all over the world. 'Mickey wouldn't act like that,' they say."

Scenes Gain Depth and Motion

As the pictures were ground out, the art of animation progressed. Characters were being drawn in the round and in perspective, as contrasted with the first flat figures. But Walt was never satisfied.

"I knew that locomotion was the key," he told me.

> We had to learn to draw motion. Look, pull your hand across your face and you'll see what I mean. You don't see a single hand; it's sort of stretched and blurred. We had to learn the way a graceful girl walks, how her dress moves, what happens when a mouse stops or starts running.

Disney set up an elaborate school for his artists. "It was costly, but I had to have the men ready for things we would eventually do."

What "we would eventually do" was *Snow White and the Seven Dwarfs,* the first feature-length cartoon. When word of this project got around Hollywood, many movie people said Disney was making his biggest mistake.

"They were thinking of the shorts—thought we were just going to string some together," Walt said. "But we had a story to tell. They couldn't get that through their heads."

While his artists were training, Walt had technicians working on a new kind of camera he planned to use for *Snow White*. He was no longer satisfied with just round figures; now he wanted the illusion of depth. To achieve this, he developed the radically different "multiplane" camera—and won an Academy Award for it.

In photographing animated films, three separate drawings are usually involved, each done on a sheet of transparent celluloid. One shows the foreground, one the animated figures, and the last the background. Before the multiplane camera, the three celluloids were simply stacked together and the camera shot through them all, giving a flat image. With the multiplane, more than three celluloids could be used, and they could be placed in different planes, sometimes as much as three feet apart. The camera could focus in and out among these planes to give an astonishing effect of depth and motion.

Snow White brought up a new problem. "We had to learn how to put personality into the characters," Walt told me. "Up to *Snow White*, we'd just had stock characters."

A Disney artist enlarged on the theme. "Remember in *Snow White* when the dwarfs had the pillow fight and Dopey ended up with a single feather?" he asked. "Remember how he fluffed it out and lay down with it under his head? It *was* funny, but more, it was Walt's way of expressing what kind of character Dopey is, and creating audience sympathy for him."

Snow White cost one and a half million dollars, and the bankers became restive before it was completed. Walt reluctantly had to show a man from the bank the unfinished product to try to retain their confidence.

"We needed a quarter of a million dollars to finish the picture, so you can guess how I felt.

"He sat there and didn't say a word," Walt told me.

> Finally the picture was over and he walked to his car, with me following him like a puppy dog. Then he said, "Well, so long. You'll make a pot of money on that picture." So we got the money.

Snow White and the Seven Dwarfs went on to make theatrical history and brought many honors to Disney. In 1938 Yale gave him an honorary Master of Arts. In presenting him as a candidate for the degree, Professor William Lyon Phelps said:

> One touch of nature makes the whole world kin, and Walter Disney has changed millions of people in every part of the earth. . . . He has endeared America to the hearts of foreigners.

That same year brought honorary degrees from Harvard and the University of Southern California. (In 1960 Walt received an honorary diploma from the Marceline, Missouri, high school, which was pleasant, since he had never finished high school.)

After *Snow White* came other feature-length cartoons: *Pinocchio, Fantasia,* and *Bambi. Fantasia,* released in 1940, started out to be a kind of super *Silly Symphony* for Mickey Mouse, with Leopold Stokowski directing a full orchestra in *The Sorcerer's Apprentice.* Walt built it into something more, a brilliant combination of animation and fine music—from Beethoven's *Pastoral Symphony* to Stravinsky's *Rite of Spring. Fantasia* introduced stereophonic sound fifteen years before it was generally used in motion pictures.

"Bambi" Points Way to Nature Films

Bambi was the fictionalized story of a deer, and the animal studies it involved made it the forerunner of one of Disney's most important contributions: the True-Life Adventure films, about live animals in nature.

"One thing always leads to another around here," Walt told me. "In *Snow White,* we had cute little animals, more on the fantasy side. In *Bambi* we had to get closer to nature. So we had to train our artists in animal locomotion and anatomy."

Walt introduced live animals into the studio, deer and rabbits and skunks. "But they were no good," he says. "They were just pets. So we sent the artists out to zoos, and all we got were animals in captivity. Finally, I sent out some naturalist cameramen to photograph the animals in their natural environment.

"We captured a lot of interesting things and I said 'Gee, if we really give these boys a chance, I might get something unique!' "

But the war intervened: Walt Disney Productions became virtually a war plant for the duration. Disney training films for the Army and Navy, pictures for bond drives, and similar projects made an important contribution to our war effort.

As one of his first postwar projects, Walt sent Alfred Milotte and his wife Elma to Alaska. They sent back miles of film. In the footage—or mileage—Walt stumbled on one of the great stories of nature: the saga of the fur seals coming up from the sea to crowded island beaches in the Pribilofs, there to calve and mate.

The Milottes caught the cruel and mysterious reality of the fur seal— the courting and mating, the fury of the bulls defending their harems against bachelor seals, with babies being trampled and crushed in the turmoil. And, in the end, the eerie disappearance of the herds into the sea.

The picture was *Seal Island.* It won an Oscar as 1948's best two-reel subject.

This success was followed by another, *In Beaver Valley.* Walt will go to the *n*th degree to get perfection, and for this film he kept cameraman naturalist Milotte in the wilds for more than a year, studying the beaver's life habits as he photographed. Out of Milotte's footage came the story of a talented, fascinating animal.

The True-Life Adventure pictures used techniques learned in cartoons.

"Any time we saw an animal doing something with style or personality—say a bear scratching its back—we were quick to capitalize on it," says a Disney writer. "Or otters sliding down a riverbank—humorous details to build personality.

> This anthropomorphism is resented by some people—they say we are putting people into animal suits. But we've always tried to stay within the framework of the real scene. Bears *do* scratch their backs and otters *are* playful.

Old Indian Trick Still Works

The cameramen spent months in primitive areas, in African heat, in Alaskan blizzards, in South American jungles. A film by Murl Deusing for a National Geographic Society lecture formed the basis of many important sequences in *Nature's Half Acre,* and many of the society's lecturers over the years have contributed footage to Disney nature films.

Disney's cameramen naturalists worked with telescopic lenses, zoom lenses, time-lapse cameras, and underwater cameras; from behind elaborate blinds, high in the treetops, and from fixed platforms.

Tom McHugh, photographing a buffalo herd for *The Vanishing Prairie,* found he could not get close enough, even with a telescopic lens. Then he remembered an Indian trick. He covered himself with a buffalo skin and sneaked in for close-ups.

James Algar, the writer and director of *The Vanishing Prairie,* recalls being surrounded by the torrential rush of buffalo.

> I'd always heard of the thundering herd, and the herd thundered all right. But what I had never heard of was the sibilant, silken swish which accompanies the stampeding buffalo. It was even more terrifying than the thunder.

Alfred and Elma Milotte spent almost three years in Africa photographing *The African Lion.* One of their notable sequences shows a rhinoceros bogged in a water hole, helpless and raging. The exertions and grunts of the doomed rhino attracted an audience of jungle creatures. Birds added their raucous cries. Antelope watched. An elephant surveyed the scene, panicked, and ran away. A baboon sat on the bank thoughtfully, as though trying to contrive some plan that would be of help.

Enraged Rhino Charges Benefactors

In the film the rhino was left to die. Actually, the Milottes decided to rescue him. Dodging the desperate animal, they got a stout rope under his head and rump, tied the line to a truck, and pulled him free.

The rhino was ungrateful. Once on dry land, he charged the truck, and they barely managed to get away.

The Milottes brought back much distinguished footage. They recorded a leopard lurking in a thorn tree above a herd of wildebeests, showed him drop on a calf and drag it back into the tree for his meal. They also filmed the kill of an antelope by a lion.

Other outstanding film records were produced by Disney's naturalist photographers: a bobcat in hot pursuit of a marten; the private lives, births, mating, and the search for food of the pine squirrel, golden eagle, raccoon, and crow; a goshawk striking a flying squirrel in mid-air.

They also recorded a goshawk slamming into photographer Paul Kenworthy's shoulder as he worked high in a tree to film close-ups of its young.

As the technique improved, the photographers worked in compounds—sometimes as big as fifty acres. "It was a short cut," a writer told me. "We're not faking nature. We gave the animals the opportunity to appear before the camera.

Take the spectacular shot of the screaming bobcat scrambling to the top of a saguaro in *The Living Desert.* It may have been taken in a compound—but it wasn't faked. The cat streaked up that cactus because he was frightened by wild pigs.

When we followed the animals underground, we of course expose their tunnels. In *Perri,* the squirrel goes underground. We spend days conditioning her to the bright lights needed for color photography. Then, when we came to shoot, she didn't pay any attention to us. We wondered if she had needed conditioning at all.

"Our naturalist photographers probably wound up knowing as much about animals they photographed as anyone around—including the scientists," Walt said. "I don't think there's an animal on the North American continent we don't have coverage on."

Merely documenting the lives of wild creatures was not enough. The cameramen's footage contained drama, but it took the dramatist's hand to make it coherent.

A fascinating fragment of one of Walt Disney's critiques taken down during a screening of *The Living Desert* survives and shows him at work:

In sequence where tortoises are courting, Walt said: They look like knights in armor, old knights in battle. Give the audience a music cue, a tongue-in-cheek fanfare. The winner will claim his lady fair.
. . .

"*Pepsis* wasp and tarantula sequence: Our heavy is the tarantula. Odd that the wasp is decreed by nature to conquer the tarantula. When her time comes to lay eggs, she must go out and find a tarantula. Not strength, but skill helps her beat Mr. Tarantula. . . .

Then the hawk and the snake. Our other heavy is the snake. . . . With wasp and tarantula it's a ballet—or more like a couple of wrestlers. The hawk should follow. Tarantula gets his and then Mr. Snake gets his. . . . *Pepsis* wasp doesn't use brute strength, but science and skill. Should be ballet music. Hawk uses force and violence. One could follow the other and have a different musical theme as contrast.

Nature Documentaries with a Plot

Walt has an amazing capacity to dramatize his work. When he is in a story conference, he takes the parts himself. Before *Snow White* he gave a four-hour performance of the entire picture, taking all the parts from Snow White to the smallest rabbit.

"That one performance lasted us three years," an animator told me. "Whenever we'd get stuck, we'd remember how Walt did it on that night."

Next Walt Disney laid plans for a new kind of animal picture. "We decided to combine nature's truth with fiction," Walt told me. "We would use the documentary material straight from nature, but give it a plot."

Perri, the story of a squirrel, by Felix Salten, who also wrote *Bambi,* was the first of these. Naturalist photographers spent three and a half years in the Uinta Mountains of Utah, filming the life cycle of every animal in the cast. They sent back more than two hundred miles of film!

"Just viewing their films took weeks," Winston Hibler, the coproducer, told me. "Then it took painstaking editing to fit the film to the story. And by adding music and animation, we produced a paradox—a true-life fantasy."

Perri was followed by a continuing series of similar pictures that tell stories about animals in relation to man.

"The animals have names and we kind of pull for them," a writer told me.

> Stories are believable as long as the audience knows the things actually happened. We have to contrive to get the animals to do what the plot calls for without their appearing to be trained animals. But we aren't asking them to talk.
>
> In *The Legend of Lobo,* for example, the script called for the main character, the wolf, to walk a narrow log spanning a deep chasm. This was achieved by training the wolf, first to walk across a log near the ground, then to continue to cross the log as it was raised higher and higher.
>
> When the picture was shot, the wolf actually crossed a log about seventy-five feet long spanning a chasm several hundred feet deep.

From animal pictures Walt Disney has gone on to live-action pictures about people on an astounding variety of subjects.

Disney stuck to timeless pictures at first: *Treasure Island, Robin Hood,* and *Davy Crockett*—films which can be released many times. "Then I got to thinking, when it comes to making comedy, we're the ones; so we did *The Shaggy Dog*. So far it's been seen by fifty-five million people." The live-action comedies closely follow the Disney cartoon techniques. "We've always made things fly and defy gravity," Walt told me. "Now we've just gone on to flying flivvers, floating football players, and bouncing basketball players."

The geographic scope and variety of the Disney activities are awesome. Besides a company in the Burbank studio filming a new movie called *Summer Magic,* Walt had camera crews in Florida, Yellowstone Park, and New England, a complete production unit in Canada for *The Incredible Journey,* a production unit in Majorca and another in Vienna, a feature cartoon in the works, plus four television cartoons, and a Western being shot at the studio ranch.

I had been told that Walt makes all major decisions on all his pictures, and I wondered how he kept track of things.

I found out when I sat in with him as the "dailies"—excerpts from various pictures—were projected. About fifteen of the staff—musicians, directors, song writers, producers, and writers—came in.

We listened to Burl Ives sing "The Ugly Bug Ball" a dozen times as the camera covered him from different angles. Sad Sam, the original shaggy dog, appeared on the screen with a caterpillar on his nose. We saw a scene from a Western played over and over from different points of view. The dogs in *The Incredible Journey* went through their paces.

Disney himself, in full color, flashed on the screen in a lead-in for his television program, *The Wonderful World of Color*. He began suavely and then blew his lines.

"I'm not only getting wrinkles," he said from the back of the room, "I'm losing my eyesight, too." He told a cameraman, "Don't use that diffusion on me. I look out of focus. Let the wrinkles show."

We were in the projection room two hours. This, I learned, was how Disney keeps on top of his many projects. His men send their product to be appraised. A shipment of film from Europe arrives every Tuesday. Walt also makes frequent trips to Europe and flies key personnel to the studio for conferences. He is not a memo-writing man.

"After we tie down the shooting script, it's up the boys to make the pictures," Disney told me.

> If they run into trouble, I always tell them, "If you bring me a problem, have a solution." Lots of times, their solution is the answer and it's just a matter of saying OK.

Magazine a Friend to Researchers

On one of my first trips around the studio, I saw the *National Geographic* almost everywhere I went: in the animators' offices, in the machine shop, on writers' desks. I saw it in the wardrobe department, where it's used in designing the correct clothing for various countries, and in the staff shop at Disneyland, where the realistic animals are cast for Adventureland.

"Looks like I planted them," Walt said, but we really use the *Geographic*. We couldn't be in business without it."

When I dropped into the library to inquire about the meticulous research that backs up every Disney picture, Koneta Roxby, the chief of research, told me: "The *Geographic* is one of our basic research sources. We use it almost every day.

"We certainly used it when Disneyland was being built," she went on. "This library was a madhouse. There would be ten or fifteen people waiting in line for research materials and, of course, the phone rang every minute."

Disneyland really started more than twenty years ago, when Walt got the idea for an amusement park that grown-ups as well as children would enjoy.

"I had all my drawing things laid out at home, and I'd work on plans for the park, as a hobby, at night."

At the time, amusement parks were dying all over the country. "I talked Disneyland, but no one could see it," Walt recalled. "So I went ahead and spent my own money."

In 1954, for the site of his kingdom, Walt bought 244 acres of land— mostly orange groves—225 miles from Los Angeles, near Anaheim, California. "I wanted flat land that I could shape," he said.

He surrounded the entire park with a high earth embankment. "I don't want the public to see the real world they live in while they're in the park. I want them to feel they are in another world."

When the preliminary plans for the park were completed, the cost estimate was $4,700,000, but Joe Fowler, who is in charge of Disneyland, says, "That was only a guess." The overall cost to date is approximately forty-four million dollars!

Disneyland: the Geography of Imagination

At the Disneyland opening, in July, 1955, a year after the first orange tree was uprooted, Walt said, "Disneyland will never be completed. It will grow as long as there is imagination left in the world." It seemed, at the time, a pleasant sentiment, but few took it literally. Walt did, and that is why Disneyland remains unique; he is forever enlarging it. Now he is building an old New Orleans Square, complete with a bayou boat ride.

Disneyland, on a fall day, is full of warmth and zest. I paid my respects to the giant portrait of Mickey Mouse, in living flowers, that adorns the slanting earth embankment at the park's main entrance.

I stepped into the Town Square—and right into Walt Disney's childhood: the square with its redbrick Victorian elegances is a distillation of Walt's early memories of Chicago and Marceline and Kansas City shortly after the turn of the century.

A gaily cockaded band was tootling. A horsecar rolled along, the horse's rubber shoes making muffled thumps; a double-decked bus stood at the curb; and a balloon seller, hidden behind a great cluster of his wares, looked like a gigantic chrysanthemum. Over a loudspeaker from the Santa Fe and Disneyland Railroad station came the measured voice of the train announcer:

" . . . now leaving for Adventureland, Frontierland, Fantasyland, and Tomorrowland—all aboarrrd!"

Main Street, USA, sets the tone and pace of Disneyland: It is a place for strolling. People stop to peer into the windows of the apothecary shop and the old-time general store, and to look over the shoulder of a sidewalk artist as he sketches a portrait. Most of the visitors are grown-ups. As the park statistics prove, adult guests outnumber children three and a half to one.

Visitors Fooled by Live Swans

At the end of Main Street, faraway jungle noises made me turn to the left and enter Adventureland.

I took the jungle river cruise aboard the sturdy river boar *Ganges Gal*, which chugged past menacing crocodiles, a ruined temple, and a group of bathing elephants. Gorillas and a tremendous African elephant roared from the tropical vegetation which choked the banks of the stream.

There was some discussion among the passengers about the animals. Were they real? (They were, of course, animated.) But in Disneyland, it is sometimes hard to know where fantasy ends and reality begins. A little later, I watched a pair of ladies peer intently at the live swans sailing on the moat of Sleeping Beauty Castle.

"They are not real," one lady finally said with authority.

I met Bill Evans and Ray Miller, landscape architects for the park, and complimented them on the effects they have created along the jungle stream. They have made Disneyland a must for visiting horticulturists. The park has close to seven hundred species of plants. It takes at least thirty gardeners to keep them in trim.

We wandered to the base of the Swiss Family Tree House, which opened last fall. I asked what kind of tree it was.

"It was modeled after the banyan tree, *Ficus benghalensis*," said Ray

Miller, "but we call it *Disneyodendron eximius,* which means an out-of-the-ordinary Disney tree."

The seventy-foot tree is a copy of the Swiss Family Robinson's tropic domicile, complete with furniture salvaged from their ship.

I took a short cut through Frontierland just in time to be caught in the middle of a running gun fight between a rootin'-tootin' sheriff and a Western bad man. Happily, they were using blank cartridges, or the slaughter would have been awesome.

The *Mark Twain,* the stately white river packet, was just leaving her dock for a cruise on the Rivers of America. Across the water, I saw some energetic boys romping on Tom Sawyer Island, while others helped Indians paddle war canoes or rode the high-sided keel boats, the ones used in Disney's *Davy Crockett* movie and television series.

In Fantasyland I found myself face to face with larger-than-life-size impersonations of famous Disney characters: the Big Bad Wolf, one of the Three Little Pigs, Minnie Mouse. The Mad Hatter, his rubber jowls quivering, was trapped in a corner. He was having a hard time defending himself against a mob of children.

The Most Marvelous Submarine

In Tomorrowland, I boarded the submarine *Skipjack,* one of eight submersibles in the Disney fleet. It took me on one of the incredible journeys of the world, though it was made in a mere six million gallons of water rather than an ocean.

The sub "went under" in a swirl of bubbles and sailed serenely (guided by sonar, the skipper said) through treacherous coral reefs ablaze with animated tropical fish. Giant turtles dined on sea grass. Barracudas, sharks, and a dangerous moray eel loomed from the shadows. In a plunge to the abyss, we saw phosphorescent creatures of the deep.

We passed through the hull of a sunken ship and glimpsed chests filled with gleaming treasure. And, as the skipper explained that we could not expect to see mermaids since they were only figments of imagination, we nosed impolitely into a mermaids' boudoir.

The sub visited the lost continent of Atlantis, went under the polar ice cap, and finally passed what may be the largest sea serpent in the world. Certainly the largest *cross-eyed* sea serpent.

When I talked with Joe Fowler, the retired admiral who is vice president for Disneyland operations, he said his former Navy colleagues are delighted with the submarines. One, a sub skipper, said, "That's the only time I've ever been on a sub and could see where I was going."

"We were apprehensive that some guests might suffer from claustrophobia in the subs," Fowler told me. "But in my Navy experience, I had learned that few people suffer from claustrophobia if you have moving air and something to see. That's why there's an air jet in front of every porthole."

How to Build a Mountain

Fowler has one besetting problem: "Almost everything we undertake in the park has never been done before," he told me.

He cited the Matterhorn as an example. The 146-foot-high mountain, which is one hundredth the height of the real Matterhorn, contains five hundred tons of structural steel, and almost no two pieces are the same length, size, or weight.

The Disney Matterhorn is a close copy of the real mountain. Disney designers studied hundreds of pictures of the rugged peak, pictures taken during the filming of *Third Man on the Mountain*. Like the original, it also has its mountain climbers, athletes in alpine attire who scale and rappel it eight times daily.

Whereas the real Matterhorn is extremely solid, the Disneyland version is hollow and houses an exciting bobsled ride.

I rode one of the bobsleds and was lifted high inside the mountain. Then my bobsled dipped over a sharp edge and I was on my own— moving around curves, through icy grottos, past waterfalls, and under the Skyway's ski-lift buckets, which take visitors through the mountain for a view of the ice caves. Finally my bobsled dashed into a tumbling mountain stream, which braked it, and the ride was over.

One of the greatest attractions is the Disneyland-Alweg Monorail System which loops in and out of the park. Disney and Alweg engineers collaborated in the design, and the trains were built at the Disney studio. The monorail is the first of its type—a "piggy-back" design in which the cars are locked to the track.

I rode the monorail from the Disney Hotel to the park several times. A uniformed girl handed me aboard the long silver train. It started gently, smoothly. We glided over the magic kingdom at twenty miles an hour, silently surveying the wonders below like some satellite from space. Most passengers, myself included, leave the monorail convinced it is the answer for rapid transit of the future.

I wandered backstage at Disneyland to visit Bud Washo, the head of the staff shop. There I got a glimpse of the Disney future, though its subject matter in this case was the dim past.

At WED Enterprises in Glendale, where all the design work for Disneyland is done, I had watched Blaine Gibson modeling a series of small-scale dinosaurs, cave men, and other prehistoric creatures. Now Bud Washo took me into a barnlike room where Gibson's dinosaurs were being re-created—life-sized. An enraged Tyrannosaurus rex with a two-foot mouthful of six-inch teeth is something to stand beside—even if it is just clay.

Once the clay figures are completed, plaster molds are made, and then the carefully detailed skin is cast from 3/8-inch Duraflex, which Washo described as a "hot-melt vinyl reformulated for strength."

"Hardly anything affects it," Washo said. "It can take weather, most oils, or gases. It's enormously flexible and durable."

When the casts are finished, the figures are trucked carefully to the studio machine shop, where their animation machinery is installed.

Dinosaurs Will Go to World's Fair

I pointed to a sail-backed dinosaur which was being fitted into its skin and asked: "What will that one do?"

"It will be able to swish its tail from side to side, open its mouth, flex up and down like a lizard, and the sail will sway," Washo said matter-of-factly.

"Where will the dinosaurs and cave men be used?" I asked.

"They're for the Ford Motor exhibit at the 1964 World's Fair in New York," Bud said.

Plastic Birds Come to Life

One day after lunch, Walt grabbed my arm. "Come on," he said. "I want to show you something."

We walked in the bright sunshine between the stages on the movie studio lot and turned into the machine shop. Four elephants without skins sat in a row, gravely nodding their heads. On a bench lay what looked very much like a human hand, closing and opening silently. Farther down, a prehistoric man waved his arm; someone had incongruously placed a handkerchief in his hand.

On the machinists' benches stood a variety of plastic birds, opening and closing their beaks, turning their heads, and flipping their tails.

Walt stopped to talk to a machinist. I looked at one of the birds. Without its feathers, the creature was a mass of wiring and air tubes. As I watched, this unearthly bird puffed out its chest and began to sing.

A machinist told me that every bird contains five air lines and four sets of wires, plus a tiny loudspeaker.

"This is the latest thing we've done with Audio-Animatronics," Walt said. "We are using the new types of valves and controls developed for rockets. That way we can get extremely subtle motions."

"About that word," I said, "Audio-Animatronics."

"It's just animation with sound, run by electronics," he smiled. "Audio-Animatronics. It's an extension of animated drawings."

> We take an inanimate object and make it move. Everything is programmed on tape: the birds' movement, lighting effects, and sounds. We turn on the tape and the birds do their stuff. At the end, the tape automatically rewinds itself and starts all over again. With tape we could present a program of an hour and six minutes without repeating anything.

"Is anyone else doing this kind of thing?"
"I don't know anyone crazy enough," Walt laughed.

Disney Birds Sing Popular Songs

Several weeks later, Walt invited me to the studio for a showing of the completed mock-up for the Enchanted Tiki Room, scheduled to open in the park this summer.

Now all the birds had been bedecked in colorful feathers, and were individually lighted. Four macaws opened the show with a line of chatter and then swung into a lively calypso number followed by Offenbach's *Barcarole*. A fountain jetted in time to the music under colored lights.

The fountain sent up a particularly high jet and, as it fell back into the bowl, a Bird-Mobile slowly descended from the ceiling, bearing yellow and white cockatoos. They broke loose with "Let's All Sing Like the Birdies Sing," and brought down the house.

There was much more: songs sung by orchids and bird-of-paradise flowers; a rain storm; chants by tikis—carvings representing various native gods—accompanied by animated drummers. It is a tremendous show—the climax of more than two years' work at a cost of approximately a million dollars.

Abraham Lincoln Comes to Life

I went out into the street again with Walt and Wathel Rogers, who supervised the Enchanted Tiki Room. We entered another building and I got a shock; I almost bumped smack into Abraham Lincoln!

The illusion was alarming. The tall, lonely man sits in a chair much as in the Lincoln Memorial in Washington, DC. But this is no cold stone figure; this Lincoln is man-size—and so realistic it seems made of flesh and blood.

Wathel Rogers made adjustments at an electronic console, and Lincoln's eyes ranged the room. His tongue moved as if to moisten his lips and he cleared his throat. Then with a slight frown, he clasped the arm of his chair, stood up, and began to talk in measured tones.

"What constitutes the bulwark of our own liberty and independence?" he asked.

And then he answered: "Our reliance is in the love of liberty which God has planted in us. . . ."

To get an idea of the tremendous animation job this is, try it yourself. Sit in an armchair and pull yourself to your feet, observing how many muscles are called into play and the subtle balance required.

The Lincoln skin is the same Duraflex that has worked so well on the other Audio-Animatronic figures.

"Duraflex has a consistency much like human skin," Rogers said. "It flexes as well as compresses. Rubber, for example, will flex, but won't compress correctly for our needs."

Rogers described the mechanics: sixteen air lines to the Lincoln head, ten air lines to the hands and wrists, fourteen hydraulic lines to control the body, and two pairs of wires for every line.

Rogers ran the Lincoln face through some of its fifteen expressions. Lincoln smiled at me (first on one side of his face, then the other). He raised each eyebrow quizzically, one at a time, then, fixing me with a glance, frowned and chilled my marrow. And just to show he wasn't really angry, he ended by giving me a genial wink.

"Lincoln is part of a Disneyland project called *One Nation Under God*," Wathel Rogers explained.

> It will start with a Circarama presentation of great moments in constitutional crises.
>
> Circarama is a special motion picture technique Walt developed for Disneyland and the Brussels World's Fair. The Bell Telephone Circarama now at Disneyland tells the story of the great sights of America. It has a 360-degree screen. The audience is surrounded by the continuous action, as if they were moving with the camera and able to see in all directions.
>
> The Circarama for the *One Nation Under God* showing will have a two hundred-degree screen. After the Circarama showing, a curtain will close, then open again to reveal the Hall of Presidents. The visitor will see all the chief executives modeled life-size. He'll think it's a waxworks—until Lincoln stands up and begins to talk.

Audio-Animatronic figures are now being planned for Disneyland's French Quarter square in old New Orleans. They will also add chilling realism to the Haunted Mansion now under construction in Frontierland. (Visitors who ask about the mansion are told, "Walt's out capturing ghosts for it now.")

Never Do the Same Thing Twice

What next? Walt enjoys the past but he lives for the future.

"The fun is in always building something," he told me. "After it's built, you play with it a little and then you're through. You see, we never do the same thing twice around here. We're always opening up new doors."

I asked him a doleful question, "What happens when there is no more Walt Disney?"

"I think about that," he said. "Every day I'm throwing more responsibility to other men. Every day I'm trying to organize them more strongly.

"But I'll probably outlive them all," he grinned. "I'm sixty-one. I've got everything I started out with except my tonsils, and that's above average. I plan to be around for a while."

National Production

5

Disney's Business History: A Reinterpretation

Douglas Gomery

As we begin the 1990s no media enterprise seems more successful than the Walt Disney Company.[1] Through the 1980s Disney, with its ever increasing profits, has been held up as a quintessential American business success story; no Japanese takeover here. Its theme parks—in Florida, California, France, and Japan—attract millions of visitors per year; revenues from film, TV, and consumer products contribute millions more to the bottom line. Disney's current corporate leaders, Michael Eisner and Frank Wells, have come to represent two of America's most successful executives, with their faces regularly splashed across magazine covers from *Time* to *Parade*.

It seems as if this dynamic Disney enterprise has been with us forever, always a paradigm of corporate success. Based on the fertile imagination of Walt Disney, the company has proffered quality entertainment, we are told, to generation after generation. Profits and power seem to have always been the name of the game for Disney.

Closer examination reveals that the Disney company has had a rocky corporate history. The corporate balance sheets have not always been positive. Why? By analyzing the history of Disney as a business, we shall see that this heralded company, like all others, has had its ups and downs, and has never been able to buffer itself from the realities of technical change, the vagaries of the business cycle, and the wrenching effects of war.

An Initial Golden Age, 1922–1946

From its founding (as Laugh-O-Gram Films) through the close of World War II, the Disney corporate enterprise grew from a marginal operation to a successful niche company, specializing in one phase of movie-making, animation. At the beginning, Walt and brother Roy Disney, in Kansas City, were just two of many movie entrepreneurs trying to make it in an industry then beginning to consolidate around eight major studios. By 1946 the Disney brothers had fashioned a moderately successful, yet still marginal Hollywood company.

The Disney operation struggled to find an appropriate business niche. At first Disney only proved that there simply was no great market for short, animated, advertising films or local newsreels. In time the Disney brothers moved to Hollywood, enabling their fledgling company to participate in a national market rather than a smaller regional one. But it took a fundamental technical change—the coming of sound—to prevent the Disney company from going under.

Disney needed a base on which to build its innovation of sound; it needed distribution agreements with powerful studio patrons—first through Columbia Pictures (1929 to 1931), then United Artists (1931 to 1936), and then RKO (1936 to 1954)—to fully exploit marketing leverage. Without these corporate sponsors to distribute its products around the world, the Disney company surely would have gone the way of any number of now-long-forgotten, marginal, Hollywood companies.

Indeed, the success of the Disney enterprise can be precisely measured as it moved up the ranks from an alliance with a small studio (Columbia) to a more powerfully connected one (United Artists) to a member of the "Big Five" (RKO). Only with RKO was the Disney company able to take advantage of the power associated with a fully integrated (production, distribution, and exhibition) major studio.

Corporate success began, at a moderate level, in 1931 with Disney's linkage to United Artists. Disney produced about twenty-five cartoons per annum—roughly half under the Mickey Mouse banner and the rest under the "Silly Symphony" name. The Disney company operated under razor-thin profit margins, but was able to make a go of it because United Artists could book the short subjects in the best theatres around the world. But in 1936 Disney moved from United Artists to RKO.[2] With RKO's network of first-run movie theatres from New York to Los Angeles, the Disney company was for the first time fully able to milk revenues from short subject hits. It is no wonder that Disney quickly moved to make its first animated feature, *Snow White and the Seven Dwarfs*. Then success came. *Snow White and the Seven Dwarfs* was the biggest hit of 1938, and for a brief time stood as the highest-grossing feature film in Hollywood history. RKO enabled Disney to reach its initial Golden Age.

Walt and Roy Disney recognized that to keep their partner happy they must offer something unique. Disney accomplished this through product differentiation—first with innovative use of sound and then with the celebrated handling of Technicolor. With the coming of sound the Disney company created its first star, Mickey Mouse. With *Flowers and Trees,* an entry in the *Silly Symphony* series, Disney won the first Oscar ever given for animated short subject because of its skilled use of Technicolor. The Technicolor company would have preferred to ally itself with a larger studio, but Disney proved an ideal partner. This tiny niche company had the flexibility to test the then-new three-strip Technicolor process.

Yet the 1930s were lean times. For example, despite an exclusive three-year agreement, from 1932 to 1935, United Artist' executives thought so little of Disney's experiments that they refused to advance any money. So the Disney brothers picked up additional monies by which to finance motion pictures by merchandising their characters. In February 1930 Roy Disney signed the initial contract for merchandising, granting the George Borgfeldt Company the right to manufacture and sell items embodying Minnie and Mickey Mouse. The Disney company received a two-and-a-half percent royalty on items selling for fifty cents or less, and a five percent royalty for more expensive products. Borgfeldt, in turn, initially sublicensed the images for handkerchiefs first set out for sale during the Christmas 1930 selling season.

By the depths of the Great Depression the Disney company was generating hundreds of thousands of dollars per year. General Foods, International Silver, and Ingersoll Watches paid Disney royalties. Lionel trains claimed it sold two hundred thousand wind-up hand cars simply because it attached Mickey and Minnie Mouse figures. "Who's Afraid of the Big Bad Wolf?" became a hit song in 1933, boosted by the attendant Oscar-winning cartoon.

With this initial success the Disney company set up a division of corporate management that would last thirty more years. Walt Disney produced; indeed he stopped drawing altogether and managed studio output. Roy Disney handled the finances and other "mundane" details, freeing Walt to "be creative." It was Roy Disney, for example, who insisted that United Artists hand over future TV rights in 1936; and it was Roy Disney who then skillfully took the Disney company into the protective arms of RKO.

It should be recognized that in the 1930s mere survival did not mean vast earning power. The celebrated Disney studio rarely earned profits of more than five hundred thousand dollars per annum. And Walt insisted on spending all of that on current product, including his noted indulgence, *Fantasia.* Thus, in 1941, as the US was preparing to enter World War II, the Disney company teetered on the edge of corporate extinction. The company had poured too much money into *Pinocchio* and *Fantasia,* boosted by the unexpected financial success of *Snow White and the Seven Dwarfs*. Through 1941 and 1942 the Disney company lost a total of one million dollars.

Additional pressures—including moving to a new studio lot, still in use, in Burbank—provoked a bitter strike in 1941. Walt Disney felt he was giving his one thousand employees an opportunity not available elsewhere in Hollywood; they felt they were not being given full credit, either in terms of publicity or money. These generally young animators (average age 27) wanted to share immediately rather than simply plow all profits into Walt's latest vision. The American Federation of Labor had made Disney a target of a unionization drive, as the lone Hollywood studio without union coverage.

The result of that 1941 strike, settled after several bitter months, named the Screen Cartoonists Guild as the official negotiator for studio employees. *Bambi* was delayed by three months; the studio shut down completely for a time; union activists quit. World War II saved Disney. The Federal government needed an ambassador of goodwill, and Disney offered a name beloved everywhere. Few allies (and enemies) did not embrace Mickey Mouse as Michel Souris (in France), Topolino (in Italy), Miki Kuchi (in Japan), and Miguel Ratoncito (in Spain). It was estimated that one in three inhabitants of the planet had seen a Disney film.

The US government awarded Disney filmmaking contracts and authorized valuable access to chemicals to make movie film. From 1942 through 1946 the Disney studio produced numerous films for training and instruction. Disney serviced the departments of Agriculture, Treasury, and State, and also the Army and Navy. Hundreds of thousands of feet were created on a wide variety of topics—from the topography of enemy-held islands, to support of new income taxes, to the surveillance of airplanes and ships. Disney came to rely on the government.

This government work changed the Disney enterprise. *Bambi* proved to be the final animated feature for almost a decade. Although Donald Duck, Mickey Mouse, Pluto, and Goofy animated shorts emerged, they did so at a far slower rate than during the 1930s. Live action replaced animation. For example, to "boost wartime morale" and improve relations with Latin America, Disney produced two part-live action, part-animated features: *Saludos Amigos* and *The Three Caballeros*.

The war taught Disney the value of its film library. To make extra money the brothers began to rerelease features. In 1944 the reissue of *Snow White and the Seven Dwarfs* accounted for all Disney's corporate profits outside of government work. The government may have kept the factory working, and met day-to-day expenses and payroll, but it was from the film library that Disney—from this early date—realized additional pure profit.

By the end of the war, Disney had cut the studio's million-dollar debt to less than three hundred thousand dollars, and in 1946 successfully released *The Song of the South,* a combination live and animation feature. But a significant challenge loomed ahead. Could the company survive in the postwar world? It almost did not.

Reorganization and Revitalization, 1946–1966

Initially the postwar economic environment disagreed with Disney. During 1948 and 1949 losses reappeared on its balance sheets. Again the Disney company teetered on the brink of insolvency. The postwar years proved particularly difficult. In 1953, for example, the Howard Hughes-inspired demise of RKO forced Disney to borrow millions to form its own movie distribution arm, Buena Vista.

It became a struggle to fill this new channel of distribution; Disney stepped up production and release of live action films. Indeed, the first effort for the new Buena Vista was no animated classic, but a documentary, *The Living Desert.* Made for three hundred thousand dollars, *The Living Desert* quickly grossed more than one million dollars; in time it passed four million dollars in grosses. Disney turned to mainstream, live-action, adventure films aimed at family audiences, beginning with *20,000 Leagues Under the Sea* in 1955. Still the problem remained; the Disney movie-making operation could not grind out feature films fast enough and often enough to support its distribution arm.

Disney did fully annex the family film genre. Such films as *Old Yeller (1957), The Shaggy Dog* (1959), *Toby Tyler* (1960), *The Absent Minded Professor* (1961), *Son of Flubber* (1962), *The Misadventures of Merlin Jones* (1964), and *That Darn Cat* (1965) entertained a generation of baby boomers dragged to the movies by their parents. But this was simply not enough to sustain a major motion picture studio. Disney needed to do something else to create corporate survival.

Innovation came through television and theme parks. By 1960 the Disney company would seek bottom-line salvation not as a film studio, but as a mass-culture maker of theme parks and television shows. Through the 1950s the Disney company reformatted basic corporate strategies.

In April, 1954 Disney with the struggling ABC network announced plans for a Disneyland TV series. But television was a means to an end for Walt Disney. Sensing the baby boom and suburbanization, he wanted to build a park for families. Roy had approached banks but could not convince conservative officers that Disney would not build another "Coney Island." They turned the company down cold.

Disney tried a new tactic. Maybe it could work with a TV network. David Sarnoff at NBC and William Paley at CBS were not interested.

Leonard Goldenson of ABC, with a bankroll of millions from theatres he had to sell, agreed to back Disneyland if the Disney company would produce a one-hour television series. Goldenson, who had merged the former Paramount theatres with ABC, was looking for new investments. Indeed, it was the forced sale of theatres, particularly in Texas, that enabled Goldenson to advance the necessary monies.

The Disney TV show went on the air on Wednesday nights beginning in October 1954; it moved to Sunday nights in 1960, and would remain a Sunday night fixture for more than two decades. ABC had its first top-twenty ratings hit, as the Disney show finished sixth overall for the television season that ran from September 1954 through May 1955. Thereafter, the Disney TV show finished fourth in the 1955–1956 season, thirteenth the following season, and then dropped from the top twenty only to reappear every year from 1964 through 1975. In October, 1955 Disney followed with its afternoon *The Mickey Mouse Club.*

These TV series in turn kindled interest in the Anaheim, California theme park, which opened in July 1955. ABC took a one-third interest in the park, as well as all profits from food concessions for the first ten years, for financing. Disneyland proved an instant hit, forever transforming the Disney company. Walt Disney sought to follow up with an even greater park, and in the years preceding his death in December 1966 he began a complex in Orlando, Florida that would culminate with the October 1971 opening of Walt Disney World. Walt even planned the EPCOT (Experimental Prototype Community of Tomorrow) Center which would not open until October 1982.

The *Disneyland* TV series served as a weekly advertisement for Disneyland and later, Walt Disney World.[3] Over the years the Disney feature film library, plus "specials" about parks, plus a mixture of new cartoons, live-action offerings, and "true-life" documentaries added up to the weekly Disney series. At first there was a four-part rotation based on the divisions of the California park (Frontierland, Fantasyland, Tomorrowland, and Adventureland), but later that obvious connection was quietly dropped.

One segment of that Disney TV effort surpassed all expectations. The December 1954 *Davy Crockett* series, shown during *Frontierland,* created a national obsession, one that signaled the beginning of a new Golden Age of Disney corporate profit making. By mid-1955 "The Ballad of Davy Crockett" had become a pop hit, coonskin caps were on all baby boomer heads, and Fess Parker had become a star. Walt and Roy became rich men for the first time in their lives.

Yet even during this Golden Age it should not be forgotten that Disney frequently made corporate misjudgments. For example, the company could never replicate Davy Crockett's success, as hard as Walt tried. Who remembers TV's *The Saga of Andy Burnett?* Or *The Nine Lives of*

Elfego Baca? Even Fess Parker could not make a go of his next series, *Westward Ho! The Wagons. The Swamp Fox* sported a foxtail three-cornered hat, but few baby boomers pressed their parents to buy this latest TV icon. The long-run Disney "magic" on TV consisted of fashioning a popular series that symbiotically promoted its core theme parks into world-class attractions.

Adding somewhat to profitability were regular theatrical releases of *Snow White and the Seven Dwarfs* and *Pinocchio* in markets around the world. The Disney brothers increasingly looked to foreign film markets. They asked: "How will it play in Finland?" or "Will it do well in Brazil?" With its film production costs fully amortized, the Disney Company freed its animated features at approximately seven-year intervals to hit new generations of children. Other studio films might be shown on *Saturday Night at the Movies,* but Disney feature-length animation classics could only be seen during the holidays in theatres.

And the results could be spectacular. For example, *Snow White and the Seven Dwarfs* was rereleased in 1952, 1958, and 1967, and gathered nearly fifty million dollars more from worldwide markets. Foreign monies could be downright spectacular. Consider that in 1976 *Snow White and the Seven Dwarfs,* long fully amortized, took in nearly two million dollars in one release in West Germany alone.

There also were the modest monies from ancillary operations. During the 1950s thirty million fans paid a dime for each installment of *Walt Disney Comic Books.* Songs from films sold millions in records and sheet music. And by 1954 more than seven hundred other companies were releasing some three thousand other "Disney" items, from Mickey Mouse weather vanes to Donald Duck hats to Minnie Mouse pencils. Sales were spectacular, but profit participation by Disney never matched the millions coming in from Disneyland and Walt Disney World.

Walt and Roy Disney saw a record twelve million dollars earned in 1966 from revenues of $110 million. Their company was valued at one hundred million dollars. During the heady days of the late 1950s and early 1960s, the Disney company moved from a simple niche moviemaker to a corporate theme park giant. The Disney company had successfully transformed itself from a marginal operation into a core business in American mass culture. We may think of the 1930s as the initial Golden Age for Disney animation, but for making money a Golden Age did not begin until the building of Disneyland and the promotional success of the TV series.

Walt Disney died in 1966 and Roy five years later. Who would replace them? Could anyone replace them? Sadly—for the company—no one was found for nearly two decades. A treacherous era of economic calamity commenced.

Looking for a Successor, 1966–1984

Walt's and Roy's immediate successors nearly took the Disney company down. All sought to "do what the founders might have done." Control passed to Ron Miller, Walt Disney's son-in-law. But neither he, nor other MBAs he hired, proved able to match the success of the team of Walt and Roy Disney.

Miller left theme park operation to others, and with that, guaranteed that the company would continue to make money. He concentrated on reviving the moribund film division, properly reasoning that the long-run corporate future lay in generating new material. Initially Miller had some success. His *Herbie Rides Again* and *Castaway Cowboy* made money in 1974, in the days before Steven Spielberg and George Lucas transformed Hollywood. But thereafter nothing seemed to work. *Tron, Running Brave, Condorman,* and *Night Crossing* all proved box office busts. The worst year came in 1983, when Miller agreed to subtract more than ten million dollars from the company's bottom line for *Something Wicked This Way Comes* and *Trenchcoat.*

Miller's Disney seemed to have lost touch with making money making movies. In 1975 Steven Spielberg gave the world *Jaws;* in 1977 George Lucas followed with *Star Wars.* Both generated film grosses in the hundreds of millions of dollars. The teenage, repeat-viewing audience made them blockbusters. The Disney Corporation tried to maneuver into this new movie marketplace, and always failed, but not for a lack of trying. *Midnight Madness,* an imitation of *Animal House,* took in less than five million dollars. The horror film, *The Watcher in the Woods,* was so universally panned that Miller pulled it from distribution and substituted *Mary Poppins.* For his *Star Wars* Miller anted up the twenty million dollars for *The Black Hole* which promptly died during an active 1979 Christmas box office season. By the early 1980s the Disney share of the movie audience had slipped to less than four percent.

Slowly the core corporate fabric began to tear apart. During the 1970s the Sunday night TV show continued, now on NBC, but always to lower ratings than the year before. Each year the Disney renewal became more doubtful, until NBC finally announced the show's cancellation during the spring of 1981. During the early 1980s attendance even began to fall— ever so slightly—at the company's mighty Florida and California theme parks.

The Disney company still made plenty of money; indeed the 1970s saw profits move ever upward, past eight million dollars in 1977. Net income crested in 1980 at $130 million and the company stopped growing. By 1983 company profit had dropped to one hundred million dollars per year, a figure equal to the 1977 net income. The movie division was now a major profit drag; the new cable and home video ventures were losing millions in start-up costs; the theme parks—with bad demographics and a painful recession—could not continue to subsidize the other parts of the enterprises Walt and Roy Disney had so carefully crafted a generation earlier.

There simply was nothing new coming through the pipeline. Wall Street pundits predicted that the Disney corporation would be taken over simply for its valuable film library, massive real estate holdings, and marquee name. By 1983, as the Reagan "go-go-economy" was heating up once again, the faded Disney profit-making reputation reached a nadir. This was best symbolized when the final Walt Disney vision, the billion-dollar EPCOT Center, failed to add to the bottom line. Rumors flew about corporate raiders; Saul Steinberg was paid three hundred million dollars in "greenmail" to stay away. Could a "white knight" be found, or would another great corporate enterprise be lost in a game of "mergers and acquisitions?"

Yet Another Golden Age, 1984–1990

Disney was not sold because a friendly investor, Texas billionaire Sid Bass, anted up nearly five hundred million dollars to place Disney on firm financial footing.[4] Bass worked with his board of directors to find new management and in September 1984 hired former Paramount executive Michael Eisner and former Warner's executive Frank Wells. In what has become an oft-repeated tale of rags to riches, 1980s-style, Eisner and Wells are credited for revising a great American institution. From late 1984 through late 1990 these new Disney managers recorded one record profit statement after another. Unlike Universal and Columbia Pictures, they did not sell out to the Japanese. But it is important to keep in perspective that Eisner and Wells hardly started from a base of zero, or with an altogether new enterprise. They took a company which was underperforming and began to fully exploit its rich assets during one of the greatest peacetime economic expansions on record.

Eisner and Wells brought a rich base of experience to Disney. Eisner had begun his career at ABC, and then, with Barry Diller, helped make Paramount the top studio during the late 1970s and early 1980s. In 1978, two years after Diller and Eisner had arrived, Paramount had moved to the head of the major studio race, with a quarter of the box office, led by *Grease, Saturday Night Fever,* and *Heaven Can Wait.* Wells was an experienced Hollywood deal maker who at Warner Bros. had promoted such diverse films as *Superman* and *Chariots of Fire.* Even though Eisner and Wells knew each other only slightly, they would work well together.

And they had help. For example, they hired Hollywood's new "Irving

Thalberg," Jeffrey Katzenberg, barely thirty, to make movies under the two new "brand names:" Touchstone Pictures and Hollywood Pictures. Katzenberg represented the new breed of moviemaker, a compulsive, driven studio boss fond of saying, if you don't bother to show up on Saturday, then don't bother to come on Sunday and anytime thereafter. Hard work seemed to move ahead of creative spirit and inspiration.

With the Disney movie division in deep trouble, Katzenberg went immediately to work. With no marquee stars he fashioned *Down and Out in Beverly Hills,* an R-rated film; *Ruthless People* became the highest grosser of his first three years in office. *Three Men and a Baby* pushed beyond one hundred million dollars in box office take, the first Disney film to pass that vaunted goal, and finished atop the theatrical box office race in 1987. *Three Men and a Baby* symbolizes the new Disney methods of making movies. Its stars—Ted Danson and Tom Selleck—came from TV. Its narrative source, a French film, guaranteed instant appeal in foreign markets. Katzenberg looked for any way to save money in movie production.

In time he was even able to convince others to finance his films. Through Silver Screen limited partnerships, doctors and dentists and other upper-middle-class Americans were able to "get into the movie game" by purchasing ten-thousand-dollar shares of future Disney "blockbusters." E.F. Hutton's vast network of brokers quickly sold these offerings, and millions poured in at lower-than-market rates of interest. The "partners" shouldered most of the risk and gave away most of the profits. By the end of the 1980s more than 140,000 investors had signed up for Silver Screen, accumulating a pool of a billion dollars for Disney filmmaking.

By 1987 Katzenberg had the Disney film unit again adding to the corporate pot of profits. In the fiscal year that ended that September film revenues neared three hundred million dollars, almost five times the figure on balance sheets when Eisner, Wells, and Katzenberg took over. And more hit films also meant more product for home video. Soon tapes of *Down and Out in Beverly Hills, Ruthless People,* and *Three Men and a Baby* were adding millions more to Disney's growing profitability.

Eisner and Wells instructed Katzenberg to remake Disney into a TV power. Centered on the initial hit, "Golden Girls," on NBC, and "The Disney Sunday Movie" on ABC, success seemed to come easily. Disney expanded into the TV syndication business by hiring "film critics" Gene Siskel and Roger Ebert to "review" movies, including ones from Disney. The Chicago Tribune Company, employer of reviewer Siskel, immediately took him off the daily reviewing beat and made him a "mere" columnist. The pay-TV Disney Channel, through a seemingly infinite set of cross promotions, by 1990 had five million subscribers and began to make money.

Innovation also became the byword in the core theme park business. George Lucas agreed to produce a 3-D short, *Captain EO,* a $17 million extravaganza starring Michael Jackson, to attract a younger audience. For the September 1986 *Captain EO* opening Jane Fonda headed a Hollywood-like premiere; a few industry watchers shook their heads, imagining Walt Disney on the same dais with former radical Fonda. Rock groups from The Jets to Paul Revere and the Raiders entertained Disneyland and Walt Disney World crowds. For the first time beer and wine were allowed in Walt Disney's theme park utopias.

Eisner and Wells gained a third park when in April, 1983, at an investment of three hundred million dollars, Disneyland in Japan opened its doors to throngs. Eisner and Wells set in motion Euro Disney, a park located outside Paris which opened in 1992. But for all of Eisner and Wells' supposed inventiveness, the pair took up common textbook business strategies, in pushing the Walt Disney Company to grow. Consider their two core strategies:

Strategy one: if a corporation is languishing, sell some of the assets. Eisner and Wells did this in spades by packaging and proffering the "classics" of Disney animation in the expanding home video market. These video revenues provided an immediate boost to the corporate bottom line. In 1986 alone, home video revenues added more than one hundred million dollars of pure profit. In October 1987 when *Lady and the Tramp* was released on video, the Disney company had more than two million orders in hand before it ever shipped a copy. By the late 1980s *Bambi* and *Cinderella* were added to the list of the all-time-best-sellers on video. Eisner and Wells placed even *Fantasia* into "video sell through," that is, pricing the tape so that every family could afford to buy a copy.

But there is a price for this "success." Now Disney cannot rerelease *Pinocchio* or *Sleeping Beauty* in theatres, as the company had done for every new generation of kids from the early 1940s through the early 1980s. The cupboard is bare. Eisner and Wells have placed the pressure directly on Katzenberg's film division to create new "classics." They sought to permit him to demonstrate that he was indeed the new "Irving Thalberg." And with *Who Framed Roger Rabbit?* and *Beauty and the Beast* he has added to the cast of Disney favorites.

Strategy two: do more of what you are already making money with. So Eisner and Wells expanded Disneyland in California and Walt Disney World in Florida. They added the Disney-MGM Studios tour as part of the Florida complex. They added new rides. But there they stopped. So, for example, after three years of studying the idea of adding a second theme park in Southern California, Eisner and Wells simply reproduced EPCOT Center in Disneyland—as WESTCOT Center.

Eisner and Wells began to exploit corporate sponsors for these existing theme parks. When Eisner and Frank Wells arrived in 1984, they learned the company was pulling in nearly one hundred million dollars per year from selling participation in EPCOT Center. Giants of American business (from AT&T to Exxon to General Motors) annually anted up for the right to run pavilions. These "sponsors" paid all the costs, and Disney simply took a cut. Frank Wells took on the job of further exploiting this existing corporate strategy. For example, he pressured Kodak, which sought to renew its license for Walt Disney World, to pay part of the cost of making *Captain EO*. General Motors, to renew, agreed to "share" in Walt Disney World advertising. Wells jettisoned Eastern Airlines as Disney's official airline because Delta agreed to advance forty million dollars more. Within two years, Wells had doubled the take from participatory agreements, but in the process had soured long-standing working relations with corporate America.

Eisner and Wells made the Disney balance sheets glow. From mid-1985 through late 1990 the company broke profit records for more than twenty straight quarters. Based on the good times of the 1980s, operating margins and cash flow tripled. It was no wonder that, in order to honor the company's founder, Eisner and Wells changed the formal company name to The Walt Disney Company.

As 1991 opened the Walt Disney Company had become a true corporate power. It ranked in the top two hundred of all US corporations in terms of sales and assets, an outstanding forty-third in terms of profits. In terms of its stock value, Disney had grown into a $16 billion company, with mind-boggling sales of six billion dollars per annum, and profits approaching one billion dollars per year. This was a media corporate powerhouse of a rank with Time Warner or Paramount, no longer a marginal enterprise.

And Eisner and Wells were well rewarded. In surveys of the ten best-paid US corporate executives done in 1990, Michael Eisner ranked in the top ten. Between 1986 and 1990 he had been paid nearly one hundred million dollars for his efforts. The Walt Disney Company hit an embarrassing publicity apex in May of 1989 when it was revealed that Michael Eisner was the highest-paid executive in the US for 1988—at more than $40 million—and Frank Wells had come in second—at more than $32 million. At that point they ranked as the highest-paid professional managers in the history of American business.

Pundits began to ask: could this duo keep it up? Was it possible for Disney to eliminate the effects of recessions? Could these new, skilled managers move Disney into all phases of popular culture production?

Facing the Future, 1990 to the Present

The answer seems to be no. And the seeds of problems had always been there, once one looked closely. For example, in 1988 Florida state regulators charged Eisner's economic miracle with improperly storing paint, solvents, and other hazardous materials used in theme park expansion. Two years later US environmental officials ordered the Walt Disney Company to stop its use of a Florida wetlands sewage treatment area. This particular Walt Disney World expansion was producing more dangerous substances than the already-overcrowded Orlando, Florida ecosystem could handle.

And the basic Sunday night TV show, revived with Michael Eisner hosting as the new "Uncle Walt," had to be canceled. Indeed, despite a prized 7 P.M. Sunday time-slot on ABC, with a new cycle of TV movies, CBS's "60 Minutes" squashed the Disney show and remained atop the ratings race. *The Magical World of Disney,* as it was then titled, went off the air ranked only seventy-sixth among the season's ninety-six prime-time shows.

Disney's TV syndication efforts were not minting money. For example, in 1985 Disney issued *Today's Business,* an early-morning show which, although it aired initially in half the television markets in the US, lasted but a few painful months. The Walt Disney Company pulled it, eating a five million dollar loss.

Eisner and Wells created an unhappy work force. In early 1985, after three months on the job, they had fired more than four hundred studio employees, from painters to carpenters to assistant directors. Indeed, during their first days on the job, they embarrassingly bungled a three week walkout by two thousand "cast members" at Disneyland. This strike, complete with picketing covered extensively by TV news, saw workers plead for a small raise. Eisner and Wells responded by hiring scabs as ticket takers, ride operators, and street sweepers, and broke the strike. The new Disney management had proved that it could (and would) be tough with anyone who tried to spoil their leap toward corporate glory.

Sometimes Michael Eisner and Frank Wells did not rise to the task in corporate negotiations with equals. For example, when Eisner and Wells purchased the Wrather Corporation for its valuable land next to Disneyland, they later had to admit that they were outmaneuvered, and paid millions more than they would have liked. But their opponent in these negotiations is rarely mentioned. Bonita Granville Wrather, child star of the 1930s, should be credited with taking the Disney boys for more than one hundred million dollars. The mythology of the new Disney miracle does not have women, particularly former child stars, outwit its male business wizards.

And in the long run the Wrather deal soured. Eisner and Wells pledged to turn Wrather's other asset, its Long Beach facilities, into the "Port Disney" marine theme park. Local activists challenged the plans. In 1991 Eisner quietly canceled the project and wrote off some twenty million dollars that had been spent planning "Port Disney."

Eisner and Wells incurred the wrath of many a breadwinner as they steadily raised the prices at Disneyland and Walt Disney World. In 1984, when Eisner and Wells arrived, a day at a Disney theme park cost less than twenty dollars. They instituted a five-dollar increase almost immediately, knowing that every dollar added to ticket prices would add more than thirty million dollars to corporate profits. By the late 1980s the price for a day at Disneyland or Walt Disney World had soared well into triple figures.

Eisner and Wells survived all these complaints, protests, and price increases. What would do them in was the double blow of the 1990 to 1991 recession plus the Gulf War. In the fiscal year ending September 1991 the Walt Disney Company reported—for the first time in the Eisner era—declining profits. Specifically the Walt Disney Company finished with nearly a twenty five percent drop in net profits, even though revenues had climbed six percent. Ever-increasing corporate prosperity had come to an end; in December 1991 Wall Street experts were recommending selling the formerly high-flying stock.

Eisner and Wells officially blamed bad times and war, but there existed other reasons. Katzenberg stopped supplying blockbusters after *Pretty Woman* in 1990; the lukewarm receptions for *Dick Tracy, What About Bob?* and *The Rocketeer* came to symbolize the new, languishing Disney studio. Indeed, during the summer of 1991, the lone Disney movie hit was the rerelease of *101 Dalmations.* No one expected a tale of cuddly pooches would outgross *Snow White and the Seven Dwarfs* and become the most successful animated hit ever, even when adjusting for inflation.[5] Even the relatively large grosses for new animated features—*Beauty and the Beast* and *The Little Mermaid*—inspire major headlines, but all too little in the way of needed profits.

The Walt Disney Company in the 1990s has seen a mediocre record in television, despite spending a rumored one hundred million dollars over five years. With busts such as *The Carol Burnett Show, Good & Evil, Nurses,* and *Pacific Station* (all canceled), only *Home Improvement* could be counted as anything close to a hit, with the long-run potential to mint millions through syndication sales. *Golden Girls* can still be judged the company's lone long-term TV hit.

Eisner and Wells' strategies of the go-go 1980s seem inappropriate in the austere 1990s. We can best understand this by closely examining the failed Disney deal with Jim Henson Productions. It had looked as though an alliance between Henson and Disney would make both rich. But when Jim Henson died unexpectedly the deal fell apart. Henson's heirs called off the negotiations and charged Eisner and Wells with bad-faith dealing. An angry split of law suits and accusations flooded the press, further tarnishing the Disney image.

The "Henson affair" underscores the Disney company's ever-growing reputation for penny-pinching. By going back to the old days of micromanaging film and TV projects, Jeffrey Katzenberg was able to keep costs low—as long as the hits kept coming. By the 1990s the Disney "no stars" formula seemed to sour; Hollywood gossips labeled Disney as just another greedy corporate miser. The lean and mean Disney corporate machine had turned just mean.

Eisner and Wells looked to new avenues, frequently with little immediate success. For example, they poured millions into a new music company, Hollywood Records, and paid the rock act Queen some twelve million dollars for an album. Choosing not to buy an existing label, Disney signed The Scream, WW III, The Dead Milkmen, Raw Fusion, and Sacred Reich. The Queen album failed to sell more than half a million copies. The other acts generated precious little revenue. Rumors swirled that Hollywood Records might close down, taking forty million dollars against the bottom line. Eisner and Wells seem unable to expand into this popular culture market.

Eisner and Wells also plunged the Walt Disney company directly into the operation of an over-the-air television station, another facet of show business with which the Disney company had no prior experience. The Walt Disney Company paid more than three hundred million dollars for an independent station in Los Angeles, renaming it KCAL. But, as of the end of 1991, KCAL-TV was still the lowest-ranked station in the Los Angeles TV market. Even in its backyard Disney seemed to be unable to lure television watchers to a Disney channel.[6]

If these new start-up ventures are any indication, the future for the Walt Disney Company in the long run looks bleak. As the 1990s begin, the Walt Disney Company seems to be just another overextended media conglomerate. Eisner and Wells cannot seem to effect a long-run turnaround; they have exploited all the assets in the Disney closet. Indeed, if history is our guide, the Disney company would seem ready for a cycle downward. Eisner and Wells have proven human after all.

Lessons for Media History

As we view the Walt Disney Company from the perspective of the early 1990s, at least four important lessons seem evident.

One: The Disney company has not been a success story from the beginning. Like other capitalist operations it has had its ups and downs, heavily influenced by the uncontrollable factors of technical change, the business cycle, and war. Walt and Roy Disney, and Michael Eisner and Frank Wells all had to deal with these real business conditions. So will their successors.

Two: We can properly ascribe much of Disney's business success to skillful use of new technologies. In the 1930s it was sound and color; in the 1980s it was home video and cable TV.

Three: In the long run Disney corporate enterprise achieved its economic success by becoming a theme park company. The niche company of the first three decades was a marginal operation at best. Disneyland made Walt and Roy rich, not filmmaking. And for all the change they have wrought, Michael Eisner and Frank Wells simply expanded the theme park core business while achieving uneven success—in the long run— with movies, television, and records.

Four: In the end we need to abandon the "great man" version of history. Walt was no genius, nor is Michael Eisner. We are the fools if we ascribe all the actions and strategies of a company to one man or woman. The Disney company is simply another capitalist enterprise with a history best understood within the changing conditions of twentieth-century America.

6

Disney After Disney:
Family Business and the Business of Family

Jon Lewis

Hollywood can't do anything but do what Hollywood always does, as a community, which is hope that everybody who is doing well gets caught in some secret nightmare . . . This is a town that doesn't just want you to fail, it wants you to die.

David Geffen, Producer

An Old Mob Saying: Fish Stinks from the Head

On January 11, 1991, Disney Studio Chairman Jeffrey Katzenberg distributed a memo to his fellow Disney executives; its grandiose title: "The World is Changing: Some Thoughts on Our Business." To those in the know, the memo seemed a panicked response to "the new Disney's" first, brief downturn,[1] and further fueled industry rumors that Katzenberg, who had just turned forty, had finally (thank God!) burnt out.

It is fair to say that Katzenberg's memo did little to make friends or influence people at Disney (or elsewhere in the industry), but his principal argument—that at one hundred million dollars, *Dick Tracy* was too expensive—was hard to dismiss. On the subject of *Dick Tracy,* Katzenberg wrote

We should now look long and hard at the blockbuster business . . . and get out of it. The number of hours it required, the amount of anxiety it generated and the amount of dollars that needed to be expended were disproportionate to the amount of success achieved. *Dick Tracy* was about successful filmmaking, it was also about losing control of our own destiny. And that's too high a price to pay for a movie.[2]

However well-taken Katzenberg's argument was, the key problem with the memo was its tone. Even by corporate Hollywood standards, "The World is Changing: Some thoughts on Our Business" was astonishingly fatuous, unselfconscious, and aphoristic. Indeed, the memo was so cloying, so pompous that someone—and nobody is saying who—leaked the memo, and after a couple of days, everyone in Hollywood seemed to have a copy. That Katzenberg and Disney became the brunt of a good amount of unkind humor was predictable, but "the most remarkable effect of the memo," Hollywood journalist Peter Boyer aptly points out, "was the illumination of Disney's place within Hollywood's entertainment subculture . . . [the memo] seemed to burst the dam on a reservoir of pent-up ill-will too vast to be explained by mere success envy."[3]

In a recent poll published in *Esquire* magazine, screenwriters dubbed Disney the studio they least like to work for. Aljean Harmetz summarized the situation as follows: "Screenwriters are venemous about the dumb Disney executives who treat you horribly and give you pages and pages of notes written in Pidgin English."[4] John Gregory Dunne puts it even more succinctly: "I'm not in this to pass judgment, but writers who have worked for Disney call it Mouschwitz."[5]

On a recent Larry King show, Bill Murray had much the same sentiment for his former employer. Appearing "in support" of the Disney release *What About Bob?*, Murray and King put matters in perspective with the following dialogue:

> KING: What's it like working with the Disney people?
>
> MURRAY: Well, you know they have a terrible reputation.
>
> KING: What?
>
> MURRAY: Well, you know they have a reputation of being very difficult to work with and very tough with a buck, and stuff like that.
>
> KING: And?
>
> MURRAY: It's all true.

Over the past eight years, Disney management has found itself at odds with a Who's Who of Hollywood producers, directors, stars, and screenwriters. These feuds generally feature Katzenberg, whose work habits and people skills have earned him the nickname "the golden retriever" (because he's so relentless and because he's so loyal to management). Barry Diller, who hired Katzenberg at Paramount in 1975, tells a particularly revealing story about "the golden retriever's" first days at the company. "He was so aggressive and impossible, he ruffled so many feathers I couldn't keep him [in the production division]." So Diller sent

Katzenberg to Paramount's Marketing Department "to see if he could survive those people."[6] Katzenberg not only survived, he prevailed, working his way up to third in command at Paramount by the end of the decade.

Since coming to Disney in 1984, Katzenberg has locked horns with (and this is a partial list): Warren Beatty (they haven't talked since the release of *Dick Tracy*), Alec Baldwin (after *The Marrying Man,* Baldwin called Katzenberg "the eighth dwarf: Greedy"), and Barry Levinson (which cost the studio *Rain Man*). But perhaps the bitterest battle of all wages on between Disney CEO Michael Eisner and his former boss and mentor Barry Diller. After Disney opened its motion picture theme park in Orlando, Diller accused Eisner of stealing "his" (actually MCA President Saul Sheinberg's) idea. The two CEOs no longer speak; Diller won't occupy the same room or contribute to the same charity as Eisner.

Though it is less a feud than an astounding bit of nastiness and stinginess, the story Hollywood insiders most like to tell about the new Disney concerns Peggy Lee, and the company's attempt to cut her out of her share in the profits of the video release of *Lady and the Tramp.* Lee, who recorded six songs and provided the voice for four characters in the film, eventually had to take Disney to court to get satisfaction. Lee, confined to a wheelchair, made a convincing witness on her own behalf and exited with a $2.3 million settlement.

But Lee holds one of the few victories over the litigious studio. Disney's bad reputation, it is fair to say, begins, like everything else at the studio, with its legal department. Led by Helene Hahn, aka Attila the Hahn, Disney's Business and Legal Affairs Department sets the tone from contract negotiation, to the studio's inevitable final cut, to payment (or nonpayment) on residual and ancillary accounts. As one ex-Disney executive puts it: "The whole tenor [at Disney] is, let's go beat them up."[7]

Disney's most convoluted and most acrimonious intraindustry legal battle—and here I am choosing from quite a list—centered on the proposed Disney/MGM motion picture theme park in Orlando. On June 27, 1985, lawyers from Disney and MGM/UA closed a deal, spelled out in a thirty-one-page contract, which enabled Disney to begin work on the park. The agreement gave Disney rights, for a nominal licensing fee, to borrow liberally from the MGM/UA film library, including *Gone With the Wind, The Wizard of Oz, Rocky,* several Woody Allen films, and most of the James Bond series.

Weeks later, when Kirk Kerkorian, the "hands-off" CEO at MGM/UA, finally got around to examining the deal closely, he couldn't believe what his lawyers had done to him. He called Disney President and former entertainment lawyer Frank Wells to renegotiate, but Wells quickly deferred to Hahn. If Kerkorian wanted satisfaction, Wells made it quite clear, Kerkorian/MGM/UA could, like everyone else in the business, see Disney in court.

When Disney announced plans to begin construction on the park, Kerkorian was joined by MCA (Universal Studios' parent company) CEO Saul Sheinberg, who four years earlier had announced his intention to build a Universal Studios (Tour) East in Florida. Indeed, by 1985, Sheinberg had already bought the land and had begun courting Florida Governor Bob Graham, who, pending pro forma legislative approval, promised to lend MCA thirty-five million dollars a year for five years to help get the project off the ground.

But once Disney announced its plans—after all, they were already a force in the area with Walt Disney World and EPCOT—a Tallahassee lobbyist and former Disney employee named Bernie Parish began making the rounds, asking Florida legislators to vote against Graham's loan to Sheinberg/MCA. Within weeks of Parish's appearance on the scene, the "MCA Bill" was killed in committee.

Sheinberg, of course, threatened to sue, and then things got weird. When Sheinberg's lawyers took on the case, they discovered what Hollywood insiders already knew, that Diller (then at Fox) and Eisner were already feuding about the Florida theme parks. The Eisner/Diller feud recalled an incident back in 1981 when Sheinberg was still looking for a partner for a proposed studio theme park in Florida, and had run the idea by then-Paramount President Diller and, according to both Diller and Sheinberg, Diller's right-hand man Eisner.

Eisner, who claims he was never at any meeting where Sheinberg's plans were discussed—Diller, who was at the meeting, insists he was— brushed off the accusations of impropriety as groundless. When MCA decided to go ahead with their plans anyway, Eisner told the press that he was glad; tourists coming to Universal Studios East would certainly patronize at least one of the Disney parks in the area.

While it seemed inevitable that MCA and Disney would find themselves in court, Disney hardly played things close to the vest. Eisner countered all the accusations by announcing Disney's plans to build a theme park in Burbank to compete with the original Universal Studios Tour. And while Sheinberg boasted to *Business Week* that he would not be intimidated, it was clear (in a language all studio executives understand) that he would not say he wouldn't be intimidated unless he was. By the time the two Orlando studio theme parks opened, Sheinberg had an even more serious problem; the Disney/MGM Studio Tour was better. And though he got in a dig at Eisner/Disney in the *Jaws'* ride (which featured Mickey Mouse ears floating in the shark's waters), *Time* dubbed Sheinberg's park: "Universal's Swamp of Dreams."

Disney's willingness—indeed its anxiousness—to take on *the* major players in the industry again surfaced in their well-publicized dispute with Rupert Murdoch. Murdoch, then in control of Fox, and Disney locked horns over Murdoch's Sky Television service in Europe. At first Disney was a partner in the venture—or at least a major investor—but when Murdoch began making significant decisions without consulting Disney management, Eisner withheld seventy-five million dollars in protest. When Murdoch pressed for the cash, Eisner referred Murdoch to Hahn, and all Murdoch got out of the deal was one less headache—partnership with Disney—and a TV service without the popular Disney Channel.

The new Disney's penchant for not paying bills—or for withholding payment until it gets its way in a dispute—is widely acknowledged in the industry. In 1989, for example, Disney ran up and then refused to pay more than eight million dollars in film processing bills to its own subsidiary, Metrocolor Labs. When Metrocolor pressed for its money, Disney blamed Warner Communications, which had just bought and shut down Disney's partner at Metrocolor, Lorimar. Warner then refused to patronize Metrocolor, as Lorimar had been bound to do by contract. Complicating matters even further, when Disney tried to unload Metrocolor Labs to the Rank Organization, which offered $130 million for the property, it discovered that Lorimar had promised New York investor Ronald Pearlman the first thirty-eight million dollars in the event of a Metrocolor sale. This not so minor detail led Disney to back out of the deal, and when Disney and Warners could not agree about what to do about the Ronald Pearlman problem, Disney flatly refused to pay its bill and forced Warners to file suit (asking for $118 million in damages). Disney countersued for forty-eight million dollars and the suit was eventually settled out of court, with Disney walking away from the venture entirely, without, of course, ever paying the bill.

When dealing with Disney, a rather simple rule of thumb applies: Disney's terms are the only terms. In an astounding move made soon after Eisner took over, Disney Distribution Chief Dick Cook informed exhibitors that the studio would refuse to accept anything less than its percentage on a full-price ticket. If a theater wanted to offer senior citizen discounts, for example, that was their business; Disney still got its take from a full-price ticket. Disney then refused to send its prints to theaters that screened advertisements. When theater owners boycotted Disney— led, not incidentally, by MCA-owned Cineplex Odeon—the Disney sales force showed their grit and willingness to fight back. On one occasion, Disney rented a local Elks Lodge and screened a film on a bedsheet rather than give in to disobedient exhibitors.

In another well-publicized corporate skirmish, Disney took on the Wrather Corporation, which, thanks to a blunder by Walt Disney back in 1953, owned and operated the Disneyland Hotel. When Wrather began faltering financially, and allowed the hotel to suffer a visible decline, Eisner made an offer to buy the property. But Wrather refused to discuss the matter. Eisner countered by threatening to dramatically increase the fare for the Monorail which connected the hotel to the theme park—the Monorail was of course owned and operated by Disney. Wrather then promptly sold out, industry insiders point out, for significantly less than the property was worth.

All this said, Disney is at its most anxious, its most litigious (and that *is* saying something) when it comes to its copyrights. On this score, the Disney Business and Legal Affairs Department is fierce and at times bizarre. For example, Hahn *et al.* filed suit against the small town of White River, in Ontario, Canada, over the community's plans to celebrate the seventy-fifth birthday of Winnipeg the Bear (Winnie the Pooh's namesake). The town planned to erect a statue in the likeness of the A.A. Milne character. When news of this plan reached Burbank, Disney lawyer Robert Ogden informed White River's mayor that the statue would violate Disney's copyright.

The story caught on in the mass media—with Disney aptly portrayed as a bully, and more than a little bit ridiculous—but despite thousands of letters reaching Burbank in protest, Disney clung to its bottom line regarding its copyrights. Finally, Disney and White River struck a deal: White River could have its statute, but only in the likeness of the bear drawn by the original book's illustrator Ernest Shephard, and not the far more familiar Pooh drawn by Disney animators.

Equally unpopular was Disney's much-publicized battle with three day-care centers in Hallendale, Florida, all of which featured the unlicensed use of Disney characters painted on their exterior walls. Once again the media revealed Disney's seeming lack of heart and perspective. But Disney refused to back down. Wells dealt with the issue like a lawyer: "We have no choice [but to sue] if we are to continue to own the rights to Mickey Mouse. It is among the most valuable rights this company has." Katzenberg, predictably, was more grandiose—"We are held to a higher standard in every area"—while revealing Disney's bottom line— "I am not sure the consumer is aware [of this higher standard but] I think our shareholders appreciate how concerned we are with the way we spend their money".[8]

The day-care centers were eventually forced to remove the Disney characters from their walls. With the help of the MCA theme park's Public Relations Department, studio painters arrived on the scene and painted the MCA-copyrighted Flintstones over Mickey Mouse and friends, and then threw a party for the children. Indeed, while Disney held its copyrights to be inviolate, Saul Sheinberg for once got to laugh last.

Copyright was also at issue when Disney took on the Motion Picture Academy for its use of the Snow White characters in an awful production number at the 1989 Academy Awards Show. By 3:30 P.M. the day after the broadcast, Disney had already filed suit in Federal Court, claiming copyright infringement. When the Academy publically apologized, the studio dropped the suit. But it had made its point again. Disney is ready and willing to go to court against anyone. And when it comes to copyright, Disney has no sense of humor at all.

To put Disney's litigious bent in perspective, consider the following. In 1987, Disney filed seventeen *major* lawsuits, naming some seven hundred defendants in the United States and another seventy-eight overseas. The following year, one suit alone named four hundred defendants, claiming copyright infringement, and then, after *Dick Tracy* hit the theaters, the studio filed another suit against fifteen hundred vendors selling "fake" Dick Tracy paraphernalia. By 1989, Eisner biographer Ron Grover quips, "it was difficult to find a Hollywood company with which Disney was not involved in a lawsuit or a public relations fight." Indeed, when *Show Biz News* editor Alex Ben Block proposed a special issue on legal battles in Hollywood, he dropped the idea when he discovered that "Disney was involved in almost every one of the fights."[9]

Disney's 1988 Annual Report to its stockholders proclaimed "a year when dreams become a reality." By and large Disney made good on that promise, as studio revenues exceeded one billion dollars (a thirty-one percent increase over 1984). And while the good news was that three Disney films—*Who Framed Roger Rabbit?*, *Good Morning Vietnam,* and *Three Men and a Baby*—all grossed over one hundred million dollars, the even better news was that the newly diversified film unit drew sixty percent of its considerable revenues not from films per se, but from videos, TV syndication, and cable.

What the annual report did not include was what Disney did back in 1984 by way of saving money in order to get so good in 1989. Within months of their arrival at Disney, Eisner and Wells fired over four hundred employees, many of whom had worked with Walt. The new executive team then dramatically increased ticket prices at the theme parks; broke a strike that they had inherited at Disneyland by threatening, in a move Walt would have tried himself, to hire an entirely new work force; and restructured the company along the lines of Charles Bluhdorn's Gulf and Western/Paramount, seducing sixty Paramount executives to jump ship. Katzenberg, Hahn, Ricardo Mestres, Bill Mechanic, Richard Frank, and Bob Jacquemin, who comprised the New Disney power structure, had all worked with Eisner and Diller in the still quite recent good old days at Paramount.

The Paramount connection extended beyond the boardroom. Shelly

Long, Ted Danson, Danny DeVito, and Robin Williams, all of whom starred in Paramount-produced television shows, signed contracts with Disney. Jim Abrahams and David and Jerry Zucker, who directed the very-low-budget, big-box-office *Airplane* at Paramount, signed on to shoot *Ruthless People,* and superstar television producer Garry Marshall, who made Paramount a lot of money in the seventies, made the transition to superstar movie producer at Disney.

Only Frank Mancuso, who was named Paramount's Chief over Eisner after Diller left, and his very successful marketing crew rejected Eisner's offers to join the new Team Disney. In their place, Eisner hired Stephen Rose and Gordon Weaver, who had worked at Paramount until allegations surfaced that they had received kickbacks from companies that did advertising and production work at the studio. At the time, Rose and Weaver protested their innocence; but to be fair, Eisner was hiring them because of their work on *Raiders of the Lost Ark* and their connection to Paramount, and not because they were in any way innocent. Indeed, seven years later the IRS went after the kickback "income" that Rose and Weaver claimed they never received, and in 1991, the two marketing executives pled guilty to tax evasion in Federal Court in order to avoid jail time. The point here is not so much Eisner's willingness to do business with Rose and Weaver (at family-oriented *Disney!*), but the extent to which Eisner was willing to go to reassemble the old Paramount at the new Disney, and to conduct business as usual in the form and with the formula that had proven so successful for him—and his former mentor and now archenemy Diller—at Paramount.

The new Disney/old Paramount method—its formula for success—is simple: talk tough, talk cheap, and keep total control. To its credit, as a result Disney tends to market films instead of stars (or "packages") and has at least shown an effort to shift the balance of power in the new Hollywood away from the powerful agencies. But in doing so, Disney's tough/cheap talk reveals a fundamental inequity and hypocrisy; with the exception of Eisner and Wells—who, for example, in 1988 and 1989 took home over fifty million dollars per year, apiece—Disney skimps when it comes to paying virtually everyone else. Turnover at the lower management level is encouraged to (as Eisner says) "keep bringing in new employees who look fresh and exciting."[10] And when casting its films, the studio seeks out ex- or soon-to-be stars who are willing to work for far less than star compensation; a way of doing business that prompted Robin Williams to jibe that Katzenberg likes to cast his films at the Betty Ford Clinic.

The casting of *Down and Out in Beverly Hills,* the new Disney's first big hit, supports Williams' funny and accurate quip. Bette Midler hadn't had a hit film in over five years, and was fresh off the disastrous *Jinxed,* a film that not only hurt her credibility as star, but earned her a reputation for being "difficult" because of her behavior on the set. When Katzenberg approached "her people" for what was then called *Jerry Saved From Drowning,* Midler's asking price was $750,000. Katzenberg offered $600,000. When her agents balked, Katzenberg remarked; "Her career is in the fucking toilet," and since Midler's people could offer nothing convincing in reply, they acquiesced to Disney's terms. Richard Dreyfuss, who had appeared in three of the biggest hits of the seventies (*American Graffiti, Jaws,* and *Close Encounters of the Third Kind*), was asking $1.2 million. But it was clear to Katzenberg that Dreyfuss could be had for significantly less, since he too had not had a hit in five years and, more importantly, had a recent history of drug abuse that was well publicized in the media. Katzenberg offered and Dreyfuss accepted $600,000.

The highest-paid actor in the film was Nick Nolte, who was fresh off a huge success in (Paramount's) *48 Hours.* Nolte eventually signed for $750,000, hardly stellar, by Hollywood standards. In all three negotiations, the stars signed at Disney's price. Indeed, after the fact, ICM superagent Sam Cohn, who represented both Dreyfuss and Nolte, quipped: "There's no way to overestimate their stinginess."[11]

As to an obsession with total control, Disney executives plead guilty. Indeed, all the memos, the meetings, the script changes, and editing changes are part of what Katzenberg calls "managing ideas," and Disney executives are quick to point out that, unlike the other studios, *they* take responsibility for *their* movies even when they bomb.

The bottom line at Disney these days is the company's reputation on Wall Street, which has never been better. As Christopher Knowlton points out in a recent article in *Fortune* magazine:

> So far Disney's bad behavior has had zero effect on its prospects. The main question about Disney's balance sheet is how much stronger can it get. Along with Coca Cola, American Express and a handful of other companies, Disney stands as one of America's undisputed international success stories . . . the company has become the archetypal American corporation for the 1990's: a creative company that can move with agility to exploit international opportunities in industries where the US has a competitive advantage.[12]

Knowlton's analysis rather typifies the Wall Street line on the new Disney. Indeed, financial analysts predict somewhere in the neighborhood of eleven billion dollars in annual sales at Disney by 1995, a doubling of the company's size from 1990. And if things go according to Eisner's 1990 five-year plan (and so far things have), the studio will be making thirty films a year, the retail division will sport over one hundred Disney merchandise stores, the entertainment division will expand into main-stream records and publishing, and the company will further international-ize its theme parks and move further into the hotel business, with a goal of thirty hotels and twenty-six thousand rooms by 1995. Disney, if it isn't already, would very much like to be *the* entertainment juggernaut on this planet by mid-decade.

If they get there, analysts agree, they must return to the new Disney/old Paramount formula. Indeed, Disney's recent foray into the blockbuster market has, as *Business Week* so glibly put it, left the company "looking a little fragilistic." Disney stock, which had peaked in the $140 range, fell under one hundred dollars when *Dick Tracy* failed to be the next *Batman*. And when Chief Financial Officer Gary Wilson resigned after a long and bitter battle with Eisner, Disney's usually imperturbable stock fell $4.50 in a single day—hardly a vote of confidence for management.

But despite finally showing a little weakness, far more convincing evidence points toward Disney following through on Eisner's plan. In 1990, for the second time in three years, Disney topped the industry in motion picture ticket sales, and in 1991, with *Green Card* and *Arachnophobia*, Disney went back to making smaller movies and big profits. Indeed, at this writing, in 1992, Disney is still the most powerful, the most feared, the most disliked and the most profitable studio of them all.

From Family Business to the Business of Family

The first major crisis at the Disney family business took shape in 1952 as Walt Disney announced his plans to build Disneyland. Roy, Walt's older brother and business partner since the early 1920s, opposed the project, and with the backing of the board successfully blocked Walt's pursuit of conventional financing. When Walt pressed Roy for company funds, Roy offered ten thousand dollars. It was meant as an insult and was taken as one.

Walt responded to the insult in predictable fashion. He borrowed against his family's life insurance, and formed WED (for Walter Elias Disney) Enterprises, a holding company set up to oversee the planning of the Disneyland venture, and Retlaw (that's Walter spelled backwards), to merchandise the name *Walt* Disney. With WED, Walt effectively cut Roy, the corporate board, and his own wife Lilly out of the Disneyland project. With Retlaw, Walt finessed approximately five percent off the top of virtually every Disney merchandising deal. The formation of Retlaw was a particularly bold move for Walt, not only because it cut him off from the rest of the family, but because he risked the ire of the Disney shareholders, since it looked as if he meant—indeed it was his intention—to divert corporate funds into his own pocket.

Roy and Walt feuded for almost a year about WED and Retlaw, talking to each other only through their secretaries. At the time, Roy was fond of telling the story about how Walt used to wet the bed they shared as kids. "He'd pee all over me," Roy would say, "and he's still doing it." Walt, when he heard what his brother was saying about him, begged to agree: "I pissed on him then and I'm still pissing on him."[13]

The resolution of the Disneyland controversy came almost entirely on Walt's terms. When ABC agreed to back the project in exchange for a weekly Disney television show, Roy brought Walt an offer on behalf of the board of five hundred thousand dollars for Walt's share of Disneyland.[14] Walt countered by agreeing to sell half his interest for that price, or, if Roy Jr., whom Walt glibly referred to as "the idiot nephew," agreed to work as a clown at the theme park, he'd cut his stake to twenty-five percent. Roy Jr., who looks eerily like his uncle, declined, but Walt, having made his point, eventually agreed to cut his share to 17.25 percent.

The crisis over Disneyland is important for several reasons. On the surface of things it showed who was really running the company. It boosted Walt's participation in the corporation's profit structure, and Disney became a significantly more diversified company, involved in amusement parks and television. But more importantly, the crisis and its resolution fragmented management; there were, after 1952, "Walt men" and "Roy men." And nobody, especially Roy Jr., seemed willing to forgive and forget.

In 1966, when Walt died, Roy Sr. took over the company. Donn Tatum was named President and Card Walker became Executive Vice-President in charge of operations. In a deliberate effort to move the company away from the autocracy his brother had maintained, and to update the management style of what had been far too much of a family business, Roy Sr. established an executive committee to run things at Disney, comprised of himself, Tatum, Walker, Walt's son-in-law and chosen heir Ron Miller, Roy Jr., and producers Bill Walsh and Bill Anderson.

Roy Sr. proved a very successful CEO; Disney's last until Eisner. By 1972, the year of his death, Roy Sr. had doubled the company's net worth. But he was somewhat less successful in mending fences between the two warring factions in the company.

In 1967, literally over his brother's dead body, Roy Sr. secured a seat for his son on the corporate board. And as Roy Jr. finally began to show interest in the family business, Roy Sr. made him a Vice-President (in charge of 16mm). But despite his father's grand final gesture—Roy Sr.'s last official act as CEO was to change the name of Disney World to Walt Disney World—there were still too many "Walt men" at the studio for the "idiot nephew" to emerge as his father's successor.

After Roy Sr.'s death Tatum became CEO, and Walker (whom Roy

Sr. had once tried to fire) emerged as the hands-on manager of the studio. The executive committee, now comprised of Tatum, Walker, Miller (all "Walt men"), and Roy Jr., forced the "idiot nephew" to the periphery. And after six years of bitter infighting, in March 1977, after a row with Miller over a parking space, Roy Jr. resigned.

Roy Jr. then refocussed his attention on the stock market. With superstar Hollywood entertainment lawyer Stanley Gold, Roy Jr. formed Shamrock Holdings and parlayed a one-hundred-million-dollar capital investment into well over seven hundred million dollars in a matter of a couple of years. Meanwhile, Disney, without him, began to fall apart.

By the end of the decade, the film studio's market share fell to four percent, the lowest of the seven major studios. *The Unidentified Flying Oddball* and *The Apple Dumpling Gang,* two old-Disney-style live-action features, exposed just how out-of-date the studio had become. Compounding the decline were Walker's refusal to move Disney into hard-PG and R rated film production, and his rigid policy against affording independent producers and directors profit participation in Disney releases—a policy that cost the studio both *Raiders of the Lost Ark* and *ET: The Extra-Terrestrial.*

Things went from bad to worse in September 1979. As Walker prepared to take over from Tatum, Don Bluth, one of Disney's premier animators, quit to protest incessant cost-cutting at the studio. Following Bluth's lead, sixteen Disney animators followed him out the door. Long dependent on the animation studio for predictable revenue—indeed, they hadn't had a live-action hit since *Herbie the Love Bug* in 1969—Disney entered the 1980s in deep, deep trouble.

During Walker's tenure, the film division became a significant liability. *Tron, The Devil and Max Devlin, The Last Flight of Noah's Ark, Condorman,* and *The Watcher in the Woods,* the live-action films released while Walker was at the helm, all bombed. Income from the film division fell fifteen million dollars and earnings per share of Disney stock dropped ten percent.

In 1983 Walker retired, and named Miller and real estate tycoon Ray Watson to succeed him. But it was already too late. During Miller and Watson's brief tenure, the film division posted losses of $33.4 million, studio overhead reached thirty-five percent (compared to the industry average of twenty percent) and while efforts to diversify via a Disney cable channel began to take shape, the film division was in need of a miracle.[15]

Over a year earlier, as Walker contemplated shutting down the film division altogether, Miller approached Eisner and offered him the top job at the studio (and third in command at the company). Though he confessed to being "a fan" of Disney, at the time Eisner saw no reason to make a parallel move to a far less successful studio, and turned Miller down.

That Eisner would be Roy Jr.'s man less than two years later is at once ironic and unsurprising. Despite their considerable personal differences, Miller and Roy Jr. had much the same vision for the company, but both at the time, and for different reasons, found themselves hamstrung by the late Walt Disney, who still guided the faltering company's every move.

For those few "Roy men" left at the company in 1983, it seemed a kind of poetic justice that, just as Walt's heir gained control at Disney, he and it were doomed. Best of all—and here we are taking things from the point of view of a "Roy man"—just as the company seemed a prime candidate for takeover, Roy Jr., by then a very successful businessman, seemed the most likely player in such a scenario. Indeed, as 1983 rolled on, the battle for control at Disney—still essentially a family problem—had only just begun.

Wall Street and the Battle for Disney, or Monopoly in Fast Forward

In November 1983,[16] only eight months after Miller and Watson "took over," Disney stock fell to $58 a share. With little debt, a huge pool of unused assets (the film library, all that Florida real estate), undervalued stock, and over a decade of weak management, it was hardly a secret that Disney was an attractive takeover target.

In an effort to block a potential raider, Miller and Watson hired Stan Ross of the Kenneth Leventhal Company to assess the situation. Ross's assessment was hardly encouraging: a raider could easily leverage the company's assets to more than cover the outstanding stock's net worth (at the time, approximately two billion dollars). As to a strategy that could save the company, Ross had no good advice. Watson suggested taking the company private, but Ross pointed out that even if the executives offered as much as $65 a share, they could not "maintain a principaled objection" if a raider countered with an offer of $66. Moreover, if it came down to a bidding war—and no doubt it would—they were bound to lose, and just to stay in the game, they would have to sell off pieces of the company—precisely what they feared a raider would do.

At the same time, Roy Jr., who held 1.1 million shares of Disney stock (worth about thirty million dollars less than a year earlier), decided to do his own research. But unlike Miller and Watson, Roy Jr.'s investigation revealed several good options: he could launch a proxy fight to force a change in management; he could pursue a hostile takeover himself (he even had a better chance of taking the company private than Miller and Watson did); or he could convince a multinational to buy Disney, under the assumption that it at least would run the company better than his cousin's husband. From a purely selfish standpoint, the third option was Roy Jr.'s best. One thing in common between Charles Bluhdorn and Gulf and Western's purchase of Paramount, oil billionaire Marvin Davis and commodities trader Marc Rich's takeover at Fox, Kerkorian's buy-out at MGM/UA, and funeral parlor entrepreneur Steve Ross's merger with Warner Brothers (forming Warner Communications), was that they all made money for their stockholders. Though hardly just a major stockholder, Roy Jr. had every right and reason to protect his investment.

In a move that was (and was taken to be) at once symbolic and strategic, on March 9, 1984—ironically, the release date of *Splash,* Miller's one big success and Disney's first high-concept film—Roy Jr. resigned from the Disney board. Within hours of his resignation, he made a second move, purchasing additional stock, upping his stake in the company to 4.7 percent. Roy Jr.'s resignation and stock purchase prompted a flurry of rumors on Wall Street naming, in addition to Roy Jr., Rupert Murdoch and Coca-Cola as potential players in an unfriendly takeover of Disney.

While Roy Jr. assembled his "Brain Trust," comprised of himself, Gold, his wife Patty, Mark Seigel, Cliff Miller, and Frank Wells, to plan his next move, on March 29, Saul Steinberg, on behalf of his Reliance Group Holdings, filed a Schedule 13D with the SEC in order to purchase a 6.3 percent interest in Disney. The Wall Street rumor circulating at the time was that Steinberg's interest in Disney was piqued by Coca-Cola, which, it turns out, never made a move. Steinberg hoped, at the time, to establish a position vis-à-vis Disney that would allow him either to take advantage of a potentially advantageous buyout price, or to take a run at the company himself.

But there is another, funnier story about why Steinberg went after Disney. Sometime in mid-March Steinberg told his aides to "go after Watson." He didn't mean Disney's Ray Watson; he was referring to Thomas Watson, the President of IBM. But once his staff generated the numbers on Disney, Steinberg couldn't help but like what he saw.

Following Steinberg's "lead," the following day arbitrageurs began stockpiling Disney stock in anticipation of a takeover battle. Meantime, Roy Jr. hired Michael Milken of Drexel, Burnham and Lambert to put together a financing package for a leveraged buyout of Disney. By 1984, Roy Jr. was hardly a novice when it came to corporate takeovers. Shamrock Holdings had "gone after" corporate giants Polaroid and Faberge; both battles resulted in lucrative greenmail settlements for Roy Jr.

Milken's research provided Roy Jr. with more good news, delivered in quintessential Wall Street-speak: "It's do-able," Milken told Roy Jr., "it's a do-able deal. I can see the numbers."[17] But when Roy Jr. looked at the big picture, it was clear that he would have to sell off huge pieces of the company to execute the deal, a detail that did not seem to bother Milken as much as it did him.

On April 1, Miller and Watson met with Joe Flom of Skadden, Arps, a law firm specializing in takeover battles. Flom's advice was simple: accumulate debt. Eight days later, as Disney executives contemplated Flom's advice, Steinberg upped his stake in the company to 9.3 percent, at a total cost of one hundred fifty million dollars.

Eleven days later, in a seemingly unrelated incident, Bass Brothers Enterprises, run by Fort Worth billionaire Sid Bass, accepted greenmail and backed off in their leveraged buy-out of Texaco. For not buying the company, Bass Brothers netted a twelve percent premium on their stock, grossing $1.2 billion (a pretax profit of four hundred million dollars). In what turned out to be a shrewd move, Bass then met with Watson and suggested that Disney buy Arvida, a Bass Brothers real estate company in order to accumulate debt, and thus forestall Steinberg and/or Roy Jr.

But it is likely that Bass had far more on his mind than assisting Watson. Indeed, with the stock swap outlined in the proposed Arvida sale, Bass stood to gain almost a nine percent stake in Disney, and with all that cash left over from the aborted Texaco deal, Bass could well take a very strong position himself vis-à-vis a takeover. And though Richard Rainwater, Bass's top aide, tells a different story—that Bass went to Watson as a "white knight" to save the company from less friendly parties—however you look at it, Bass emerged, literally out of nowhere and overnight, as a major problem for Steinberg, Roy Jr., and perhaps for Miller and Watson as well.

By the time the Arvida deal received board approval on May 17, Roy Jr. had secretly given up any hopes of taking over the company himself. But he remained committed to ousting Miller and Watson, so much so that he agreed to let Milken turn over the Drexel, Burnham financing package to "another client," knowing full well that the other client was Steinberg. As to the Arvida deal, Bass's emergence irked Roy Jr., just as Miller and Watson had hoped it would, so much so that Gold hardly held back when *Business Week* asked him what he thought of the Arvida deal: "Disney needs those twenty thousand acres of Arvida land like they need another asshole."[18]

On April 25, Steinberg filed an amended 13D in order to up his stake to twenty-five percent. Meantime, MCA President Saul Sheinberg—this well before his well-publicized problems with the new Disney—offered to be Disney's white knight, neglecting to tell Miller and Watson that he had already met with Roy Jr. and had offered to help him take over the company. Watson turned Sheinberg down, partly because he was committed to an accumulation of debt strategy, and partly because the company was beyond Sheinberg's ability to save.

On May 25, Steinberg filed suit against Disney to block the Arvida deal, claiming that the deal "served no proper or valid corporate purpose" and then filed an amended 13D in order to purchase 49 percent of the company. Ten days later, at Roy Jr.'s son's wedding, Disney General Counsel Dick Morrow brought Roy Jr. a peace offering from Miller and Watson. But as Roy Jr. examined the possibility of joining the very management team he had been working to force out, Arthur Bilger of Drexel, Burnham called Gold and asked if Roy Jr. wanted a piece of Steinberg's action.

Complicating matters further was the announcement that Disney planned to purchase Gibson Greeting cards, a deal so transparently disadvantageous it proved a completely ineffective "poison pill." Indeed, all the proposed Gibson deal accomplished was to convince Roy Jr. that Miller and Watson were incompetent and insensitive, since it brought up the question of merchandising rights to *Walt* Disney's name once again.

On May 31, Roy Jr. opted to back Steinberg—he was the more likely victor anyway—and offered $350 million for the studio, film library and, of course, merchandising rights. Steinberg promptly rejected the offer as "incredibly low." Four days later, Gold learned through the grapevine that Steinberg was ready to make an offer for Disney without Roy Jr. With second level financing in place—thirty-five million dollars from Minneapolis millionaire Irwin "Irv the Liquidator" Jacobs and seventy-five million dollars from Kerkorian (who secured an option to buy the film studio and library for $447 million should Steinberg succeed)— on June 8, Steinberg, under the aegis of the MM (for Mickey Mouse) Corporation, presented Miller and Watson with a two-tiered offer: $67.50 per share for the company "as is" or $71.50 per share if Miller and Watson agreed to kill the Gibson deal.

As Miller and Watson considered their options—really, they had only two: pay greenmail or sell out—Roy Jr., by then cut out of Steinberg's plans, offered to help Miller and Watson take the company private. But once again Miller and Watson snubbed him, and hashed out a thoroughly disadvantageous greenmail deal with Steinberg. In the end, Steinberg walked away with $325 million (selling out at $77.50 per share), "earning" a net profit of $31.7 million by not buying the company.

On June 11, the first day Disney shares traded after the greenmail deal was announced, the stock fell by $3.78 per share. On Gold's advice, Roy Jr. purchased an additional one hundred thousand shares. Taking advantage of a surplus of undervalued Disney stock, Roy Jr. was at once taking a position vis-à-vis a second (and inevitable) takeover attempt and, like any smart businessman, buying low, hoping to eventually sell high.

Through the following week, Disney stock continued to fall. On June 20, as it hit a low of $46 per share, Roy Jr.—the major investor who had seen his stock's worth dramatically decrease . . . the jilted nephew who never forgave his uncle for what he did to his father—finally put a gun to management's head. Allying himself with the company's three other major stockholders—Bass, Jacobs, who held onto his stock when Steinberg settled for greenmail, and Ivan Boesky, an arbitrageur who purchased over a million shares of "undervalued" Disney stock on credit after Steinberg filed his first Schedule 13D—Roy Jr. pressed the company board to: kill the Gibson deal; remove his old nemeses Tatum and Walker from the executive board; give him three seats on the corporate board, taken by Gold, Roy Jr.'s brother-in-law Peter Daily and himself; and force the resignations of Miller and Watson. Faced with either a bitter proxy fight led by all four of the largest stockholders, or worse, yet another takeover battle, the board gave in.

Meantime, Irwin Jacobs, himself a well-known corporate raider, kept buying more and more stock. By July 30, he owned six percent of the company. Buoyed by Miller and Watson's resignations on September 8, which caused Disney stock to take an immediate turn for the better, and the subsequent transitional disarray in leadership at the company, Jacobs upped his stake to eight percent. But in a move he would soon live to regret, Jacobs asked Bass to join him in his bid for the company. Bass responded by buying out Boesky and refusing to share the wealth with Jacobs, who then had no choice but to sell out to Bass. By the end of September, Bass was the company's major stockholder, owning 24.8 percent of the company's stock.

According to Jacobs, Bass became Disney's principal stockholder by reneging on their deal to pool their resources and take over the company. Bass, though, tells a different story. According to Bass, on September 25, he and Jacobs met with the newly hired Eisner and Wells. The meeting went so well, Bass says, that he decided to buy up as much Disney stock as he could, and told Jacobs he thought he should do the same. Bass then called Milken and went after Boesky's 1.52 million shares (which Boesky was very anxious to get rid of) and literally stole them for sixty dollars per share—$3.25 over market value and over forty dollars less per share than they would be worth by the end of the decade. When Jacobs demanded half of Boesky's stock as "part of their deal," Bass refused. "I put up my money," Bass concluded, "and now post facto you don't get fifty percent." Jacobs then offered to buy Bass out for sixty-five dollars per share, but Bass declined. Finally, Jacobs accepted sixty-one dollars per share for his stock, grossing $181 million on the deal. Bass then promised to stand pat for five years; a decision that turned out well for him and for Disney.[19]

The New Disney: A Brief Conclusion

On September 8, 1984, two weeks before Eisner left Paramount for Disney, and the day after Miller officially resigned, Barry Diller decided to leave Paramount for Fox (and three million dollars a year plus a twenty-five percent participation in any increase in value he could bring to the company). Though Diller's deal with Fox was not yet final, details of the move were leaked to and published in the *Wall Street Journal*. Eisner, then second in command at Paramount, found himself in an awkward spot: Diller never confided in him about the Fox offer so he hadn't made any of the right moves; the "offer" from Disney seemed to change every day; and he had a clause in his contract assuring him Diller's job should he leave, but Marty Davis, Bluhdorn's successor at Gulf and Western, disliked and distrusted him and Eisner had every reason to believe that Davis would not adhere to the contract. Unbeknownst to Eisner, Davis had already tried to get around the clause by asking Diller to fire Eisner, but Diller never followed through.

Two days later, Diller officially resigned from Paramount. Davis then called Eisner to New York and made it clear that he had no intention of giving Eisner Diller's job. At 4 A.M. the following morning, Katzenberg called Eisner with more bad news: the *Wall Street Journal* was publishing a story identifying marketing chief Frank Mancuso as Paramount's new studio chief. By the end of business on Tuesday, September 11, Eisner resigned, as Davis agreed to forgive a $1.2 million loan on Eisner's Bel Air home in consideration of Davis's decision not to honor Eisner's contract.

Temporarily out of work, Eisner received offers from several studios including Fox, but remained patient for all of two weeks with all the tumult at Disney. He was Roy Jr.'s man, but that hadn't meant a whole lot in the past. And despite Roy Jr.'s new-found power, the majority of the board favored former Fox Chairman and Times Mirror Vice-President Dennis Stanfill, a "numbers man" not unlike Roy Sr. Eisner got the nod only after "numbers man" Frank Wells agreed to take the second spot, and Bass and Rainwater were sold by Roy Jr. on the necessity to have a creative man (like Walt!) in the top spot. When the board met to officially hire Eisner and Wells, the nomination came from the unlikeliest of characters, Card Walker.

During Miller's brief tenure as chief executive, the company launched the Disney Channel and set in motion his five-year plan, which included diversifying the film division with Touchstone Pictures, and exploiting Disney's considerable film library, for example, by putting the classics on videotape. It was Miller who purchased the rights to *Who Framed Roger Rabbit?*, and work began on the project under his leadership.

Finally, Miller's one big live-action film, *Splash,* was the studio's first hit in over fifteen years, and effectively moved the film division into production directed at both adult and adolescent audiences.

In what is yet another ironic twist, Miller essentially set in motion the very changes Roy Jr. proposed a decade earlier, which led to his resignation in 1977. But like Roy Jr.'s exit, Miller's ouster was primarily symbolic. He had to go because of his ties to the old regime, and his exit had to be at the behest of the last "Roy man" left standing, ironically and importantly, the only blood-relative Disney capable of and interested in the day-to-day operation of the family business.

To be fair here, Miller had vision but little ability to run the company. Roy Jr. was a far better businessman, and with Hollywood's move into the Reaganomic eighties, his way of doing business tended to carry the day. Indeed, while Roy Jr. became something of a major player on Wall Street—his exile made him strong enough to return his side of the family to power at the company—Miller, who spent his life at Disney, was shockingly naïve about the new corporate Hollywood. This naïveté is evident in, for example, Miller's decision to pull the Disney television show off the air. Richard Nunis, a far more savvy player at Disney, advised strongly against pulling the show; despite poor ratings it at least afforded the company free advertising for the theme parks and merchandise. Miller, eager to move off-network so as not to compete with the Disney cable channel, ignored Nunis's advice. But looking back, Miller realized that Nunis was right. In a typical bit of self-effacement, Miller reflected: "I just didn't get where he was coming from. I mean, what the hell, no one was watching the damn thing anyway."[20]

This is all to say that the reconciliation of the family business and the business of family at Disney offers an object lesson on the new Hollywood and, alas, on doing business with one's own family. Indeed, though Roy Sr. and Walt reconciled before Walt's death, for Roy Jr. the last few years have been sweet revenge. We can only guess at how good it felt when, in 1987, as Eisner and Wells had the studio poised to take the number one spot in the industry, Roy Jr., who could never draw, was named head of the animation department.[21]

7

Painting a Plausible World: Disney's Color Prototypes

Richard Neupert

Technicolor Inc. introduced a three-strip color motion picture process in 1932 which improved upon their earlier two-strip process by adding a blue component to what had previously been only a red and green system.[1] However, problems of resolution and accuracy with the earlier two-color process made Hollywood's major studios leery of color. The *costs* of Technicolor increased producers' hesitation toward live-action feature filmmaking. According to *Variety*, in 1930 the industry warned that the added cost of color must be limited to about ten percent above black-and-white costs before it could be widely accepted. They cite Warner Bros.' *Gold Diggers of Broadway* (1930) as an example: in black and white the daily rushes would have cost $23,000, in Technicolor they were $115,000; in black-and-white release prints would have been $63,000, in color they were $451,000.[2] Technicolor was therefore seen as an outrageously risky expense.

Thus, while the new 1932 process may have been more accurate, it now compounded problems of expense by requiring *three* strips of film being simultaneously exposed in the rented Technicolor cameras. Moreover, producing in Technicolor also meant you had to have a Technicolor camera operator, plus a Technicolor color consultant present throughout all stages of production, and finally, expensive Technicolor color-matrix processing for the negatives and release prints. Because Technicolor needed an immediate influx of capital (their 1932 sales of five hundred thousand dollars were only one-tenth of what they had been in 1929, and their 1932 deficit was $235,000),[3] they looked to animation and industrial clients to pay their bills and prove to Hollywood that the new process was indeed worth the extra investment.

While Technicolor would have welcomed a cartoon contract with a major studio like Warner Bros. or MGM, the major studios were unwilling to increase the expenses of cartoons, which they saw as a marginal line of production at best. Instead, Disney became the first studio to exploit commercially Technicolor's three-color cinematography process.[4] In order to shift over from black-and-white to color cartoons, Disney had to change its animation procedures. However, since the earlier two-color Technicolor had failed to satisfy Hollywood standards of efficiency and quality, the unproven three-color process posed immediate risks and challenges. Thus, in addition to technical inventions and innovations (such as new inks, paints, lamps, and three sequential exposures of each frame),[5] aesthetic innovations were required as well.

Disney, therefore, embarked on a program to train its animators and story writers alike in color theory. As a result of this *aesthetic* innovation during the years 1932 to 1935, the *Silly Symphonies* cartoon series became an unlikely prototype for Technicolor's subsequent live-action feature films. Moreover, as we shall see in the cases of the cartoon compilation *Academy Award Revue* (1937) and the feature-length *Snow White* (1937), Disney also provided successful blueprints for the marketing of color.

In an address to the Society of Motion Picture Engineers in 1938, Herbert Kalmus, President of Technicolor, paid tribute to Disney Studio's patronage and creative application of the three-color process. Kalmus admitted that in 1932 Technicolor needed to try the new process out in animation "to prove the process beyond any doubt," and that only Disney was willing to undertake the added expense and risk of color cartoons. He also mentioned that a good topic for debate would be whether Technicolor helped Disney more, or whether it was the Disney Studio that did the biggest favor by boosting Technicolor. Either way, Kalmus concluded, each relatively small company expanded greatly thanks to the other's contributions.[6]

In addition to describing the history of Technicolor, however, Kalmus discussed Disney in order to prove that three-color Technicolor was indeed viable, both commercially and artistically. Kalmus told the industry that whenever producers asked how much more it would cost to shoot in color rather than black and white, he told them the concrete costs, but then added that not all aspects of the question concerned such tangible elements:

> You have all seen Disney's *Funny [Little] Bunnies;* you remember the huge rainbow circling across the screen to the ground and you remember the Funny Bunnies drawing the color of the rainbow into their paint pails and splashing the Easter eggs. You will admit that it was marvelous entertainment. Now I will ask you how much more did it cost Mr. Disney to produce that entertainment in color than it would have in black and white? The answer is, of course, that it could

not be done at any cost in black and white. . . . A similar analogy can
be drawn with respect to some part of almost any recent Technicolor
Feature.[7]

It is important to note that while Kalmus admitted at the end that similar
examples *could* be pulled from Technicolor features, he preferred to
discuss a color cartoon made in 1934, rather than to describe color in
any of the fourteen features produced during 1935, 1936, or 1937, or
any of the fifteen features released in 1938, the year he was speaking.
Disney remained a vital selling point for Technicolor even after the three-
component live-action features were playing in theaters across the country.
It is common knowledge that before Pioneer Pictures (which owned a
healthy portion of Technicolor's stock) produced the first live-action feature, *Becky Sharp,* in three-color Technicolor in 1935, Disney Studios
had already won four Academy Awards for its color use in the *Silly
Symphonies.* What is even more startling is that those same color cartoons
were still being used by Technicolor to win over clients three years after
the first live-action features had been released.

Two questions obviously arise: first, why was color so essential to
Disney's animation; and second, what could *Funny Little Bunnies* and
Mickey Mouse offer the industry that *Becky Sharp* could not? The first
section of this article describes how Disney's cartoons in the early 1930s
established codified norms for color use that did satisfy historically proven
demands of the Hollywood system. As David Bordwell writes, Technicolor had always supplied its own research prototypes for the industry to
prove it could meet Hollywood's various demands.[8] Similarly, Disney's
early practice and the industry's enthusiastic discourse made its cartoons
a sort of ideal prototype, pointing the way for subsequent color stylistics
throughout the industry. However, close adherence to Disney's model
raised new problems when applied rigorously to Technicolor's live-action
features in the middle 1930s.

To begin with, we should briefly summarize how color reinforced
Disney's own theories of animation. Up until the move into color, Disney's
product was widely praised for several seemingly contradictory traits:
first, as Disney's own marketing discourse emphasized, its product was
dedicated to creating a convincing "illusion of life," even in the most
unreal realm of the cinema. Second, the cartoons followed classical models
of narratively motivated action in which character traits and goals organized the story events, initiating and maintaining a strong emotional
attachment and identification for the audience. Finally, Disney's "artistic
spectacle"—its attention to detail and stylistic flourishes—presented a
third important dimension. Thus its "magical art" was plausibly motivated
by the diegetic world of the stories. Disney's earlier innovation of sync-

sound serves as a perfect example of this balance of plausible illusion, narrative motivation, and spectacle.

Color certainly continued Disney's emphasis on these three aspects of its theories of representation. Color schemes were designed around the central characters' "personalities." Roger Noake, in his 1988 book on animation, writes for instance that Disney's significance lay in tying sound and color to "close attention to narrative and characterization."[9] In addition, the painted backgrounds were harmonious with the central figures' colors. Disney animators Frank Thomas and Ollie Johnston write that the background painters "support the action" by minimizing detail or bright colors that could distract from the action, thus the background palette is said to reinforce characterization and the action's effects subtly and plausibly.[10] Yet there were always segments that foregrounded dynamic color arrangements to reinforce exciting and fast-paced moments in the action.

Perhaps color's greatest single contribution to Disney's mode of animation, however, was its ability to aid in the illusion of depth. Psychologists and perception theorists cite color as one of the most active cues for depth perception and spatial orientation. In his article "Color in Contour and Object Perception," for example, Robert Boynton writes that when we open our eyes in an illuminated room we are bombarded with the images of forms that quickly become "differentiated and separated from one another through differences in their colors. Colors are what fill in the outlines of the forms; they are the stuff out of which visual phenomena are built."[11]

Obviously, a black-and-white film image uses a host of other cues to convince us of depth (such as overlap, familiar size, and atmospheric perspective, all of which Disney used). However, contours and variations in color intensity are among the most reliable visual cues for implying the edges of objects and for constructing pictorial or finally scenographic space.[12] While lending depth and spatial cues, color also supplies additional illusory cues in flat pictorial representations. The illusion of various planes can thus be created by choice of color. For instance, cooler colors and tints tend to recede, while warmer colors and shades appear to advance in a flat color image. Simultaneously, brighter colors seem *larger* than darker objects of similar size and shape, which also reinforces the perception of various planes where there is only a two-dimensional surface.[13]

Thus while the addition of color to Disney's world certainly provided new narrative tools for reinforcing characterization, and new opportunities for spectacle, it was the ability to supply stronger *perceptual* cues for reading depth into the flat surface that really helped Disney's images create an even more complete and complex scenographic space. For Herbert Kalmus at Technicolor, Disney's color use did even more. It created an illusory world that could not exist in such convincing detail in black and white. Color allowed animators more cues for creating an illusion of depth, and consequently, color made black and white's depth cues less convincing. Once Disney's characters danced their way deep into an illusory color world, the black-and-white cartoon did not become obsolete, but it did become more stylized and artificial-looking by contrast. Even Disney found it necessary to stop filming Mickey Mouse in black and white.

Technicolor's problem was precisely the opposite. The early live-action features were being criticized within the industry, as well as by film critics and historians, as artificial and distracting. It is important to remember that, unlike sound and its rapid diffusion by the major studios in 1928 and 1929, color's diffusion was very slow.[14] Moreover, Technicolor's earliest efforts were only moderately successful financially, and were thus considered by the industry merely as early stages in a slow evolution. Only Disney's cartoons were universally praised for their color innovations. For example, Lewis Jacobs, writing for the *New York Times* in 1935, criticized *La Cucaracha* (Pioneer's 1934 live-action short subject) and *Becky Sharp*, but labeled Disney's cartoons "moving examples of the astute mechanical perfection and creative possibilities of color films. . . . Disney alone understands the problem of color on the screen."[15] Similarly, Eric Rideout complained that *Becky Sharp* was often artificial, *Trail of the Lonesome Pine* (1936) "betrayed the vicious possibilities" of the Technicolor process, and even *The Garden of Allah* (1936), while less distracting than previous Technicolor films, occasionally "directed attention to the process and destroyed the atmosphere."[16] Critics were thus warning about color's interference with the films' continuity, as well as its disruption of the story and action.

Disney's cartoons, on the other hand, were seen as unified works that made color an integral element reinforcing the larger story and narration structures. Disney's narrativized colors and balanced harmonies established carefully motivated and pleasing schemes that became the norm for how color could be used in the cinema at large. In order to answer our second question, therefore, about why Disney's cartoons were so much more successful than the live-action films, we must consider what makes any new technology viable in the highly capitalized and narrativized Hollywood cinema.

Three general causes can justify technological change: efficiency, product differentiation, and/or adherence to standards of quality, according to Bordwell, Staiger, and Thompson in *Classical Hollywood Cinema.*[17] Color did differentiate films like *Becky Sharp*, but it was not at all efficient: it increased production costs by roughly 30 percent, required more lighting, demanded "cumbersome" cameras,[18] and created long delays for receiving rushes. Clearly, this sort of inefficiency was less of a hurdle for an animated short, which required less film stock, was comparatively easy to light, had a fixed camera anyway, and whose "shooting" was purely mechanical, so that delayed rushes caused fewer problems. Thus, while three-color Technicolor caused problems on the set for live action, once it was adopted by Disney, it became quite routine to use it to shoot cartoons.

More importantly, Disney's color satisfied and even surpassed industrial standards by narrativizing the colors and supplying a very marketable visual spectacle. Color became a new, expressive, yet naturalized element, and Disney tied color use to character, setting, and action, following the same cause and effect rules employed by the classical Hollywood cinema. Christian Metz's definition of the word *plausible* applies here. According to Metz, "the Plausible . . . is an *arbitrary* and *cultural* restriction of real possibles; it is in fact, censorship: Among all the possibilities of figurative fiction, only those authorized by previous discourse will be 'chosen.' "[19] Similarly, the range of color's possibilities (or free play) was reduced by arbitrary industrial and cultural conventions. Even in the idealized world of fantasy cartoons concerning big bad wolves blowing down pigs' huts, the color was "plausibly" applied so that the wolf's color would gradually shift to reveal the "real" strain in generating such a force of air. Hollywood norms were satisfied and the audience, critics, and industry alike were won over.

It is logical, then, that Technicolor paid close attention to Disney's successful aesthetic innovations in color use. One of Technicolor's own aesthetic strategies was to provide (or promise to provide) more pleasing and narrativized colors for live-action productions, since that was what the industry and critics alike were demanding. Natalie Kalmus, director of Technicolor's Advisory Service, outlined strict guidelines in 1935 that regulated policy for live-action features. Almost point for point, those guidelines echo the color *practice* already provided by Disney's *Silly Symphonies*.

One problem, however, was that while Natalie Kalmus's ideas sprang from animation and painting, they did not always seem to suit feature films. For example, her philosophy for a unified Technicolor style stood on a three-tiered argument similar to Disney's: color should be naturalized; color should follow established conventional standards of harmony, contrast, and cultural connotations; and color should be narrativized to add to the story without distracting the audience.[20] She appealed for "natural colors" which did not tax the eye, and added that "even when Nature indulges in a riot of beautiful colors, there are subtle harmonies which justify those colors."[21] Her policies, as Bordwell writes, insisted on cool colors for sets and costumes, "the better to set off the tones of the characters' faces," and thus she dictated heavy use of pastels which were "less harsh and distracting."[22]

All these general and specific rules already characterized Disney's work. For instance, Disney enforced strict rules of color harmony, but added great variety and detail to the resulting animation cels. One color design strategy that helps guarantee such harmony and color balance, even in a "riot of colors," is to use adjacent colors for the color scheme (such as blue, blue-green, and green), with each hue sharing similar values. In addition, the largest color area (such as the sky, a grassy area, or a wall) generally has relatively weak chroma, while smaller areas in the foreground use more saturated colors. In this way, one has a balanced color harmony within the image and a great potential for deep "space" (brighter objects appear closer).

In *Funny Little Bunnies* these strategies are quite clear—the pale blue skies (often mixed with blue-violet and gray clouds) and the pale blue-green grass help distinguish the deep blue overalls on the rabbits. The brighter costumes and white faces are thereby set off from the background and function to focus our attention on the characters while simultaneously suggesting planes of depth. Similarly, during the most colorful shots (such as the rainbow and the colored eggs being loaded into baskets) all significant objects share similar values and chroma, but they are also brighter than the backgrounds. Contrasting colors (here red and yellow) are used on the details in the foreground, or on the central figures. To further lend harmonious balance, bright objects in the foreground (such as yellow flowers) are often paired with paler objects in the background, creating a "plausible" color shift reinforcing the representation of depth. Thus, the Disney image typically uses a pale background with colors that allow the main characters to be painted with brighter harmonious colors but also bright spots of contrasting color, lending distinction, personality, and depth. Disney animators even mention that color reduced the number of close-ups they could use, because close-ups flatten the image with their large expanses of color.[23]

However, while Disney supplied an overall color strategy for composing narratively functional and extremely harmonious images, such balanced harmony in live-action often looked highly staged and artificial. For instance, during the famous Waterloo Ball scene in *Becky Sharp,* the guests are divided into high society people or soldiers. The socialites all wear pale gray, blue, or blue-green, and are barely brighter than similarly colored backgrounds (walls, curtains, potted plants), while the soldiers sport red uniforms. The suspense that builds as Napoleon's cannon fire nears is paralleled so obviously by the gathering of more and more red uniforms in the frame that the scene becomes comical. Either a character is the color of the potted plants, or else he is a soldier running around to add some contrasting red to the mise-en-scène. Such overly simplistic color schemes were meant to support the dramatic action, but in reality they actually detracted from both the action and its plausibility. Many critics noticed (and resented) the color design being sketched out in clumsy fashion before their very eyes: cool harmonious colors were used for the vulnerable people in contrast to the bold soldiers' blood red uniforms, which paralleled the rockets' red glare.

Disney's color use appeared much more vibrant and both narratively and aesthetically pleasing than much of the live-action Technicolor product. Admittedly, by 1937 Technicolor's reputation with live-action was improving with each film. Most major color productions from David O. Selznick's production of *A Star is Born* (1937) on, including pictures like Walter Wanger's *Vogues of 1938* (1937), Paramount's *Ebb Tide* (1937), and Selznick's *Nothing Sacred* (1937), were touted by *Variety* as among the "best tinting jobs yet." But while ads like that for *Vogues of 1938* may have declared "From now on all pictures will be in color,"[24] critics and other producers were not quite ready for such a color revolution. For example, the review for *Nothing Sacred* is quite revealing about the continuation of color's wary reception: "It's one of the best of a few outstanding color jobs of the past year. . . . The prismatic features of *Nothing Sacred* are pleasing to the eye, not unrestful, and not disturbing."[25] Color had to prove itself pleasing, restful, and integrated, and in the late 1930s Disney was still the only consistent source of such color.

While Disney's aesthetic innovations of three-color Technicolor were thus setting the standards by which live-action would be judged, its marketing and financial successes were also pointing a direction for Hollywood. For instance, Disney's string of Academy Awards and its marketing barrages exceeded individual live-action features in both scale and success. While a particular film like *Nothing Sacred* may have encouraged the industry about Technicolor's potential, the three-strip system was still being evaluated on a film-by-film basis. Disney's product, by contrast, was constantly equated with color quality.

Disney decided to sell each new color cartoon with great emphasis on technical wizardry, but it also kept reminding the public and industry (much like Kalmus himself) about its *past* triumphs. As early as 1933, Disney and United Artists advertised the Technicolor *Silly Symphonies* as "acclaimed by everybody the finest motion pictures ever made, critics are playing them up ABOVE the features on the same bill!"[26] By 1937, when other animation studios had access to three-strip color, Disney further emphasized its color expertise by rereleasing its most celebrated color *Silly Symphonies* as *Walt Disney's Academy Award Revue*. This compilation lasted forty-three minutes and featured *Flowers and Trees, Three Little Pigs, The Tortoise and the Hare, Three Orphan Kittens,* and

The Country Cousin. Each cartoon had won an Academy Award for Color Cartoon in consecutive years. (Disney's cartoons continued to sweep the short cartoon awards until 1940, but the special category of "color cartoon" was discontinued.)

Disney's practice of rereleasing later feature cartoons every seven years, and its tactic of protecting the market value of motion pictures on videotape by pulling them from distribution and then rereleasing them, or offering videos like *Fantasia* or *Jungle Book* for sale during "limited time" periods,[27] is obviously in keeping with Disney's long practice of preserving future revenues, even from market conditions or alternative technologies not yet on the horizon. (Disney, for instance, broke its distribution contract with United Artists in 1936 over contractual disagreements concerning future TV revenues at a time when United Artists, like the rest of the industry, had no clear idea how TV might affect the industry.)[28] Disney's marketing plans for color cartoons provided both a key to understanding its own promotional savvy, and a blueprint for success (followed by Selznick's promotion of *Gone With the Wind*) in pushing color itself.

Studios had always done a good job of pushing their top features and looking for tie-ins, but Disney/United Artists provided what seems to have been one of the most successful promotional campaigns of the 1930s with *Snow White,* and *Academy Award Revue* was in some ways *Snow White's* prototype. "Dollarize with Disney" became the battle cry from United Artists in trade ads, with an insert from one *Variety* ad, quoting from Phil M. Daly's column "Along the Rialto," making full use of the slogan:

> Dollarize with Disney . . . that will be the slogan for you exhibs when you book this Walt Disney novelty feature with its sure-fire B.O. pull . . . this novelty cartoon will be backed with a nation-wide newspaper campaign . . . an exploitation campaign along the lines of a Chaplin feature . . . tie-ups with more than a hundred Disney licensees who will plug the event with newspaper ads, window displays and radio mentions . . . a special pressbook . . . and a series of coast-to-coast broadcasts for several weeks prior to the release date, with scenes from the Revue put on the air and Walt Disney himself speaking to the nation in the final broadcast . . . it is a cinch that this Quintuplet Quintessence of Quality from the Cartoon Master will Bowl Over your B.O. in a Disney Deluge of Dollars.[29]

However, while *Academy Award Revue* did in fact generally receive feature billing, either singly or in a double bill, and while United Artists and Disney did get feature rentals for the compilation, the box office returns were disappointing. The lesson seemed to be that a cartoon could be billed and rented as a feature (even at only forty-three minutes), but that the rereleased cartoons could only really pay well at second-run houses. Nonetheless, Disney had earned additional revenues from color cartoons that had already returned a handsome profit years earlier, and proven that a cartoon could be handled like a feature, even with nothing "new" to sell. The marketing campaign therefore was quite successful; the product simply did not have legs in competition with other first-run products (like Technicolor's *A Star is Born,* which premiered at the same time and drew much new praise for live-action color).

The second and certainly more significant marketing coup for Disney, and its new distributor RKO, arrived for the Christmas season that same year but lasted long into 1938. Disney's first feature-length cartoon, *Snow White,* "wowed" everyone, becoming the most popular American film of all time (until profits from *Gone With the Wind* began to soar in 1940). In city after city during its very long first run, *Snow White* broke all records in attendance and the only reason it failed to break box office records in some markets was that a large portion of the audience was composed of children paying a lower ticket price.[30] RKO was indeed successful with its overall strategy, however, since its *Snow White* contracts brought it fifty and even sixty percent of the receipts.

In New York, *Snow White* held the distinction of being the first film ever held for more than three weeks at Radio City Music Hall; it lasted five weeks, and was only moved out because of contractual obligations. In fact, even during its fifth week at Radio City, *Snow White* took in $102,000 (for a five-week total of $525,000), while Selznick's color *Tom Sawyer,* which followed, only drew $85,000 its first week. (RKO's take from the five-week run was also a record for the highest amount Radio City had ever paid out to a distributor.) Moreover, *Snow White* went directly to the Palace, where it played for three more weeks, for a total Manhattan run of eight weeks (while it simultaneously set home records in Brooklyn). Similarly, the "tinted cartoon" ran eight weeks in Los Angeles. *Variety's* theater column even notes that *Snow White's* business was so good that it was hurting vaudeville. Furthermore, several cities complained that Disney's film was draining children's piggy banks so they would be less likely to go to other "kid pics," like *Tom Sawyer,* in the near future.

How did Disney's film attract such an overwhelming and immediate wave of enthusiasm? As the "Dollarize with Disney" ads to theater operators demonstrated above, Disney's strategy combined excellent name and quality recognition with both a media blitz and local tie-ins. In Louisville, the local *Variety* stringer proclaimed "It's *Snow White* week. Groceries, drug stores, etc. are cooperating by special window displays, and various *Snow White* tie-ups with merchandise."[31] Even New Yorkers helped Disney sell his movie: "Another feature of the Disney picture is the way merchants, newspapers, etc. want to tie in with the film. That's unusual."[32] Thus, in addition to radio and newspaper interviews and stories, the sales of *Snow White* dolls, sheet music, and other ancillary products allowed local stores to profit. Disney and RKO had every sales angle covered, and locals were *asking* for movie posters to place in their windows.

The results of Disney's successful color productions went beyond filling its own coffers and those of RKO. They established Technicolor as a great potential box office advantage. While *Snow White* was still reaching smaller cities for its first run in early March 1938, Paramount-Fleischer announced a new contract for a Technicolor feature cartoon. Perhaps more significantly, MGM signed a contract with Technicolor for six pictures in three years; MGM had previously only shot Technicolor sequences (or employed MGM's own sepia process).

It is important to note, however, that while Disney and Technicolor were both credited with *Snow White's* aesthetic and financial success, color was still being hotly debated by many live-action producers. Just after *Academy Award Revue,* Joseph M. Schenck and Darryl F. Zanuck were still reluctant on color, as *Variety* declared: "Neither can see color as an inevitable 'must,' despite the local hullabaloo."[33] Similarly, all during 1937 there was mention in the trade press that Selznick was not yet sure whether *Gone With the Wind* would be in color or black and white. Even after *Snow White,* when Selznick and John Hay Whitney were considering buying United Artists, they stated that they were pretty sure they would *not* spend the estimated five hundred thousand dollars extra to shoot their epic in Technicolor.

Thus, even with the successes of live-action color features like *A Star is Born,* Wanger's *Vogues of 1938,* or *Nothing Sacred,* and in spite of predictions that an "all-color Hollywood" was just around the corner, Technicolor was advancing slowly in the battle to capture producers' confidence and prove itself at the box office. Walt Disney's effects on the industry, therefore, should not be overemphasized in terms of immediate results. Nonetheless, Disney's cartoons were continually cited as convincing models both critically and economically, and remained the shining example for Technicolor and the trade press. When Selznick decided to shoot *Gone With the Wind* in Technicolor, it was as much due to Disney as to Whitney's personal influence (and Whitney and Selznick's common interest in Technicolor's stock and future). Moreover, when Melanie and Ashley stand at the open window at Twelve Oaks, and outside the pastel costumes and setting provide a perfect backdrop, the shot owes a debt both to Natalie Kalmus's still-developing theories of color application, and *Snow White's* harmonious color composition and narrative purpose. As for Selznick's ad campaigns, we need simply look back to "Dollarize with Disney" to see where Disney's campaign provided a base, particularly in media and color tie-ins.

Conclusions

Disney's color schemes in the *Silly Symphonies* helped point the way for codified color use that would reinforce classical Hollywood norms for motivation, clarity, and spectacle. Color schemes were designed to satisfy conventional aesthetic norms of harmony, balance, and variety, while keeping the central figures as focal points for our attention and as unifying points for the color pattern. However, live-action filmmakers found that their own color patterns tended toward simplified color connotations or featured overly distracting rather than pleasing harmonies. Natalie Kalmus and her color consultants tried to counter the artificiality of the process, but in the end, the most successful color films became those genre films which, like the cartoons, allowed for a great deal of spectacle.

Technicolor never wanted to become a process only for the musical, costume drama, and cartoon. It had to prove it could satisfy economic, technological, and aesthetic standards across genres, but Disney's work both helped and interfered with that challenge. Disney's cartoons proved more appropriate than Technicolor's own prototypes like *La Cacaracha* and *Becky Sharp* as models for demonstrating color's aesthetic virtuosity. Yet, while Disney's cartoons did provide a helpful guide for how to satisfy classical Hollywood standards, the industry would eventually have to *adapt* Disney's model rather than *imitate* it. Four years before Kalmus's speech of 1938 extolling the *Funny Little Bunnies*, Kalmus had told *Fortune* magazine that if Disney would only make a live-action feature, Technicolor's problems would be over.[34] Ironically, Disney Studios, and cartoon shorts like the *Funny Little Bunnies*, which had proven color could be innovated for animation, were still needed to boost Technicolor's diffusion process at the end of the decade.

8

The Betrayal of the Future: Walt Disney's EPCOT Center

Alexander Wilson

Among Walt Disney's many contributions to American popular culture, his theme parks call for special attention, because they form the landscape against which Disney's visions meet the historical and political realities of America.[1] Disney's most lavish theme park to date is EPCOT, the Experimental Prototype Community of Tomorrow. It was opened in late 1982 as a self-contained park within Disney World, southwest of Orlando, Florida. EPCOT was a vision that obsessed Disney from the opening of Disneyland in California in 1955 until his death. Like Brasilia and countless other modernist projects, it was to be a community built "from scratch." In a film made shortly before his death in 1966, Disney outlined his eccentric and worrisome vision of the future.

> EPCOT will be an experimental city that would incorporate the best ideas of industry, government, and academia worldwide, a city that caters to the people as a service function. It will be a planned, controlled community, a showcase for American industry and research, schools, cultural and educational opportunities. In EPCOT there will be no slum areas because we won't let them develop. There will be no landowners and therefore no voting control. People will rent houses instead of buying them, and at modest rentals. There will be no retirees; everyone must be employed. One of the requirements is that people who live in EPCOT must help keep it alive.[2]

Sixteen years after his death, EPCOT Center opened at Walt Disney World. As an announcer proclaims when you climb out of the monorail on arrival, "EPCOT is technical know-how combined with Disney showmanship—550 acres exploring the innovations of tomorrow and the wonders of enterprise."

In 1956, Walt Disney Productions of California purchased 28,000 acres of land in Florida for $5.5 million—"enough land to hold all the ideas and plans we can possibly imagine," gushed Disney at the groundbreaking. And just as the prolix Disney publicists remind us, those ideas and plans just keep coming. At present, Walt Disney World contains not only EPCOT and the Magic Kingdom (the resituated Disneyland from California) but several hotel and convention complexes which, like furniture, come in themes such as Polynesian, Contemporary, Sport;[3] two large artificial lakes made to look like the Caribbean; several golf courses; lots of landscaped freeways and parking lots; a Wilderness Campground with an "Ol' Swimmin' Hole"; two airports; and a 7,500-acre conservation area.

Almost all of the workings of Disney World are hidden from the spectator, much as productive forces are concealed in the image of the commodity. Miles of underground corridors—"utilidors" in Disney parlance—transport workers, supplies, utilities, and telecommunications to the various parts of the "Total Vacation Kingdom." Staff cafeterias, laundries and dry cleaners, costume and dressing rooms, and storage facilities are all located underground throughout the site. Pneumatic tubes "whisk refuse away like magic" to compactors. Service roads are concealed behind berms. On-site jet generators and solar collectors power the entire park. Nurseries and greenhouses propagate a quarter of a million species of flora. Through special legal arrangements with the State of Florida, this postindustrial infrastructure operates outside of the jurisdiction of municipal and regional laws regarding zoning, traffic, development, power, and waste. The Disney fiefdom is designed to withstand challenges to its global vision of the future.

Disney World employs thirty thousand workers, depending on the season. Unless they are hired at the professional or managerial level, all staff must begin at the bottom—sweeping streets or taking tickets for minimum wage—and advance rung by rung to their desired station. Staff are trained in "efficiency, cleanliness, and friendliness"—the hallmark of the organization—at the on-site Disney University.

The Market in Futures

EPCOT specifically addresses the future in a way Disney's other parks do not. Its publicity says it is dedicated to the imagination, to our fantasies and our "dreams for better tomorrows." Disney publicity makes it seem as though a brighter future were just a matter of "creative thinking" and "futuristic technologies." The widespread sense of impending ecological or military catastrophe that people have today is thoroughly absent. At EPCOT we're told what the future is going to be and that it is a hopeful one. Here technology figures large as an agent of history. Progress, development, expansion, growth—these will ensure (some day) leisure and well-being for all.

Most of the exhibits at EPCOT flaunt new technologies and make great, if vague, claims about their liberatory potential. At the Electronic Forum, five hundred of us sit in an auditorium to participate in "the largest ongoing public opinion poll in the world." We learn that this room is called the Future Choice Theatre. By pressing buttons on the arms of our chairs we can say whether we're "for" or "against" the nuclear freeze, whether we believe social security benefits should go "up" or "down," what we think of video games, and whether we will buy an American or Japanese car this year. Excerpts from Reagan's and Kennedy's speeches help us decide some of our answers, which are then tabulated and announced. We're told that these opinions will "help shape the future" and then politely ushered out.

"Spaceship Earth" is an immense goedesic dome sponsored by Bell Telephone. Once we are through the winding line leading up to the "Spaceship," we get into rail cars and move off into darkness. Speakers in the headrests start saying something about volcanoes and magma. We pass pterodactyls and cavemen, then ancient Egypt, Greece, and Rome, which was "ruined by the flames of excess." It is hard to tell what this is supposed to be about. Geology? Gluttony? Mention is made of language, counting, and "information." We pass Phoenicians, Arabs, the invention of mathematics, Gutenberg. There is no presence of Chinese or Africans.

Then capitalism whizzes by—factories, smoke, child labor—and suddenly we're in the present. "New machines such as the computer help us chart our course through a world of boundless information." Bell switching rooms light up, a spacecraft moves across a planetarium ceiling (the top of the dome) and a voice says "we must take command of Spaceship Earth." As the car creeps down a near-vertical incline to the exit, there are more blinking lights, and finally this ominous sendoff: "From primal caves we have constructed vast communications networks. Ours is the age of knowledge, the age of choice and opportunity. Let us dare to fulfill our destiny."

This ride leaves us in a group of buildings called "Communicore," where Bell, Exxon, Sperry Univac, American Express and Walter E. Disney Enterprises (WED) sponsor hands-on exhibits of new high technology. At the Exxon display there are examples of coal, and slides of dinosaurs dying in tar pits. There is also a little show on strip-mining. Exxon calls it surface mining, and it seems that on balance the land actually benefits from the "renovation" that follows extraction. Then there is a video game about conservation which somehow manages to convey that, even though we're using less and less energy, we'll need more and more by the year 2000.

The Bell exhibit is called "Futurecom," and it too has many video games. At the entrance is a sculpture of plastic and mylar that focuses on the postdivestiture research at AT&T: teleconferencing, fiber optics, digital satellite hookups, new software. We're invited to "reach out and touch the network of Bell services." One game lets us play telephone operator during a snowstorm. Another has a voice synthesizer hooked up to a keyboard. I enter the word "fuck"; the synthesizer is silent. An immense electronic map of the United States lets us "dial" any state we want. The state lights up, some tourist photos appear on a screen, and a voice reads some statistics. The man next to me dials Missouri, where he's from: "The Show-Me State . . ." the narration begins. He hangs up and the program automatically picks California: "Land of Sunshine . . . ," pictures of orange groves, cable cars. We leave, but not before a voice tells us that "these technologies allow you to participate more fully in the world around you."

Future World is full of such "participatory" exhibits. The most inventive and genuinely pleasurable are probably the ones at the Kodak pavilion, "World of Imagination." Here there are sound and laser games, electronic kaleidoscopes, and my favorite, a bank of video screens you can draw on with "pens" of various colors. Yet these exhibits are exceptional. Most of the high-tech games and displays are tedious, even when they're supposed to be fun.

Perhaps it is no wonder people are afraid of high technology. Seldom are we left with any sense of being able to manipulate the technology ourselves. Consumption is the model here, rather than control. Will we have access to the new instrumentation? Will we be able to determine how it will be introduced to society, at what pace and with what effects? What implications does it have for the future of centralized urban societies? Is information an essential public resource or a privately owned commodity bought and sold in the marketplace? Isn't it dishonest to talk of the liberatory potential of telematics without considering the shortcomings of the society that invented it? What kinds of genuinely democratic uses are already being made of these technologies?[4] These are questions EPCOT never remotely considers; they are simply not on the agenda. Fun, however, is. EPCOT is at least as interested in entertaining its patrons as in enlightening them. Indeed, the entire project insists, as a Disney publicist told me, that "the future can be fun." Whose future is another question we're discouraged from asking, this time by the exposition's very design.

Progress and the American Landscape

The organizing principle of the EPCOT landscape is control. Direction is given to the gaze of the spectator: visual perspectives, aural terrains, the kinds of movement permitted—all reinforce and reinterpret the various themes of the Center. In this case, two areas face each other across an artificial lagoon—Future World and World Showcase. In the former, the various strategies of the futurist are paraded in a complex of pavilions set in a vaguely Beaux-Arts arrangement with Spaceship Earth as its center. In World Showcase, exoticized cultures of the past and present offer relief from what promise to be the urban (or suburban) horrors of the future displayed across the lagoon. The geographical juxtaposition of past and present—a configuration that with Disney always *progresses* through the landscape, toward the spectator of the present day—is explicit in its intentions. It reconciles, as Louis Marin argues, an ideal past with a real present.[5]

When you get off the monorail near Spaceship Earth, you hear music. "Future music," like Holst's "The Planets" or the theme from *Star Wars*. The colors are pastels, rather than the nursery-school primaries of the Magic Kingdom. As the pavilions and themed areas change, so does the music, the discreet announcements, the plantings, architecture, garbage cans, uniforms, and sewer covers. All of these shape the environment, much as Muzak fluorescent lighting, and air conditioning shape the space of our supermarkets. They mask "disagreeable" sounds (such as machinery and other people's conversations) and indicate the object of our attention.

EPCOT is a seamless environment: there is never a moment or space that is not visually, aurally, and olfactorily programmed by the Disney resort managers. (When it rains, for example, vendors appear with plastic ponchos.) You're always within earshot of an announcement, a chatty narration, a monition, or music. "Exit on your left"; "Visit the unique shops in Walt Disney Village, just a monorail ride away"; "Behind us lies the splendor of a lost civilization. . . ." The effects of this sensory blanketing are at once exhilarating and exhausting. Amid signifiers of choice and plenitude, the Disney park reduces all possible experience to a single prescribed one. The occasional semi-interactive video terminal, for example, asks us what themes of the future we're interested in, and then indicates what area we should visit next. EPCOT determines our "future" at the same time that it proscribes the unpredictable or spontaneous present. Louis Marin's indictment of Disneyland holds true for EPCOT as well:

> Disneyland is an extraordinary dystopia. It displaces the spatial habit-
> ability . . . into its spectacular representation; it reduces the dynamic
> organization of the places, the aleatory unity of a possible tour to a
> univocal scheme allowing only the same redundant behavior.[6]

The geography of World Showcase, across the lake, focuses on the American pavilion. Flanking the empire, in order of importance, are its major trading partners: West Germany, Japan, Italy, France, China, Great Britain, Canada, and Mexico, each sponsored by "local" transnational corporations. Future exhibits are planned for Israel, Morocco, and Equatorial Africa. In the latter case, no transnational, or, as they say in the Disney organization, "universal" corporation could be found to sponsor it, so Disney will do it itself. Most of the pavilions are boutiques adorned with localized architectures—an Eiffel Tower here, a Japanese garden there; some have films or ride-through stories.

The anachronistic edifices of the "international" exhibits at EPCOT serve to organize historical perceptions and social nostalgia. Here, in a departure from previous American fairs, our sentiments are focused as much on urban societies as on rural ones. What these reconstructed foreign townscapes emphasize is the function medieval and Renaissance cities continue to play as a relief from the visual monotony of modern urban society, a function reinforced by the fact that these "old world" cities are one of the few places at Disney World where you can get a drink! Here in World Showcase, the city can be taken in at a single glance, as Aristotle prescribed; its human scale and the integrity of its social and geographical structure make for a visual comprehensibility absent in the modern American metropolis. And as in all of Disney's work—he if anyone has "learned from Las Vegas"—the various architectural styles of World Showcase appropriate signifiers of luxury and well-being in order to establish status.[7]

Across the lake in Future World, however, Disney's concern with the city dissipates. Against the profound and ubiquitous American nostalgia for rural society, we're given what amounts to a postwar suburb. The city—the *polis* as a unique communitarian space that reconciles natural forces with human needs—is conspicuously absent from the ideals of the Disney imagineers, as it has been from the American landscape for quite some time. There are frequent references to a metropolis, but it appears as only a few blinking lights seen from a car at the end of innumerable rides. These models are not called cities in the publicity, but "cityscapes," would-be cities. Overall, the references throughout Future World, from the Florida landscapes of the site itself to the images in many films, are to what Andrew Jackson Downing called the "smiling lawns and tasteful cottages" of the American suburb.

For Downing, Frederick Law Olmsted, and other nineteenth-century reformers, the suburb offered deliverance from the unhealthy physical and moral climate of industrial society, a compromise between the metropolis and the frontier.[8] Yet by the mid-twentieth century, the suburb was no longer an attempt at radical alteration of the tension between city and country. Massive land speculation and housing construction in the postwar period obliterated millions of acres of forest and agricultural land that had been the attraction in the first place. As Stanley Aronowitz has shown, industrial and government planning ensured an American economy structured around the industrial park, the automobile, and the interstate highway, rather than the older and less wasteful paradigm of urban factory and waterway. This shift was immediately carried out by the swelled families of returning war veterans; eventually it would have enormous consequences for all North Americans—as well as a great many people elsewhere. Disneyland popularized the suburban topographies of shopping center and cloverleaf in an American culture just getting used to the anomalous and atomized space of what Frank Lloyd Wright had called, in yet another take on the suburb, the "country-wide, countryside city."

It is a fitting irony, then, that the largest and most popular pavilion at EPCOT, Kraft's "The Land," looks like a shopping mall. The main attraction at the Kraft construction is a boat ride called "Listen to the Land." It is billed as a "journey to a place most of us have forgotten about: the place where food is grown." But before we get there, we float by some translucent plastic sculptures of plants that highlight cellular and photosynthetic development, sort of a Tunnel of Love with *Fantastic Voyage* sets. Then we sail past examples of biotic communities. Around another bend in the river we reach the Family Farm, which smells faintly of hay and cow shit. As an idealized representation of agrarian life, all is in place: bucolic setting, fence and field, farm, barn and domestic animals, the yeoman farmer and his tightly knit family. The music is what's called in the business "soothing." Yet it can't mask the rupture that follows. "Each year," the narration intones, "the family farm is being replaced by business as farming becomes a science. With better seeds, better pesticides and better techniques, we're moving into a new era." We round another corner, and suddenly we're in a greenhouse, the blue Florida sky high above our mythic boat ride through American history. The farm has been erased from memory; this is a laboratory, and it must be the place they told us where food is grown. "This is what's called Controlled Environment Agriculture, CEA for short." We again move through several biomes, which thanks to science are all blooming this time. "Nature by itself is not always productive." There are buffalo gourds, triticale, and gopher plants—this last a euphorbia species being propagated by a synthetic fuel—growing in eighteen inches of hot sandy soil. There are demonstrations of trickle-irrigation technology, nutriculture, and growing food in outer space: to simulate gravity, lettuce is spun in a mesh cylinder round a broad-spectrum fluorescent tube.

In truth, however, the family farm was far more than the site of food production in North American society. Thus its destruction entailed not only the rationalization of the agricultural landscape, but the decimation of local communities and rural cultures. Yet there is scarcely time for such musings, for by now we're passing giant tanks of bass, eels, paddlefish, and catfish. This is something called aquaculture, we're told. The fish are taking part of their nutrition from the red lights above the tanks. We hear children's voices singing a tune obviously ripped off from Woody Guthrie; it goes "Let's listen to the land we all love. . . ."

Despite the exhortations, the message is clearly "Leave farming to the scientists." As the high priests of industrial civilization, scientists are a signal part of the agribusiness complex. The United States government for over a century has funded a system of agricultural colleges, experimental stations, and extension services at large state universities throughout the country. Their imperative has been to substitute a technical revolution in the fields for a social one. The research going on at EPCOT, under the aegis of the University of Arizona, is typical of the kind of work these institutions sponsor. The beneficiaries of this research are not farm laborers, rural communities, or even the consuming public. At the end of the day, no one has benefited from mechanized harvesting, carcinogenic pesticides, genetic engineering, monoculture, petroleum-based fertilizers, outside water-diversion projects, a dangerously simplified ecosystem, or feed laced with antibiotics and synthetic hormones; no one, that is, so much as agricultural transnationals.

At the end of the ride, once we're out of the boats, we are confronted with a shop selling plastic fruits and bright ceramic vegetable ashtrays. From here it's all downhill. The central atrium of the pavilion is taken up by the Farmer's Market, a charming amalgam of pizza-parlor decor, chain-store marketing, and corporate advertising. Here we can buy processed cheese sandwiches from Kraft and ITT, peach nectar from Nestlé, soup from Campbell's, meat alloys from Greyhound, and snack foods from Pepsico. Chairs and tables are of one-piece extruded plastic in colors like avocado and salmon. The floor is a brown "cobblestone" indoor-outdoor creation, and everything reeks of mustard and ketchup.

This is pretty well the menu all over Disney World. The monotonous and denatured form of the food is masked, or perhaps enhanced—by the various "atmospheres" in which we can choose to consume it. Just as agriculture has become an industry more than a way of life, so is preparing and eating food now more a matter of commodity consumption than social activity. On the other hand, in many North American cities, fast-food malls like this have been recuperated as public space; they are hangouts for marginal youth, much as neighborhood soda fountains were in the past. May we wish the same for the Farmer's Market.

Corporate Patriotism: History as PR

At EPCOT, the pavilion rides are called "attractions." Thus, by Disney standards, the best are precisely the ones with the highest production values. The more special effects are used, the better the publicity for the corporate sponsor. The rides in fact function in the same way, using many of the same techniques, as television advertising. The object is to transform the product—or in this case the corporate image—into a symbol of particular cultural values or norms. With Disney, such values are easy to identify: patriotism, family life, and free enterprise, together with the corporate logo, form the story of the inexorable triumph of American society.

The General Motors show is called the World of Motion. Its theme song is "It's Fun to Be Free." Again, the story begins with cavemen, and moves on to a montage illustrating the obsolescence of the past: animal power, chariots, rickshaws, the Renaissance, the Mona Lisa, carriages, Indians attacking stagecoaches, steam locomotives, robbers, sheriffs in white hats, streetcars, the tearing up of streetcar tracks, the Model T, the Sunday drive in the country, and finally a glistening and wonderful 1949 Woody, one of the zeniths of Detroit engineering and design. Again, we drop in darkness past a distant "future city" of blinking lights and emerge in the "Transcenter" where we inspect models of hovercraft hotels, "personal submarines," and three-wheeled enclosed motorcycles.

Another exhibit, "Horizons," sponsored by General Electric, is ostensibly about "family lifestyles in the twenty-first century." In a city submerged in the ocean, mothers dress school children in recirculation gills for a field trip to a kelp farm. Father is away on business in space.

These corporate narratives of progress attempt to build a consensus about the historic mission of American capitalism, thus deflecting the questions of power and control that pervade our everyday lives in consumer society. At the lavish Exxon pavilion, "Universe of Energy," we're blithely told that "together, you the public, with government and industry, will solve tomorrow's energy needs." In Disney's elaborate invasion of the future, it is precisely this spurious partnership that is proposed as the means of securing an affluent and satisfying future. Yet as we blink and look again, we see that we do not produce our future out of the material reality of the present. That future is served up ready-made, a feast of "new ideas" and "leading-edge technologies." Once history is reduced to a series of technical innovations, rather than genuine change, the past can be retold as an imperfect rehearsal for the present (as the present is for the future), full of the same old moral lessons that support the prevailing ideologies of today.

The American Adventure is the name of the pavilion that sits at the head of the lake in World Showcase. It provides a spectacular history of the heroic American nation, sponsored by Coca-Cola and American Express. The building's design is the bastardized Georgian usually associated with A&P shopping plazas and Southern cafeteria chains. This style is often employed in vernacular architecture to connote "history." "With its deep-seated patriotism, rousing inspiration and acknowledgment of the contributions of all men, The American Adventure stands as the unification of World Showcase, the host to the great nations of the world." So says the souvenir book, and indeed the exhibit is one of the most chastening experiences at Disney World.

You enter, as usual, through a side door rather than the elaborate portico that here houses the terrace of a cafeteria serving "All-American fare." Inside are plaster columns, bunting, famous quotations, and paintings of scenes from the great colonial and imperial eras of United States history—the "settling" of the West, the building of Chicago, and so on. In the center a small and multiracial *a capella* chorus sings "America's favorite folk songs." The singers are wearing "colonial" costumes, and like the Lennon Sisters on the old Lawrence Welk show, they've learned to sing while smiling. "Shenandoah," "Swanee River"—these are celebrations of an America that no longer exists; we can only respond to them as myths, just as the blacks, Latinos, and Asian-Americans in the chorus can have only a mythic relation to the clothes they're wearing. The chorus begins singing "America the Beautiful," and two thousand people join in. The crowd, as all crowds at EPCOT, is ninety-five percent white, well fed, and at this time of year, the dead of a Florida winter, middle-aged.

At last, we're ushered into an immense red-white-and-blue hall adorned with white allegorical statues bearing names such as "Truth," "Resourcefulness," and "Freedom." Technically this show is one of Disney's most ambitious. It uses walking animatronic humans, film, video, slides, atmospherics, and audio. The narrators of this adventure story are Ben Franklin and Mark Twain. They stalk around the stage while telling of the settling of the New World and the promise it held for a democratic society. The man sitting beside me gasps, then claps as the first lines of the Declaration of Independence are read out loud. Frederick Douglass pops up out of the stage to talk about slavery. The Civil War is retold against a background of cannon fire and wailing. Boatloads of immigrants arrive in New York harbor and Franklin and Twain wave to them from the observation deck of the Statue of Liberty. The new Americans disperse to the new metropolises of the Midwest, but not before Chief Joseph and Susan B. Anthony address "the controversial issues of human rights." The industrialization of the nation is unsurprisingly counterposed with nineteenth-century philanthropy and the preservation of the wilderness: Andrew Carnegie opens Carnegie Hall, and Teddy Roosevelt chats with John Muir on the edge of a precipice in Yosemite. "We were soon thrust into the hectic role of world leader and into 'The War to End All Wars.'" Then we see the Great Depression, and a black man sits in a rural slum drinking Coke.

His radio blurts out, "The only thing we have to fear is fear itself." The man beside me claps again. World War II appears out of the blue after Will Rogers has walked around the stage flinging a lasso and saying something about how "no one can push us around." Smiling women are shown working in aircraft factories. Then victory is portrayed, and a long montage of misty projected images appears that supposedly sums up the next three decades. First Ike, Mamie and her far-out handbags, then Jackie Robinson, Louis Armstrong, Elvis, Einstein, Walter Elias Disney, John Wayne, Lucille Ball, JFK (on the soundtrack, "Ask not what your country can do for you . . ." and the audience claps), John-John, Martin Luther King, Woodstock, the moon landing (more clapping), Walter Cronkite and Muhammad Ali. No Beats, no Vietnam, no Jackie O, no Chicago, no Watergate, and no today. A little too "controversial" perhaps. Franklin waves his arm and says something about how "our constitution withstands the rigors of time . . . ready for new frontiers." Yet the last invocation at this prayer meeting is reserved for John Steinbeck, who ominously warns that "no civilization founded on success, plenty, comfort, and leisure can survive." The music surges; the lights come up and a standing ovation ensues. I feel that if I boo I'll be lynched.

The American Adventure attempts to mobilize us with its sweeping pop collage of historical bric-a-brac. Like a successful TV miniseries, it gives us the impression that it has summed up the mass audience's view of American history. Yet when FDR or John Wayne or Chief Joseph can be wrenched from their context of opposition and struggle; when their mere names come to stand in for American history itself, what we have is a simulacrum of history, a middlebrow impersonation of an epic story that never took place.

There is another, momentous historical failure here, and it is one of imagination. EPCOT discards the history of genuinely utopian initiatives of the American people in favor of an ideology of growth and development. "We would hope the world of tomorrow would be like EPCOT Center," a spokesperson told me, and that is the project Disney's corporate sponsors are already at work on. But they are frighteningly incapable of moving beyond a rigid technological determinism. Indeed, theirs is a future that differs from the present only in its details; it is a future of hierarchy, continued industrialization, enforced scarcity, and a ravished planet.

A future of emancipation, on the other hand, can only be reclaimed by a society willing to debate its own survival. Walt Disney's EPCOT Center stands squarely in the way of that debate and condemns us to a recurrent and eternal present.

The Global Reach

9

"Surprise Package":
Looking Southward with Disney

Julianne Burton-Carvajal

Title Song
"We're Three Caballeros"
(Sung to the tune of "Qué Lindo es Jalisco"/"How Lovely
is Jalisco"[1])

We're three caballeros
Three gay caballeros
They say we are birds of a feather
We're happy amigos
No matter where he goes,
Where one two and three goes,
We're always together.

We're three happy chappies
with snappy serapes
You'll find us beneath our sombreros
We're brave and we'll say so
We're bright as a peso.
"Who say so?" "We say so!"
The three caballeros.

Through fair or stormy weather
We stand close together
Like books on a shelf
Guitars here beside us
To play as we go
We sing and we samba
We shout, "Ay, caramba!"
"What means 'Ay, caramba!'?"
Oh yes, I don't know.

Like brother to brother,
We're all for each other
Like three caballeros
Together we'll stay.

Through fair or stormy weather
We stand close together
Like books on a shelf
and friends though we may be
When some Latin baby
Says yes, no or maybe,
Each man is for himself!

Far From Innocence

Blatant sexual punning and predation. Inadvertent homosexual advances. Cross-dressing and cross-species coupling. Reiterative narratives of conquest in which the patriarchal unconscious and the imperial unconscious insidiously overlap. "Not in the Disney cartoons *I* saw as a kid!" you say, incredulously.[2]

Granted, cartoons are generally exempted from suspicions of propaganda, and Disney cartoons in particular are seldom accused of being a locus of lasciviousness. Yet the characteristic fun, frolic and fireworks purveyed in Disney's *The Three Caballeros*, released in 1945 when the studios' national and international fame was at its zenith, are based on all of the above.[3]

The Three Caballeros does not exhibit the characteristic censorship mechanisms so familiar to anyone reared on a diet of Disney entertainments.[4] Instead of Disney's trademark "sexless sexiness"—to borrow James Agee's apt phrase[5]—*The Three Caballeros* parades rampant (masculine) desire and the explosive results of its repeated frustration. How are we to understand this temporary suspension of a virtually emblematic inhibition? Why does this particular film differ so markedly and disconcertingly from the prototypical Disney product?

The Three Caballeros is of considerable historical, cultural and political interest because it, and the related set of documentary travelogues, animated cartoons and live-action/animation combinations which led up to it, are the product of a concerted and self-conscious effort to expiate the previous sins of Yankee cultural chauvinism, to replace hollow and hackneyed stereotypes with representations of Latin Americans ostensibly rendered on their own terms. How did this self-correcting enterprise come about?

The Scoop on "El Groupo"

As World War II loomed in Europe and Asia, the United States government registered concern about the allegiances of the Latin American nations. According to image-historian Allen Woll:

> [From 1939] with the growing threat of war with Germany, the United States appeared eager to ease any remaining tensions with South American governments in order to maintain hemispheric unity as a bulwark against foreign invasion. . . . Roosevelt explained the basis for his vigorous reassertion of the Good Neighbor Policy: "I began to visualize a wholly new attitude toward other American Republics based on an honest and sincere desire, first, to remove from their minds all fear of American aggression—territorial or financial—and, second, to take them into a kind of hemispheric partnership in which no Republic would take undue advantage."[6]

Nelson Rockefeller, director of the Office of the Coordinator of Inter-American Affairs, and his assistant John Hay Whitney, head of the Motion Picture Section, extended their functions beyond regulation and into production. They were well aware that the condescending and stereotypical images of Latinness long purveyed by Hollywood—the blood-thirsty bandido, the sexy spitfire, the somnolent peasant, and so on—struck Latin Americans as distorted and demeaning. One regional government after the other had registered protests in response to what they considered offensive representations of their citizenry: Brazil over *Rio's Road to Hell* (1931), Cuba over *Cuban Love Song* (1931), Mexico over *Girl of the Rio* (1932) and *Viva Villa!* (1934). According to Wohl, Rockefeller and Whitney "were instrumental in the hiring of Walt Disney 'as the first Hollywood producer of motion pictures specifically intended to carry a message of democracy and friendship below the Rio Grande.' " Whitney claimed that Disney "would show the truth about the American Way" in a series of " 'direct propaganda films couched in the simplicity of the animation medium."[7] Disney's South American project was thus built upon a self-conscious disposition formulated at high levels of national government to represent Latin being, culture, and experience with authenticity and respect for intraregional as well as interregional variations.

Between 1941 and 1943,[8] Walt Disney, his wife, and a score of staff members made three trips south of the border in search of the "raw material" for this Good Neighbor initiative. The material they collected was eventually rendered into nearly two dozen films, both shorts and features, both educational and escapist, both—in the prevailing terminology—"direct and indirect propaganda."[9] Entertainment shorts like *El Gau-*

cho Goofy and *Pluto and the Armadillo* and educational films like *The Grain That Built a Hemisphere* and *Cleanliness Brings Health* are, from the present perspective, minor by-products of a venture whose central importance revolves around a trilogy of films which convey a totalizing account of this cross-cultural journey: *South of the Border with Disney* (1941), *Saludos Amigos* (1943) and, in particular, *The Three Caballeros* (1945). As a composite, these films move progressively away from the literal to the figurative and from the experiential to the imaginary.

South of the Border with Disney is a thoroughly conventional travelogue, a "documentary diary" of the Disney group's original Latin American tour, which Disney himself narrates. For lack of a more qualified cameraman, Disney also shot the images of "El Groupo" (as they syncretically dubbed themselves), their hosts, and their forays. *South of the Border* exhibits only occasional scraps of animation as it depicts the "birth" of various cartoon figures who will not be fully "embodied" until the two subsequent films. Joe Carioca, the fast-talking, cigar-smoking, umbrella-toting parrot from Rio, makes his first appearance here as a series of uninked, backgroundless, two-color pencil sketches, briefly and provisionally animated to offer a glimpse of him performing an incipient samba.

Saludos Amigos retraces the same basic itinerary, but this time several animated characters assume a more central role. This anthology film, tied together with documentary footage of the Disney junket, is composed of four discrete shorts: Donald Duck's adventures and misadventures at Bolivia's Lake Titicaca in the company of animated llamas and real-life *cholas* (Bolivian peasant women in full skirts and derby hats); Pedro the little Chilean mail plane's intrepid voyage over the Andes; Goofy as egregious gaucho in the Argentine; and, finally and most rewardingly, "Aquarela do Brasil" ("Watercolor of Brazil") in which Joe Carioca introduces Donald Duck to samba, *cacaça* (cane liquor) and Rio nightclubs. This last seven-and-a-half-minute portion is animated to the strains of Ari Barroso's mellifluous "Brazil" and a second, more percussive samba by Zequinha de Abreu, and features an animated watercolor brush delineating the action in lush tropical colors and textures. "Aquarela do Brasil" is proto-music video at its finest.[10]

Finally, in *The Three Caballeros*, live action becomes fully subordinate to animation. The balance of the first film has been reversed; here personality assumes precedence over geography; and literal depictions of place give way to more mythic geographies animated by imagination and desire. Each of these three films thus (re)inscribes the process of appropriation of the "genuinely" Latin American in more elaborate and intricate ways. In each successive effort, the process of cross-cultural appropriation and refiguration is more effectively displaced and transmuted.

South of the Border with Disney

Judging from the evidence offered in *South of the Border with Disney*, the dominant assumption beneath El Groupo's good-neighborly enterprise was that culture *is* its material base and that these physical artifacts are transportable and translatable—not only subject to various means of pre- and postmechanical reproduction but also subjectable to the artistic imaginations of the visiting Disneyites whose self-appointed mandate to refigure them in transculturating gestures is to be received by the locals as tribute rather than as expropriation. Countless sequences throughout this twenty-minute travelogue emphasize the materiality of Latin American culture, the raw substance and unrestrained accumulation of exotic artifact, as the goal of the Disney expedition.

In their zeal to appropriate the "authentic exotic," distinctions between animate and inanimate, flora and fauna, human and nonhuman are set aside. In a typical sequence in the Argentine segment, the mandate "to gather more impressions, more music, more color" blinds Disney's minions to the difference between human and animal species. Two of Disney's staff come upon don Riberio Sosa, introduced in Disney's voice-over narration as "an eighty-five-year-old gaucho and a veteran of the Indian wars." The Americans begin to examine the man's footgear, and one even lifts don Riberio's right foot to give the camera a better view while Disney himself in voice-over continues his recital of "scientific" information. Over a low-angle close-up of a bewildered-looking don Riberio, the voice-over intones, "He had a sense of humor and was amused at the interest they took in his costume." After the gaucho has dismounted, both men flank him, their notebooks prominently in hand, while one fingers his hat and then unceremoniously removes it from the gaucho's head. There is a brusque cut to a llamalike animal in medium shot while the narrator, without missing a beat, recites in the same didactic tone, "The *guanaco* is found in the foothills of the Andes. . . ." This is followed by another brusque cut to a man photographing a small rodent while the narrator informs us, "At the San Martin Zoo in Mendoza, we found these Patagonian rabbits from the south of Argentina. They are a little shy but easily tamed." One is tempted to inquire, as easily as don Riberio?

This attachment to the material as the essence of the otherliness of culture is parodied—albeit rather lamely—in the closing sequences of *South of the Border*. These revolve around the visual trope of El Groupo's suitcases, beginning with a montage of pottery objects displayed in close-up against a serape background while the narrator explains, "We picked up many suggestions for picture ideas in the pottery designs of Oaxaca and Guadalajara." Over close-ups of a series of small floral paintings shot against the same serape backdrop and sequentially inserted into the frame by an unidentified hand, we hear, "In every part of Mexico, we found new picture material like these flower designs suggesting the lace headdress of Tehuantepec, the Yucateca costume of Yucatan, little Tehuanos from the Isthmus. . . ." Cut back to a medium shot in which an unidentified man, only partially visible, places a large ceramic vase in the suitcase, which is already overflowing with the objects we have just been viewing, and then makes a futile attempt to close it. Fade in from a dissolve-montage of destination stickers to a US Customs sign. "The Customs officials were really in for something," the narrator observes over images of officials rifling through ludicrously overstuffed luggage. The last suitcase belongs to none other than Uncle Walt himself, who continues to narrate in voice-over: "After half an hour of this, the officer was prepared for anything, and when he came across Walt's gaucho saddles, spurs and bridle, his only comment was, 'You might as well have brought the horse!' " A neighing on the soundtrack coincides with the final shot: a close-up of a live horse's head as if emerging from Walt's suitcase while, in the background, Walt and two companions enjoy a hearty laugh.

Appropriation and packaging lie at the foundation of the Disney endeavor here. *Surprise Package* was the original working title of what eventually became *The Three Caballeros*. Reelaborated in the metropolis of the Disney Studios, this "raw material" would be repackaged for export to its originary peripheral locales, but in barely recognizable forms and with the accrued semiotic value of its industrial refiguration.[11]

What's In a Surprise Package?

The Three Caballeros is the end product of this process of cross-cultural refiguration. At seventy minutes, it is the longest of the trio. Technically, it is the most ambitious by far. Artistically, it is indisputably the richest, containing some of the most brilliant animation sequences ever devised by the resident geniuses at Disney Studios.

Structurally, *The Three Caballeros* divides successively into threes: three progressively building parts which derive from three birthday gifts sent to Donald Duck from his "friends in Latin America"; three primary cartoon protagonists (Donald Duck, Joe Carioca, and Panchito the boisterous Mexican rooster); and three flesh-and-blood actresses who interact with them (Brazilian singer-dancer Aurora Miranda, Carmen's sister, and the Mexican dancer Carmen Molina and singer Dora Luz).

Gift No. 1 contains a movie projector and a film, *Aves Raras* (Strange Birds). Donald is the only "caballero" present in this all-animated sequence, which is didactic in a rather heavy-handed way, using three male narrators in voice-over, along with animated maps and other instructional

devices, to "teach" Donald about Latin America. This is the most distanced
sequence, both geographically (it deals primarily with Antarctica and
Uruguay) and emotionally (Donald watches passively, without entering
into the action, in marked contrast to his increasingly enthusiastic "partici-
pant observation" in the subsequent Brazilian and Mexican sequences).
This first sequence is in turn divided into three parts: the travails of Pablo,
the cold-blooded penguin who pines for and eventually attains a tropical
isle; an "interstitial" essay on Latin American bird life; and the story of
Little Gauchito who, seeking a condor, captures a flying donkey, trains
him as a racehorse, and then loses the newly won jackpot when the
donkey shows his true feathers. This last section is, rather curiously,
narrated in voice-over by Gauchito himself as an old man, giving rise to
the anomalous tag line "And so I was never heard from again. . . ."

Gift No. 2 smokes and pulses to a samba beat. Once opened, this pop-
up book on Brazil becomes a kind of proscenium stage for the Brazilian
parrot, Joe Carioca. After the two caballeros enter the book in a "through
the looking glass"-like maneuver, Joe guides Donald on a trip to Bahia,
where the first live action/animation sequences occur around the comely
cookie-vendor Yaya (Aurora Miranda), the first Latin American lass to
capture Donald's heart, and the horde of male admirers whose live-action
dancing surrounds her and to some extent buffers her from Donald's
exuberant attentions.

With gift No. 3, Panchito the Mexican rooster completes the group.
The three caballeros then "tour" Mexico via a portfolio of folk paintings
and tourist photographs, with the additional aid of a piñata and a magic
serape. Pacing and complexity also increase here, with numerous tour de
force sequences of animation and mixed action, accelerating to the final
explosive mock-bullfighting climax.

Parts two and three, the core segments of the film, combine animation
with live-action footage, and share a dual configuration that I've chosen
to call *demonstration* and *transportation*. The demonstration, hosted in the
first part by Joe Carioca and in the second by Panchito, and accomplished
through the surrogacy of the visual aids mentioned above, revolves around
a love song crooned in the syrupy style of the period, a love song ostensibly
dedicated to the place but also clearly evoking the notions of absence,
of longing, and of pairing as ideal completion: "Oh Bahia, someone that
I long to see, is haunting my reverie, and this loneliness deep in my
heart, calls to you, calls to you . . ."; and "Mexico, that's where I found
you . . . your song of romance calls me to you. . . ."

Clearly, Donald feels compelled to answer the call. In the "transportation" portions, his earlier, passive contemplation gives way to direct
participation. Donald is magically transported into the spectacle which
is being offered him—through the square-wheeled storybook train of the

Brazilian sequence which dumps him and Joe Carioca at the Bahia station, and later via the flying serape which magically enters the tourist photos displayed in the Mexican portfolio. This transport consists not only of his physical presence in "otherland" but also of his emotional transport into a state of frenzied arousal once he meets the Other's Other (that is, the women implicitly assumed to "belong" to the Latin American male).

With typical lack of restraint, Donald falls head over heels in love with every Latin beauty he lays eyes on. The text is sexualized at this point, where physical entry into the space of the other becomes possible. In both the Brazilian and the Mexican sequences, these persistently frustrated pursuits "transport" Donald in a third sense—to an altered state, an hallucination within the hallucination that is the film which, dreamlike, recapitulates and condenses all that has gone before without actually *taking* him (or us) anywhere except into Donald's "subconscious": transportation as (even more uncensored) reprise.

The Acapulco beach sequence, when Donald jumps off the flying serape to join the live-action bathing beauties on the sand,[12] marks the inception of a kind of hyperkinetic hysteria that characterizes the culminating fifteen minutes of the film. In one of the film's most incredulous blendings of live-action and animation, a circle of nubile ladies turn a beach blanket into a makeshift trampoline and toss Donald repeatedly skyward. At the close of the Acapulco sequence, Donald's hot pursuit of several dozen señoritas in a game of blindman's bluff is interrupted by his impatient buddies. Yanked back onto the magic serape, the blindfolded Donald throws his arms around Joe Carioca, thinking he has caught one of the girls at last, and begins kissing him noisily as Joe protests, "Oh no, Donald, don't do *that!*" Heterosexual, cross-species pursuit is confounded by same-species injunctions against homosexuality.

Finally, in the subsequent Mexico City nightlife sequence, watching Dora Luz sing "You Belong to My Heart" ("Solamente Una Vez"), Donald at last succeeds in making carnal contact with an object of his desire. Her willingness dissolves his former bravado into puerile reticence. Donald's long-sought release only releases him into nightmare. Overwhelmed by the simultaneous kisses of several pairs of disembodied female lips, Donald takes off like a rocket, loses his "mass" and is reduced to a mere outline of his former self, sprouts wings (an angel? a fairy?) and then a wreath of flower petals. Images of past experiences return transmuted. Donald turns green with surfeit. The syrupy love song is repeatedly disrupted by Donald's gun-slinging sidekicks and their raucous anthem of male camaraderie as Donald attempts to partner first a dancing *tehuana* (woman from the traditionally matriarchal Tehuantepec) and then a phallic female *charra* (roughly, cowgirl) surrounded by syncopated and ever more phallic cacti. The frenzy of competing rhythms and imagery continue to mount until the explosive finale.

Animating Philosophies

Precisely because of their assumed innocence and innocuousness, their inherent ability—even obligation—to defy all conventions of realistic representation, animated cartoons offer up a fascinating zone within which to examine how a dominant culture constructs its subordinates. As a nonphotographic application of a photographic medium, they are freed from the basic cinematic expectation that they convey an "impression of reality." (The phrase belongs to the influential French critic André Bazin, who theorized that images from the real world press themselves upon the celluloid like a fingerprint.)[13] The function and essence of cartoons is in fact the reverse: the impression of *ir*reality, of intangible and imaginable worlds in chaotic, disruptive, subversive collision. Animated cartoons reinforce this otherworldliness when their "subjects" are not humanoid but "animaloid," and in this category, Disney stands *über alles*.

Whatever their explicit content, cartoons are often also *about* the film medium itself and its mechanisms of representation—about, that is, what they simultaneously are and are not; about the medium which they to some degree embody and yet also, inevitably, defy. Representationality and realist conventions are persistently invoked, only to be defied. This perversely contrary self-reflexivity becomes one of the most intense (and disturbing) pleasures offered by cartoons.

Because cartoon figures inhabit a world beyond materiality, beyond mortality, beyond conventionality, cartoons can also be the site of unbridled expressions of the individual and collective unconscious, defying norms of propriety as well as physics. In philosophical terms, ontological otherliness invites axiological otherliness. Cartoons in this sense can be understood as a kind of dream's dreaming, the unconscious of the unconscious.

Cartoon figures are simultaneously, quintessentially both self and Other. Rather than dissipating, this effect is heightened to dizzying levels of intensity and confusion in those films which combine animation and live-action. (*The Three Caballeros* is the first color feature to sustain this mixture within the same frame, although Disney had been experimenting with this combination since his first cartoon series in the 1920s.)[14] It is this otherly (under)side of mixed animation that comes across so vividly and disconcertingly in *Who Framed Roger Rabbit?*, direct heir of *The Three Caballeros* (and hard-pressed at times, despite the intervening forty years of technological evolution, to outdo its eye-popping prototype).

Such hybrid cartoons produce a metaphysical effect in both senses of the word: they literally transcend the plane of physical reality, and they situate their viewers in a disquieting zone of epistemological and ethical question marks. The metaphysics of hybrid animation is morally unsettling for a number of reasons—not least among them the persistent subordination/annihilation/resuscitation of the marginals, and the explicit allusions to acts of celluloid miscegenation.[15]

The consequent moral discomfiture may account for the outrage such films elicit. John Mason Brown, writing in *The Saturday Review* in 1945, called "the mixture of drawn and real people in . . . *The Three Caballeros* one of the most unfortunate experiments since Prohibition." Barbara Deming, writing in the *Partisan Review* that same year, mused, "Walt has indeed wrought something monstrous . . . [but] *The Three Caballeros* is not Disney's private monster, his personal nightmare. It is a nightmare of these times."[16] Jonathan Rosenbaum, reviewing *Roger Rabbit* four decades later, plays with this idea of moral culpability by assuming a mock-prosecutorial tone, arguing that the film's director, Robert Zemeckis, may be "the main culprit" but that he should not be "convicted" on the basis of "circumstantial evidence."[17]

These hybrid works tend to provoke moral indignation or summary dismissal on grounds of absurdity—or both. In "The Long Pause," the chapter of *The Disney Version* dedicated to the late 1940s, Richard Schickel quotes Bosley Crowther, usually a staunch Disney fan, panning *The Three Caballeros* because it "dazzles and numbs the senses without making any sense." Schickel's own assessment mixes moral censure with terminal agnosticism:

> It is fair to say that the film reflected Disney's own mood. Nothing made sense to him. . . . Since he had never really known what he was doing culturally, he, particularly, could not find his own roots. Between him and his past he had erected a screen on which were projected only his own old movies, the moods and styles of which he mindlessly sought to recapture at cut rates in the bastard cinematic form of the half-animated, half-live-action film.[18]

What is left for the cultural critic who prefers meaning to meaninglessness, and a sense of historical accountability to arbitrary accusations of immorality? Perverse texts invite perverse readings. What better term for the attempt to extract a measure of meaning from chaotic excess, to discern the coherence underpinning an ungainly amalgamation obviously assembled by committee, to identify the ideological stance behind the innocuous comic gesture?

Ten Perverse Propositions on Desire in Disney
First Proposition: Latin America as a Wartime Toontown

In *Roger Rabbit*, Toontown is a zone of marginality inhabited by the vulnerable and the victimized, literally "an/other world"—"an/Other's world" to be entered only with wariness and dread, and seldom escaped intact. For the writers and animators of *The Three Caballeros*, Latin America is the 1940s equivalent of "Toontown," the seductive-repulsive zone of spectacular excess and excessive spectacle. In the sections depicting Brazil and Mexico, reason gives way to passion, order to disorder and incoherence, the logic of experience to the chaos of nightmare. It is this impression/projection of Latinness which unleashes both Donald's and Disney's libido. The Latin is rendered synonymous with license and licentiousness. The tendency to project onto the other what we most assiduously suppress within ourselves lies at the root of the film's indulgence in excess—an excess which is specifically, relentlessly sexual.

Certainly, I would be treading shaky ground if I were to attempt to (psycho)analyze the animators, but the uncharacteristic excess which erupts most overpoweringly in the final segment begins to seem somewhat less unfathomable once one tries to reconstruct the atmosphere at Disney Studios in the last years of World War II. Financial losses occasioned layoffs and strikes which in 1941 reduced the work force by half. By the end of that year, the studios had turned into the most extensive "war plant" in Hollywood, housing mountains of munitions, quartering antiaircraft troops, providing overflow office space for Lockheed personnel. By 1943, fully ninety-four percent of the Disney product was war-related. Disney had become a government contractor on a massive scale, thanks largely to an early and very successful wartime project commissioned by the Canadian government. The wartime restrictions on costs and equipment that applied to the other studios did not apply to Disney because animation was exempted.[19] It is not difficult to imagine, in this context of dreary war work, how the license implicit in the "surprise package" of *The Three Caballeros* project might have unleashed creative juices which had been stored too long under pressure.

Second Proposition: Spectacular Packaging

The Three Caballeros packages Latin America—or, more accurately, depicts Latin America as packaging itself—as pure spectacle. Each gift is an artifact of and for visualization: a movie projector and film, a pop-up book, a portfolio of scenes from various regions of Mexico. Parts two and three begin by emphasizing the spectacle of the Latin American landscape (ideally populated by singing, dancing natives) and ultimately progress to "bodyscape"—the spectacle of the playful, alluring, receptive Latin female.

Third Proposition: An Allegory of Colonialism

Reversing the terms of Fredric Jameson's much-challenged contention that all Third World novels are "national allegories,"[20] it would be equally reductive to assert that all first world texts are "allegories of colonialism." *The Three Caballeros*, however, happens to be an allegory of "First-World" colonialism par excellence. Every story packaged here is a narrative of conquest or of enslavement. In the first narrative from Part one, Pablo Penguin sets out from the South Pole to find "the isle of his dreams." Having resourcefully overcome numerous comic setbacks, he finally reaches the Galapagos, where he is last seen tanning himself in a hammock while a tray-bearing tortoise brings him one iced drink after another. (It comes as no surprise that the narrative of this hapless indigene's enslavement has been conveniently omitted.) In the first segment's closing narrative, Gauchito captures and enslaves the donkey-bird because the instant he stumbles upon the creature, he immediately perceives that he "must be worth a fortune!"

Fourth Proposition: Hierarchies of the Willing-and-Waiting-to-be-Conquered

The chronology of conquest in *The Three Caballeros* recapitulates a hierarchy that goes from claiming territory (Pablo's tropical isle) to capturing and taming the local fauna (Gauchito's flying donkey) to Donald's designs on the female homo sapiens. Each rung in this hierarchy is represented as simply waiting to be taken; Donald's conquests fail not because his targets aren't willing but because he is not able.

Fifth Proposition: Donald's Un-Don Juanly Ineptitude as Sop to the Excessive Machismo of His Avian Accomplices

If Donald's conquest is displaced (from geography onto the female body), it is also disguised or "de-fused" by his ineptitude, his failure to fully consummate his desires. The mechanisms of geopolitical and sexual conquest here enjoy a convenient congruence. Anxious to allay potential fears that this "neighborly" North American presence will be too potent, too overpowering, the filmmakers place the brunt of the film's humor on the sheer ludicrousness of Donald Duck as Don Juan—his impotence, his childish polymorphousness or, in baldest Lacanian terms, his lack of the phallus.

The *charra* sequence, part of the climactic second half of the Mexican segment, makes Donald's phallic inadequacy most glaringly apparent. Dressed in a feminized version of a traditionally male costume and carrying a riding crop, the phallic woman (Carmen Molina) stomps her high boots in a self-confident *zapateo*. She is surrounded by a phalanx of dancing cacti which, as they deploy and metamorphose, alternately stomp, squash, obscure, fragment, and otherwise overpower Donald. At the end of the sequence, Donald runs through a forest of elongated cacti, each with a prominent lateral appendage dangling high above him, in futile pursuit of Carmen Molina, who has herself "congealed" into a cactus before he can reach her. Green, the color of envy for the gringos and lust for the Latins, dominates the sequence. The imagery of inadequacy has seldom been more overdetermined.

In marked contrast to Donald, Joe Carioca and Panchito are more generously equipped. Each comes armed with a pair of phallic objects: a cigar and umbrella in the parrot's case (in the Mexican sequence, the umbrella more than once turns into a machine gun); and a pair of pistols liberally deployed in the case of the rooster, whose species itself is—needless to say—an emblem of male sexual prowess.

As recently as 1982, a film historian wrote apropos of this film that Donald Duck's "camaraderie with the caballeros from Brazil and Mexico symbolized the idea of hemispheric unity."[21] In fact, this male camaraderie provides a thin pretext for (and eventually a major impediment to) Donald's real interest, the (hetero)sexual pursuit of "priddy girls" of uniformly pale complexion. Donald's feathered companions are first potential rivals, later indomitable restrainers and disrupters. The Disney team apparently felt the need to reassure their Latin American counterparts that they need feel no threat to their sexual hegemony from this North American neighbor who, for all his quacking up and cracking up, is clearly incapable of shacking up.

Sixth Proposition: Doña Juanita?

The ultimate reassurance regarding Donald's nonthreatening nature is the recurrent feminization which he undergoes immediately after his attempts to "connect" with the objects of his desire—a desire no less fickle for all its obsessive intensity. Donald's surrogate femaleness at key moments is underlined by visual puns that verge on the subliminal but compel an embarrassing blatancy on the part of anyone wishing to describe them.

Seconds prior to the conclusion of both the Brazilian and the Mexican sequences, Donald is literally swept off his feet by a stream of ejaculate. His concluding appearance in the Brazilian sequence comes when he tries to imitate Aurora Miranda, whose compelling gestures "animate" her cartooned surroundings, making buildings and plazas pulse to a samba beat. In response to Donald's pathetic attempt at mimesis, a fountain shaped like an elephant's head extends its flaccid trunk into a rigid horizontal pipe and proceeds to overpower Donald with its spray.

In the frenetic climax of the Mexican sequence, which also ends the film, Joe Carioca and Panchito combat Donald in a mock bullfight. The inept Donald has trouble maneuvering the bull armature which, with the instantaneousness of nightmare, he inhabits at the instant the phallic *charra* definitively eludes his pursuit. His assailants in the bullring are considerably more agile: Pancho goads him with red flags and wisecracks which call Donald's masculinity into question, while Joe sets a cluster of firecrackers alight on his tail and then skewers him with a pair of pokers. After his ejection (ejaculation?) from the make-believe bull, which magically and terrifyingly continues to rampage unaided, Donald redirects his combative fury away from its original target (the "friends" who have so persistently thwarted his amorous efforts) and toward this emblem of masculinity, charging the bull head-on as Panchito sings a fragment of the title song in ironic voice-over, "like brother to brother/we're all for each other. . . ." The trail of spewing fireworks in the Mexican finale rockets Donald skyward; embracing this ample stream, he slides back "down to earth" and assumes one of his many feminized poses. The film's final frames (or, more accurately, cels) exhibit a demure Donald, draped head to foot in a Mexican serape and protectively flanked by his two unambiguously masculine cohorts. Donald's divisive pursuit of heterosexual couplings has been (rather punitively) restrained, and in the film's concluding instants he is made to "mimic" the gender he sought to conquer.

Seventh Proposition: One Man's Dominance is An/Other (Wo)Man's Subordination

The Three Caballeros, though appearing to challenge it, in fact fully conforms to what some theories of machismo (the cult of male superiority) call the "colonial compact." Proponents of this theory wonder what the indigenous and Creole males received in return for their disenfranchisement by their Spanish and Portuguese conquerors. After they were stripped of their leaders, rituals, sacred artifacts and traditional forms of social organization, was the promise of a Roman Catholic heaven sufficient compensation for sustained submission, even in the face of the Europeans' obvious military and technological superiority? Some of those who identify the most virulent strain of machismo as Latin American in origin trace it to the colonial experience. They theorize that the reward for male acquiescence to the will of the conqueror was his socially and civically enforced superiority to and dominance over the female.[22]

Eighth Proposition: Pity the Poor Conqueror

Predictably perhaps, the "gift" which El Groupo's Good Neighbor project offers to its Latin American audience turns out to be at their expense. The emissary turns out to be not only "a wolf in duck's clothings" (to quote Panchito) but also a conquistador in *compañero*'s clothings. Donald is a disarmingly inept but no less effective front man for the imperial machine. A discerning viewer might object here that the various conquests depicted in *The Three Caballeros* are incomplete, that they "fall short," to borrow Barbara Deming's suggestive phrase. Yet the effect of this narrative strategy is not to call acts of conquest into question nor much less to condemn them, but rather to "humanize" the agents of conquest by exposing their pathetic ineptitude and/or their inner ambivalence regarding their prize.

The perspective of the conquered is banished from this account. Deprived of subjectivity, the Latin American male is constrained to serve as informant and guide for the would-be conqueror. (The role of the female, as we have seen, is to be the compliant object of invasive desire, the exotic Other's even more exotic Other.) For want of a victim, the conqueror himself is here posited as the "little guy," the "underdog," a fellow "strange bird" who inspires sympathetic concern and playful amicality rather than dread, resentment, or resistance.

Ninth Proposition: Illusory Reciprocities and Other Deceptive Ways of Seeing Eye to Eye

The notion of reciprocity is deceptively evoked in the initial frames of the film when Donald, who has opened the first of his birthday gifts from Latin America to find a movie projector and screen, subjects the strip of celluloid to the close scrutiny of his naked eye. Cut to a point-of-view close-up of one of the frames, which animates: Pablo Penguin turns his telescope toward Donald/the camera/the viewer; its huge concentric circularity, a remote eye at its center, dominates the frame. This brief sequence embodies what might be called the "myth of the reciprocal gaze." The Other who gazes back at the gazer in fact "sees" nothing, since a figure imprinted on a single frame of celluloid cannot be either animate or sensate—except of course in a cartoon and in a cartoon-within-a-cartoon.

But *were* Pablo Penguin to *see* the one who is seeing him (Donald Duck), he would arguably be merely mirroring himself. The Antarctic penguin is a notably "de-culturated" choice, a paradoxical bird if there ever was one: so terrestrial that he seems to be the antithesis of the avian; so southerly that he conveys the quintessence of northerliness. The "rare bird" given pride of place in the film's order of presentation is thus not in fact "one of them" but quite transparently "one of us." The further we travel, the more we stay at home—or some such paradoxical platitude— seems to be the subtextual invocation here.

Furthermore, Pablo's successful colonization of tropical America is rendered innocent because he comes from an ephemeral "nowhere." Without any attachment to terra firma, he simply cuts his igloo free from the ice pack when he wants to navigate north to the tropics, and the ice floe which anchored him to his Antarctic community becomes the vehicle for his solitary migration. Similarly, he lacks the avian "ethno/specificity" conveyed by the coloration, symbolic accoutrements, and richly genuine accents of both Panchito and Joe Carioca. (To his credit, Disney insisted on native voices for these roles.) Even the frenetic Carmen Mirandaesque "song" of the mischievous and disruptive araquan bird, who appears at "random" moments in parts one and two, connotes a cultural embeddedness of which Pablo is utterly devoid. Pablo has no voice at all: Sterling "Doc" Holloway, the vibrato-voiced narrator of *Peter and the Wolf*, is called in to tell his story for him in voice-over.

Tenth Proposition: Prefigurations of Things to Come

Illusory reciprocity constitutes the very core of this film. As we've seen, the production of meanings in *The Three Caballeros* is both explicit and veiled, brazen and coy. Much of the film's fascinatingly devious elusiveness derives from the intricacy of its reversals, from deceptive reciprocities in which there is no real exchange, or in which what is exchanged is not what has been promised. Anthony Wilden, writing in *System and Structure* on logical typing and the triangulation of binary oppositions, notes how the apparent symmetry of the binary pair is often governed by an "invisible" third term which converts difference into hierarchy.[23] In this case, the "third term" between the North American and the South American may be the neocolonizing ambition of the former.

A film which reportedly set out to be an offering of friendship toward Latin America adopts the reverse as its core premise. Latin America fetes Donald Duck, showering him with birthday gifts and hosting his visits to Bahia and Mexico, much as, in relation to the film's production, Latin Americans hosted Disney and his team and much as, in relation to the film's reception, Latin America was offered up as ready host to Donald Duck's successors, the American tourists. The perverse dialectic of economic aid, which rewards the donor while impoverishing the recipient, is replicated (one is almost tempted to say prophesied) here.

Disney's "gift" of intercultural understanding turns out to be the act of packaging Latin America for enhanced North American consumption.[24]

The unspoken pact which makes that package possible rests upon the equation of cultural expression with femininity and cultural exchange with heterosexual conquest, and upon the positing of a shared assumption between conqueror and conqueree: that the female of the species is a willing target of appropriation.

Conclusion: An Imperial Eagle in Duck's Clothing

To its enduring credit, *The Three Caballeros* does utilize Latin American music, accents, performers, locales, artifacts, and modes of cultural expression more extensively than any previous Hollywood film. Disney's quest for cultural authenticity was to that extent both sincere and successful. The results are often dazzling, even by today's elevated technical standards. But all these good intentions cannot mask the discomfitting evidence which hides just below the comic frenzy and the accumulation of "authentic" cultural detail: all cultural reciprocities are not created equal.

This essay has undertaken to examine a particular instance of the intricate process of appropriation and projection through which one Hollywood dream factory constructed its Other(s). *The Three Caballeros* turns out to be an exceptional instance that, despite the best intentions and a wealth of creative talent and effort, seems to prove the rule of cross-cultural borrowing as self-aggrandizement, of Good-Neighborliness as foil for empire-building-as-usual, of innocent entertainment masking a set of interests and assumptions that are anything but innocuous.

10

Pato Donald's Gender Ducking

José Piedra

The menace of Nazism and its allied doctrines, its techniques and tactics, must be understood from Hudson Bay to Punto [*sic*] Arenas.[1] Wherever the motion picture can do a basic job of spreading the gospel of the Americas' common stake in this struggle, there that job must and shall be done.

—John Hay Whitney, director of the Motion Picture
Section of the State Department's Office of the Coordinator
of Inter-American Affairs under Franklin Delano Roosevelt.[2]

F.D.R.: "Somoza? Isn't that fellow supposed to be a son of a bitch?" Cordell Hull, F.D.R.'s Secretary of State: "Yes, but he's *our* son of a bitch."

—US legend.[3]

There's only one s.o.b. in the studio, and that's me.

—Walt Disney.[4]

Nazi Love

During the first menacing wave of Nazism in the 1930s, Franklin Delano Roosevelt created the Office of the Coordinator of Inter-American Affairs within the Motion Picture Section of the State Department. Its declared purpose was to "show the truth about the American way," and to that effect it hired Hollywood Studios to engender propaganda geared to fulfill the promise of the US's Good Neighbor policy (Roosevelt's name for the US's Pan-American policy).[5] The unadvertised reason for the US interest had much to do with the commercial exploitation of Latin lands and peoples of the Americas in the wake of a war-torn Europe. Companies such as the United Fruit Company began buying big farms in our Latin American countries, importing alien business practices, producing "raw materials," selling us back technological progress and processed products, and ultimately exporting labor and money to the US. This cycle became practically unbreakable as it fostered a federal Latin dependency bureaucratically centered in Washington. What interests me here are the sexual innuendos behind the US's well-known patriarchal fostering of Latin American dependency.

The slogan "the American way" and the notion of "engendering," not to mention the phrase "good neighbor," are loaded with biased libidinal connotations. The "American way" refers to the US's styling itself as the model for Pan-American political unity or, more dramatically, the unifying principle for the American continental unity—which included a rationale for sleeping by or with the "giant of the North."[6] I use the term "engendering," in regard to the propaganda machinery, to refer to the colonizers' highly arbitrary assignation of gender to the colonial subject as part of the local Other acquiring international Selfhood. As I will illustrate later on, the colonial propaganda scheme that the US has put in place in the Americas imposes its own simplistic libidinal dialectic. Whoever rose to "the top" represented the male, international, civilized Self ready to conquer, package, and import himself as the savior. Whoever remained at "the bottom" was relegated to being female, local, savage, and Other, someone who had to be made ready to be conquered, packaged, and exported.

Ultimately the US, self-styled as a good neighbor, stands as an incestuous *padre de familias* who, while ostensibly teaching his Pan-American children to forge their own nations, libidinally encourages their dependency. The system even teaches us Latin Americans how to become the "child brides" of the US. Thus we Latins in and around the US's backyard become not only the poor live-in neighbor but the tantalizing girl-next-door—not to mention the fruit-next-door so dear to the United Fruit Company's heart. Social and sexual politics, engendering and gendering, brotherhood and paternalism, family and colonial affairs, go hand in hand in transforming the Americas into a *falsa-panamericana* unit, which led to the construction of Latin Americans as America's Latin "minions." As the US's minions we can only take a rather hysterical form of action or assume a disposable form of libidinal power. We are recognized as being endowed with a kind of languorous hyposexuality or frantic hypersexuality that does not translate into a productive, but rather into a showy and superflous kind of libido, be it receptive or assertive. This sexually united state of affairs renders Latin America into a unit of people dependent on the patriarchal and promiscuous (model of the) United States. If I am right, some forms of colonial homogenization even lead to postcolonial homosexualization.

Throughout this century the US has placed itself at the head of a self-serving propaganda and propagation campaign geared to ensure its libidinal hold on the "American" species—in short, the US is libidinally cloning itself. Sometimes it seems convenient to persuade us Latins to make love, war, or babies, and other times it does not; the same goes for any other crop. Sterilizations, performed on Puerto Ricans, Neuyoricans, and Neo-Ricans during the first half of this century, alternate with peace, welfare, and CARE campaigns throughout the Latin continent for the duration of this century.[7] The issue was to make us believe that we needed such a control. Indeed, the balance between crop and love, or genital control, and ultimately between commercial life and death, habitually walks a colonial tightrope between alien imposition and native desire. A more recent example, the testing and use of pesticides, proves the point from another angle. In places like Costa Rica, the US export of questionable pesticides allegedly improves crops and proportionally decreases the natives' life expectancy or desire and ability to procreate, while preserving and even enriching the alien testers and users. Warmaking, lovemaking, and moneymaking intertwine colonially, as alien agents continue to have commerce on the love life and deadly wars of Latin peoples of the Americas.

The (in)famous guerrilla movements with which South of the Border nations have come to be associated lead to endemic "*coups d'état*,"— co-opted by the US if the guerrillas opt for a pro-Gringo stance. The process of rebelling "for" the United States makes this country condone the institutionalization of guerrilla movements as their surrogate up-and-coming governments. In other words, after doing the dirty work for the gringo, the Latino rebels ostensibly ask for the latter's protection, seduce the powers that be, and/or endorse solutions embedded in a Gringo cause. In short, the guerrilla leader becomes the US's "s.o.b."—no different from those exemplified in the epigraph by the surrogate tyrannies ennacted by Somoza and Disney in the name of American policy and entertainment. Perhaps the worst aspect of such a state of affairs is its hypocrisy: the US fakes (organizationally and orgasmically) being called into action by bitchy South of the Border warriors.

There were even hints early on in the century of a US-sponsored federation that echoed Bolívar's own nineteenth-century dream, and which would turn the South of the Borderlands into a federation of providers of raw materials, beginning with fruits and vegetables and expanding to other marketable products. As observed by Bolívar himself, liberty itself was included as a trade commodity in the American marketplaces, as was life itself and the pursuit of happiness—a lush variant on the French revolution's *liberté, égalité,* and *fraternité*. Tacitly, the US's take on liberty seems to include a Latin mixture of fun and profit through produce, markets, vacation paradises, gambling casinos, whorehouses, and so on. To that effect the US's anti-Nazi campaign of the thirties was as good an excuse as any to seek refuge in Latin hands. As a result, the United States posed not just as a model of Pan-American unity but as the butt of Pan-American seduction, serving, at once, as organizational principle and orgasmic hope of the deprived and depraved Latin masses. The US would export itself as a policy construct that would lead the world into a lovingly free, egalitarian, and brotherly tyranny: that of a United States of the Americas.

Consider that the entertainment industry is one ostensibly freed by its relentless pursuit of fiction from a serious commitment to telling the truth about, or pointing out the cynicism of, the "American way." It is not surprising, therefore, that such an industry would profit from the hypocritical defenses of continental American colonialism dressed up as the US's anti-Nazism and as a seductive union with Big Brother. Since very early in this century Hollywood, particularly MGM, Twentieth Century-Fox, and the Disney Studio, collaborated with the United Fruit Company and other multinationals in putting the finishing touches on the selling of the trans(en)gendering American way to the rest of the Americas.[8]

The history of the Disneying of anti-Nazi propaganda in the Americas has been sketched and protested by Walt Disney himself, as well as by George Black in a book cynically titled *Good Neighbors.*[9] The aftershocks of the US's attempt to substitute its own brand of internationalism for a variety of nationalist socialism was tackled by Ariel Dorfman and Armand Mattelart in *How to Read Donald Duck*, and stressed by David Kunzle's "Introduction to the English Edition" of that book.[10] These remarkable views about the Disney mystique address the libidinal politics that resulted from the anti-Nazi and pro-US campaign South of the Border, a topic that is more poignantly discussed in pioneering works by Cynthia Enloe and Julianne Burton-Carvajal.[11] Enloe goes further than Dorfman and Mattelart in proposing a connection between the US's exploitation of Latin American fruits and other produce and what I term the upsurge of Latin American "fruitiness."[12] The Disney model that these critics review is either heterosexual or pansexually masturbatory; homosexual activities are "corrected" by Disney as Latin American deviation from a world norm.[13] To my mind, not all such corrections are in place, successful, or even desirable. My rereading of Disney Latin American *obra maestra* prompts me to break the thin line between the intended homogenization and the subliminal homosexualizing effects of Pan-American policy. Regardless of one's feelings toward homosexuality, one would acknowledge a colonial policy that enacts a curious democratization of genders—some would choose the derogatory term "inversion" of genders. And indeed the sort of homosexuality I am referring to here might be taken to be a "foreign sort of gender inversion," as it tends to homogenize Latin Americans based on what the patriarchal system considers to be the lowest common gender denominator: the infantilized and effeminized figure of the colonized, be it a man or a woman.

If there was a concerted US strategy of political and sexual Pan-American "unification," it was condemned to backfire, creating a crew of caricaturesque/cartoonesque amigos and amigas who proved themselves capable of uncontrollable exchanges with their neighborly Americanos/as. For better or for worse the undeniable power of the Other rests between her/his legs. Perhaps the ultimate irony of such a postcolonial bedding game is that it unifies seduction, rejection, and compliance as power tricks. In spite of the ethical problems of differentiation, seduction, viewed as a unifying force, stands alone in the realm of sexual politics insofar as it hardly distinguishes between its effects (rejection or compliance) or even between its roles—the fucker and the fucked.

Seduction is a surprisingly democratic power base. The seducing agent can place him/herself on either side of the passive/active or receptive/insertive axis; what matters is who exerts the will. Therefore, seduction has little to do with the type of metasexual enforcement associated with rape. Only those who willfully accept the relative positions of fucker and fucked share the power of the libidinal union engineered through seduction. This is so in the realm of the personal as well as in the realm of the political. And yet, the illusion remains that someone or some country has seduced another and that the seduction is not mutual or reversible. The colonial realm, be it social or personal, attempts to preserve the illusion that seduction is a form of empowerment which, even if it comes from the Other, is dictated, or at least manipulated, by the Self. Thus it is surprising that a film media mogul such as Disney proposes the permanent illusion (fiction) of seduction: Latin America making the United States love it (and fuck it) in ways that would be otherwise unnatural to the gringo tradition—not to mention to the Latino/a tradition.

At any rate, Othered libidos—such as our own from South of the Border—are likely capable of reversing the most staunch of North-of-the-Border-imposed gender roles. Whereas socially or politically speaking the masculine construct of himself "on top" retains a certain power advantage, this is not so in its sexual interpretation. Summing up the situation, fear of ideological or actual Nazi invasion condoned, eased, and justified ideologically charged libidinal invasions, including the US's being on top of its Latin "charges" or being the victim of electrifyingly Latin libidinal charges. The effect of such a reversible invasion concocts a slow time bomb, whose detonation is shared between invader and invaded (fucker and fucked)—and, according to its aftereffects, it is hard to tell who is who, who is on top, or who is the hardest hit. It is up to each of us Pan-American readers to decide to what extent cultural border-crossing could become gender-crossings and transgressive sexual embraces, and whether or not the Pan-American strategy embraced by Hollywood is or is not a good thing for the Latin "natives" and for their "alien" filmmakers.

Trans(en)gendering Americana

War-torn Europe served as a backdrop for an anti-Nazi and pro-Pan-American love-thy-neighbor propaganda campaign that gave tacit permission to Hollywood giants such as MGM, Twentieth Century-Fox, and the Disney Studio to market the people of the Americas for US entertainment. MGM and Twentieth Century-Fox led the way in producing live-action films that would uphold the US's ideological, erotic, and commercial interests. At first such interests converged in a trio of "banana republics" close to the Yankee's heart and home. I am referring to the initial US engagement of Spanish-speaking islands of the Caribbean: Cuba, Puerto Rico, and the Dominican Republic. Other countries, most notably Mexico, Brazil, Chile, Argentina, as well as "vaguely defined" areas of the Amazon and the Andes, soon followed on the "second-banana" list. However, for awhile, the pioneering Caribbean "islands" of Hispanic American culture took a special place in political history and in the film industry as icons of a Pan-American federation, as well as the butt of Pan-American exploitation.

Under the aegis of Latin America's US-sponsored technical "innocence," need for money, lack of workers' rights, and gullibility for propaganda, or lack of choice in all of the above, Disney and the United Fruit Company expanded and "improved" on the Caribbean stereotypes. Disney also counted on animation's creative freedom, apparent sexlessness, and appetite for violence to project caricatured images of the friendly native South of the Border hitting (on) each other senseless(ly) in order to muster up Uncle Sam's approval. Such caricatures easily transfered into Hollywood's live-action films, Madison Avenue propaganda clichés, and the US media's simplistic slogans and jingles still with us today—for instance in the heritage of Chiquita Banana and her spinoffs. While Disney and the rest of Hollywood, Madison Avenue, the US media *et al.* exploited this continent's "fruity" character, the United Fruit Company took care of our fruits. I would like to speak first of Hollywood's libidinal exploitation of the Caribbean island trio, ostensibly for the adult film-viewing audience, so as to foreground Disney's cartoon strategy, whose subliminal eroticism was ostensibly geared to make children grow more "American."

Films such as MGM's *Cuban Love Song* (1931) proposed to package my native island as the Caribbean beachhead of US erotic, industrial, and federal landings, while songs such as "Lamento Borincano," in which the Puerto Rican composer Rafael Hernández laments the conditions of his native island, sadly became distorted as premonition for the US welfare policy toward Puerto Rico.[14] At a more specifically libidinal level, Havana was earmarked as a savage enclave, the American capital of romance, escapism, and sexism, and San Juan as a childish society, a sad capital in need of gringo consolation, parenting, and/or espousing. Cuba the noble savage and Puerto Rico the wild child stood as barely different stages in the same gringo caretaking scheme. To my mind these stages were loaded with gender implications, both the wild child and noble savage stages implying a deliberate "infantilizing," "effeminizing" of "locals." The native population was targeted to become willing victims/will-less virgins of their alien occupants. And to that effect, the US geared its propaganda machine to transform the Caribbean into a playland of subliminal sociosexual tranvestism leading to a gender-troubled colonial policy. Indeed the parallel simplistic media renditions of Cuba and Puerto Rico furnished excuses for both the social and the sexual occupation of men and women of these islands. The excuses act retrospectively, since Puerto Rico and at least part of Cuba and its constitution in principle already belonged to the US, and its people had been forced to espouse gringos and their system.

Completing the US picture of the Caribbean was a singularly biased view of the Dominican Republic, which did not seem to need Hollywood films in order to join in the US-sponsored unification or exploitation. The island was presided over by Trujillo, who at once went on periodic rampages, killing every Haitian in sight, and paradoxically worked "on his own" on the notion of a Pan-American federation, the League of American Nations—apparently leading to the United States of Latin America. As an indirect consequence of such a bloody, second-rate move toward Pan-American unity, the Dominican Republic achieved a high level of dependence, including the export of women to work in the sweatshops and the streets not only of the United States but of Cuba, Puerto Rico, even Haiti. For some reason, the exportation of Cuban women (mostly to Florida's tobacco industries) and of Puerto Rican women (largely to the New York area's garment sweatshops) never achieved the Dominican-US notoriety.

The transformation of social into sexual politics which zeroes in on the offensive treatment of Caribbean women, and of every Caribbean person as an infantilized woman, is very much alive. The Walt Disney Studio magnified the conditions of libidinal dependency to embrace the entire area of the Americas. It created a pretentiously innocent mix of infantilization and feminization with few parallels in international sexual politics. Disney's earlier efforts consisted of puritanical coatings of the

Latin powers of seduction through a series of part-film/part-animation features aimed at the children of the US, but subliminally geared toward the innocent parents of these children, and to further the not-so-innocent worldwide interest of the patriarchal Uncle Sam. My main interest is *The Three Caballeros* (1945), a technically accomplished, ambivalently gendered, sexually provocative, libidinally harassing film.

In *The Three Caballeros* Uncle Walt creates, directly or indirectly, several male and female characters who iconize a highly libidinized and violently transgendered bounty targeted to yield to Uncle Sam. Arguably none of the icons of dependency is more insidiously lasting and damaging than those of Joe Carioca and Carmen Miranda. The former is indeed the full-fledged cartoon product already brought out in an earlier Disney feature: a cigar-smoking, eye-rolling Pan-Americano pygmy trapped in the green body of a Brazilian parrot.[15] In spite of his phallic cigar and retractable umbrella, Joe is seductively feminine, even subversively queer, for instance, in his ability to sell his native Bahia and himself with the batting of his eyelashes. The female archetypal project was suggested by the Disney Studio but completed by other Hollywood filmmakers: a sometime-cartoon and sometime-actress-in-the-flesh Pan-Americana giantess trapped in the red body of a flaming whore, complete with foot-binding platform shoes and a mind-bending headdress spilling fruits. Carmen, in spite of some exaggerated secondary female characteristics, fruit and all, is decidedly a bitch goddess with ridiculous malelike fits of aggression. The film section of the State Department's blueprint for the Carmen Miranda project proposed to "create 'Pan-Americana,' a noble female figure bearing a torch and a cross, subtly suggesting both the Virgin Mary and the Goddess of Liberty."[16] Indeed Carmen becomes contagious not just as a virgin and a goddess of liberty, but as a show woman and a fruit-laden horn of plenty. As we shall see, other characters, mainly Joe Carioca and Donald, play the Carmen role with its full plethora of transgendered connotations.

The man who would light the torch of Carmen, the freedom-fighting virgin goddess, was not a local fellow but the imported Donald Duck, no glowing image of red-blooded US males. And yet, even this US duck was supposed to be man enough to pinch Carmen's fruits. Donald's masculinity or lack thereof was not the issue here, for he represented a form of commercial seduction that relies on the subliminal message and the imposition of the will, rather than on the frontal attack or bravado. Furthermore, he replaced Mickey Mouse as the "International Symbol of Good Will" following a 1935 declaration of Trujillo's US-backed League of American Nations.[17] The US torch of liberty in the Americas thus passed from Mickey Mouse to Donald Duck in pursuit of a basket of fruit and a torch singer and torrid dancer with a woman attached—the sort of Latin woman who, in the gringo imagination, makes him give up protectionist politics.

Joe Carioca is sometimes rebaptized José Carioca—as in *The Three Caballeros'* "companion" book *Donald Duck Sees South America*.[18] The role of Carmen Miranda is sometimes played by her sister Aurora—as is the case in *The Three Caballeros*. Thus, Disney made efforts to generalize the Brazilian stereotypes to the rest of Latin America. This generalization also expands on and crosses over the dialectics of gender and sexual categories. *The Three Caballeros* moves from a Carmen-like aggressive cookie vendor/vedette/bombshell to more "regressively feminine" Mexican bathing beauties and singing actresses, who tempt and reject or ignore the Donald's "masculinity." From the male regressivity of the parrot perfomer Joe Carioca, the cartoon moves to more "aggressively masculine" characters such as Panchito—the mariachi-dressed cock who tests and denigrates Donald's "masculinity," and eventually becomes the third of the "gay" caballeros. These less-than-ideal images of Latin humanity belong to a line of caricatures of which Disney emerges as a pioneering expert: the subliminally phallus-prone or unnaturally phallic Latin señorita and the unnaturally macho or subliminally sissy Latino. All of them, and some of us, live by someone else's banana policy.

Freedom to Carmen

As proposed by the Carmen prototype, Latin American females retained a role combining the model of the feisty whore with the golden heart and the willing virgin with the poisonous passion fruit—as paradoxical platforms of humanitarian activity/passivity. There is no quality control or assurance of purity in the pursuit of freedom nor in the pursuit of happiness, much less in colonial situations such as the lingering US shadow over Latin America. On the one hand, the iconic US definition of liberty for all points toward an all-consuming, French-imported, Manhattanite virgin, the Statue of Liberty. This French virginal connection pursues Carmen, who, in the film *Copacabana* (1947) adopts the part-time persona of bitch (touch-me-not) goddess Mlle. Fifí (Miss Sissi?) in contrast with her own hypersexual persona as Brazilian bombshell (Carmen the "tico-tico" queen of sex).

As she impersonates the French statue, Carmen becomes a parody of a towering, passive-aggressive, immigrant, bronze diva with a green card and patina who has stuck to the hope and to the memory of so many immigrants like myself regardless of our point of entry into the US. We all pass through, without apparently touching, her. The virgin of liberty beckons to her port, signaling the end of the ultimate trip of trips: immigration to the land of the free and carte blanche to consume—some would say prostitute—one's "native" ideals as an Other without sharing the Self's bounty. As she plays herself, Carmen becomes a piece of the show, entertaining the US crowds. But she has not only the opportunity to be touched but the power to touch her audiences. After all she is a consumable but still "erect" Chiquita Banana-type of label stuck to US-bound Latino bananas and other fruits—be they male or female in appearance and attitude. As a statuesque and aloof female of French derivation or as a fruity Brazilian populist diva in close contact with the libido of American males, Carmen's *razón de ser* is as native product in shaky transit to a foreign market.

The US colonial outlook tends to render Latinas, and above all Latinos, as sexually helpless toward their own or, at least, unable to compete with an Americana/o whom they need in order to fulfill their manifest destiny. In short, we need to be brought into the foreign market of gender and sexuality, since we all provide the natural, and even the unnatural national territory that becomes the target of the international invasion of the libido. A subliminal American fantasy, shared by masculinists and feminists alike, is to pose as the announcer or denouncer of the role of the Latin macho, and to then be forced, because of Latino inadequacy, Latina pressure, and good-old-American guilt, to impersonate that macho role him- or herself. Indeed this American tragedy is also in effect beyond sexual politics. The US military establishment and the peace movements (from the antinuclear to the ecological avant-garde) prefer to take an active part in designing—or pretending to design—the international macho monster that would require US attention: saving the poor defenseless señorita country which a local competitor is intent on devastating. The saving fantasy is endemic to the US's Latin American policy. The US is ready to defend us against the local macho—conquistadors, caudillos, guerrilleros, matadors—raping of our women, nature, systems, environment.

In 1992 the long list of Spanish macho monsters converged in the US media's recycling of Columbus as a senseless imperialist macho and genocidal maniac. The alternatives are few, but I can think of at least another type of machos-on-show: the Miami-produced homoerotic calendar *Men of Cuba*.[19] Let us remember that these unfairly competing Latinos in the world market remain poised against a rather dubious model of red-blooded American maleness, such as Donald in the role of imperialist duck. Perhaps the ultimate perversion of a feminine-sensitive—rather than feminist—society like the US, is translating the guilt of machismo to the South of the Border machos they deride. The responsibility for the hype about maleness lies with the alien Latin American machos as much as the responsibility for the hype about femaleness lies with the corresponding señoritas. Machos and señoritas made me do "it." Latin machos might be high on the scale of testosterone but low on the totem pole; Latin señoritas might be high on the pedestal but low on the scale of rights. Even our best cock and pussycat cannot compete with a lowly duck Donald or with the mousiest Minnie. And, given the currency of the clichés even among our best-meaning American liberals, I would like to return to the source—nipping, as it were, the Chiquita banana syndrome in the bud.

Carmen and I

Carmen's paradoxical genesis as the prize fruit of Latin American womanhood points to an international media tragedy. In an Anglo-Latin scene of conquest, Latinas tend to lose to stereotypical Americano invasions which presumably save these women from the local machos but ready them for worse. An alien macho will likely take the local's place. An alien señorita will likely do the same. For instance, in my Cuban primal scene, heavily sprinkled with Hollywood shooting stars, Americanos were more dashing than the local macho heroes and Americanas were prettier, faster, and worth more than the local señorita martyrs of tropical desire. This travesty of human exchange across national frontiers of gender and sex increases proportionally with alien bouts of political/libidinal domination.

It is not surprising for the worldwide history of colonialism to find that US colonizing forces have waged in film an "effeminizing" and "infantilizing" campaign toward Latin Americans, including the US's own "minority" targets. Indeed the ultimate goal of the good-neighbor policy's film propaganda campaign was to homogenize/homosexualize Latinos/as to the point of making us both palatable for the US appetite and desirous of a Pan-American union at all levels, without any procreative consequences. US media machinery, such as Hollywood, tended to "homoeroticize" us into a corner, or at least it cross-dressed and/or cross-gendered us, their amigos and their amigas, into a degenerate subservience. What Hollywood was not counting on was that its patriarchal advocates were not homoeroticizing us into a permanent corner, but rather into a transient closet, and that, in turn, their libidinal invasion strategy had an unsuspecting result. In "degenerating" Latins into gender and sexual subservience, they were also creating libidinal monsters who could entice gringos into transgendering or sexually transgressing postures. The Self coming together with the Other spelled gender trouble, under the guise of being a fictional experience limited by cartoon or cartoonlike exchanges as real rather than real danger.

In Disney's Pan-American fantasy, Latinos and Americanos wanted not only to have but also to be had; while Latinas and Americanas wanted to have, not just to be had. Thus, to a certain extent, the libidinal sphere of the anti-Nazi justified a different sort of right-wing politics: a relentless, US-centered, colonially inspired, Pan-American union that eroticized the cooperation between the US haves and the Latin American have-nots coming into a two-way embrace. The embrace is not always heterosexual. On the contrary, at least in the realm of the reel, US colonial domination is often ensured by this country presuming that there are no "real" men or women South of the Border, only Latin targets of the American libido.

In spite of the perilous balancing of genders to suit the colonial fantasy, the colonizers' libidinization of the colonized went hand in hand with a paradoxical process of gender investment that assumed gender rein-venting—some would say gender reversing. Such a process combined investing the desired target with wild and dependent qualities, a mixture of seductive danger and desire to be hugged, not to mention a daring cross-referencing of maleness and femaleness that, to maximize its titillat-ing effect, would threaten to acquire a life of its own. The process questions the very patriarchal imperialism that it cosmetically upholds—as already suggested by Black, Mattelart, Dorfman, and Enloe. But the presumably US-male-serving feminization and infantilization of the Other as wild, dependent, colonial subject, retains a fruit-throbbing bitch, à la Carmen *et al.*, as the perfect role model.

Arguably an untraditional problem for the Disney-endorsed traditional image of the colonizer is that sometimes Carmen is a man, or acts like one. And that man is not always the prototype of the colonized. Sometimes Carmen "Carmenizes" the colonizer, or challenges him with a malelike form of female aggression. Her brand of passive/passionate core, as well as defensive/offensive aggression, is likely intended to mock and disarm the imperial duck. My fantasy is that Carmen remains perfectly capable of her own independent passion and offensive campaign of self-assertion, and defies most homosexual panics, at least within the privacy of the (or my own) screening room. Furthermore, maybe Carmen and I do not *choose* to be reactive, but are instead given no choice by the circumstances in which Hollywood coined, cornered, and filmed her, or the US labels me. Her revenge is seducing me, as one of her many voyeuristic viewers and reviewers, into believing that I am seducing her, or using her as my role model and platform of revenge.

Carmen is the tip of the US trans(en)gendering Latin iceberg. There are other "hot-headed" Latinos and Latinas ready to take over Carmen and melt the Pan-American ice escapades. But whereas she embodies the virgin/whore, male/female quota with surprising ease, her male counter-parts remain largely split between two forms of testosterone poisoning: lethargy or hysteria, in the vein of the siesta-under-the-sombrero (mañana syndrome) sort of man and the Speedy González prototype of senseless activity. Both choices converge in irremediable impotence (particularly toward conquering outsiders, or even bitchy insiders—such as Carmen).

For those South of the Border types like me who do not even qualify as senseless practitioners of machismo, the alternative is worse: we might become the hyperactive rivals of, and ineffectual losers to, the imperialistically prone American Dick. Disney actually offers two basic models for the hyperactive-loser types, rendered in the bird language of *The Three Caballeros*. On the one hand there is Pablo the Penguin, who is hardworking but cold, slow to catch on (to) and to mate, but easy to catch off guard. On the other hand there is the *araquā* (araquan), an Amazonian bird whose hysterical persona might have served to shape that of the Mexican mouse Speedy González—who fluctuates between the hyperpassive and the hyperactive model.[20] The third "macho" possibility, Panchito the Mexican cock, who appears toward the end of the film, is not hyperactive, but his male strutting is unconvincing at best.[21] Non-"macho" male Latino activity is reduced to "much ado about nothing," or worse, the tabula rasa of the *lánguida y tropical* siesta under the sombrero and the "mañana syndrome" with which our "developing" economies—and in turn our "developing" or "Third World" culture—have come to be associated.

Thus begins to emerge a Disney world producing a suggestive colonial mix and match of Latino/a and Anglo-American libidos on sale. But let us assess the subversive potential for gender freedom and sexual happiness, centering on Disney's model film for the seductive colonialization of Latin America. To begin with, Miranda sometimes takes a strategically "theatrical" revenge against the consumers of her fruitiness. In *The Three Caballeros*, she assaults Donald, shrinking him with heavy petting into a flattened dot on the pavement—which later "erects" into a standing but cautious and sensitive man. She also emerges as a blue-green cardboard image in a winning Statue of Liberty-like pose, momentarily paralyzing Donald, who, at least for an instant, becomes an immigrant in need of a home port—thus empathizing with all of those other birds, from the Southernmost Pablo to the Northernmost Panchito, dying to travel "upward"—perhaps to emigrate to the US.

As liberal whore and the Virgin of Liberty, Carmen's presence has devastating effects on the male birds. Carmen the woman also triumphs elsewhere: such as at the end of the film *Copacabana*, where Groucho Marx (as an exaggerated version of a maleness-ducking American) and the leading man (the proto-macho gangster-manager-producer-owner Italo-American type) succumb to her nightclub "act." Unbeknownst to the nightclub owners, she was hired to give a split performance: as a sinuous but virginal, high-class French chanteuse (Mlle. Fifí) and as a hip-twisting and proto-whorish Brazilian samba star (Carmen herself). In the end, this double performer is integrated into a single woman who, half Fifí and half Carmen, wins over the nightclubbing mob—just as in *The Three Caballeros* she is street vendor and statuesque diva rolled into one powerful lover girl. Eventually all the men who come in contact with Carmen are Mirandized to a pulp by this gutsy Franco-Brazilian diva-in-Hollywood-residence.

The fruitful Latin woman's revenge on her ogling audience is also a feature of her male counterpart. Joe Carioca succeeds in dealing subversively with his Disney-sponsored audience. He Carioquizes Donald to a pulp, at times masculinizing and at times feminizing him, seducing or contaminating at will the self-appointed and all-consuming American duck. One would think that after the *The Three Caballeros* phenomenon was released to the world, Latin American bonding with the US would never be the same, but US-Latin American film games largely remained libidinally repressed by their audiences. Disney's films had a near perfect excuse for just such a repression: his work was ostensibly intended for children.

On Becoming an American

Arguably for Latin Americans of my parents' generation, the US of the thirties and forties was, in comparison to the Nazis, a rather progressive invader. My parents and I did not know we had to provide the fruit and to become ourselves the fruits or the hard-working and soft-bodied fruity weavers of the US loom. I attribute my own initiation into American life and world history, from the platform of a small-town Cuban childhood, precisely to such a US marketing strategy, and iconically to my viewing of the film *The Three Caballeros* and my self-conscious humming of the best-selling song "We're Three Caballeros." The film and the song made it to my hometown sometime in the late forties—perhaps too late to fight the first outbreak of Nazism, but not too late to encourage Cuba to join the US fruit basket or to encourage me to take my first lesson in my Pan-American ideological and sexual education, not to mention gender consciousness. Donald was the first gringo "bird" to invade the national territory of my libido, one of many which, if Castro and my father are right, mostly bring trouble to the locals.

My memories of the earliest period of the anti-Nazi campaign and of personal development remain cartoon and song-and-dance-like images orchestrated by three gay caballeros sanctioned by the Disney label. I was also heterosexually mystified by the blurry sight of bathing beauties lying like half-dressed sardines on the beach in Acapulco onto which Disney torpedoes the barely manly ugly duckling of a hero (pantless, feathered, and penisless—but not penniless). The "real" women in the cartoon, however, tease our duckey of a dick in a sadomasochistic "hide and seek" ritual which ends when Donald shows signs of enjoying it. Who was I rooting for?

Disney scenes and questions relate to other filmed scenes and personal/social questions. Before the TV monopoly, films were a crucial way to gain an international conscience, and for me, and I suspect many other small-town children, a favorite medium and model to judge a given culture's position in the world order. Films habitually presented such a position in terms of libidinal quotas and gender empathies.

To complete the dizzying Disneying of my conscience, I remember my excitement and subsequent soul/gender empathy search upon viewing *Flying Down to Rio*. In this 1933 film blonde female beauties fly over Copacabana beach doing acrobatics on the wing of a ("Pan American?") plane for a group dominated by foreign and local men at the mercy of these cloud-bound, intrepid performers, who in turn are both at the mercy of a Hollywood producer. The white suits and white skins, the flowery and deflowered women, heat and swaying palms put generalizing ideas into my head. This Hollywood flying-down-to-Rio fantasy could be my own town's and my own: a whitewashed generic land of tropical languor spiked by sex. Whether the men and/or the women are languorously and/or dangerously laid out on the beach—as in Disney's case—or perilously laid out on the wings of a plane or being a spectator on the side wings—as in Hollywood's case—our imagination had a choice: to play along or to play a trick on the colonial flight of the imagination. And vis-à-vis that colonial choice it hardly mattered whether we acted as women or as men.

The biggest US fear is losing the war of sedition—which remains the ultimate of conquests: to convince someone that she or he should want to be under our control. The fear of losing oneself in that seduction, of losing control of the terms of seduction, overwhelms the US fear of a Latin American sedition in the Nazi cause. In fact the politics of seduction feed on that of dependency: as the seduced becomes dependent on the seduction, with the delusion of sharing power in the transitory horizontal equality of the sexual union. Of course Latin America is not the sole seduced—and arguably passified, conquered, and "effeminized"/"infantilized"—partner. Disney and the rest of the propaganda machine seduce the insiders, the US public at large, into believing that they are "on top" of the world.

Ducking Columbus

The Three Caballeros is framed as a series of packages sent by an undetermined number of "amigo" birds to their long-distance feathered cousins in the US. The main amigos, Joe Carioca the Brazilian parrot and plain Panchito the Mexican cock, complete the trio of hot male birds that gives the film its title. To my surprise, the Caribbean is only subliminally alluded to by these model birds who share the generic heat of the Americas South of the US Border (and consequently the Hispanic/Latino immigrant within the US border). The Americas become not only a bird's nest of male bonding but a series of Southern hospitality gifts to Mr. Donald Duck, a much-deserving Northern explorer and defender of birddom or anthropologist and mourner of bird doom.

The sequences of the cartoon unwrap as a repeat voyage of discovery. Donald not only "unwraps" but also "enters" the packages, taking trips which, in a sense, become cyclical forms of repayment. His excuse for the visit is the packaged invitation which is an open-ended icon of the real (or reel) thing: Latin America itself. The duck interprets such an invitation as a summons to "help out"—at least to service the essential needs of the natives. These seductive needs are coated, sundaelike, in thick sugar syrup with plenty of nuts. Indeed the US has been seeking just such invitations to visit us, solve our misery, share our fun, and stay on terribly long vacations. Just like Columbus, Donald takes four trips that present themselves in increasingly larger packages on the occasion of his birthday, on Friday the 13th.

The US bird's first voyage of discovery, which comes wrapped in a tiny package, contains a Latin American excuse for a film camera demanding to film Pablo, Donald's penguin alter ego, who doubles as the rarest of South American amigos. The film puts Donald in charge of the camera, and thus of the situation. The duck shows off his skill and simpatico attitude toward his subject matter by building his equipment before our very eyes. He throws the gift reels into the air—to the sound of a tropical percussive melee—and they become a projector, a film, a geopolitical action? Even a duck can become a purveyor of an illusion that goes by the name of technical progress.

The politically repressive, but also libidinally repressed, duck's curiosity takes him to the southernmost realm of the Aves Raras, which appears as a sign—orally translated into English as "Strange Birds," that is, his Latin American "cousins." Pablo is the target of inquiry, a soul-searching penguin among dumb penguins, who seeks to know the world or, should I say, the US view of the world. After many unsuccessful attempts—marked by his failing traveling machinery—he manages to sail northward, bypassing the ancient Andean civilizations that only show up as colonial postcard types of resorts: Viña del Mar is "carded" instead of its counterpart, the land of the ancient Araucanos. A touristy view of Lima and Quito replaces the land of the Incas and the like.

After a touch-and-go side trip to Juan Fernández Island (still run by the ghost of Robinson Crusoe) Pablo arrives in the Galápagos, where he comes to terms in his own way with Darwin's evolutionary theories. The Penguin melts into a vacationland lethargy under his newfound sombrero. He incarnates a feathered missing link with anthropomorphic primate potential as he squeezes the peel of a golden banana into the air, to pop the white pulp into his eager mouth. Donald just provides Pablo with a "technical" opportunity to discover him, or what is the same, the Darwinian animal/cultural pyramid peaking in grade A US culture. Just as with Columbus, Cortés, and Pizarro, the Antarctic penguins are like other natives—in the Caribbean, Meso America, and Andean America, respectively—who anticipate the colonizers' arrival by attempting to reach them with all their might. As Pablo fulfills the Darwinian prophecy of the descent of man—or should we say the descent of duck—the film jumps to the next package, which is slightly larger in size, and it should be harder for the audience to follow.

The second trip, to the Amazon, is packaged in proto-Western mythological wraps. The strings attached take viewers from an Amazon iconized, even in the forties, as the last Euro-American hope to recover the ecological earthly paradise. This pristine forest ready for commerce offers Donald an anthropologizing ornithologist paradise, a kind of bird predawn of technology, where birds act out as tools—such as the scissor bird. The Latin American post-European myth of this second trip ends up at the heart of South America's own lost pampa. Disney's approximation of this landscape is by way of a winged donkey and his Gauchito (with a wide-eyed, cherubic, "take-me-take-me," plaintive look) played against a heritage of both Pegasus and Europa being swept away by a bull. This Uruguayan boy prototype and his Euro-mythical beast become an inseparable pair ready to beat the primitive system. They enter a horse race, favorite pastime of these parts, which showcases the natives' cowboy skills at a disadvantage to Euro-American ingenuity.

For the Disney Studio, the second Uruguayan passion must be boys mating with donkeys, something which is suggested at different "cloudy" levels—or literally by the appearance of an ominous cloud where some behind-the-scenes activity takes place. Perhaps the top clouded surprise presents Gauchito and his donkey's rump inside a thunderous cloud, from which the presumed horseman, or should I say donkeyman, emerges and coquettishly wonders, "who's the boss?" This love and power struggle is further underlined by another cloud scene, from which Gauchito emerges sheepishly holding the donkey's tail, which the commentator assesses as a "jockeying for position." The odd skills of this Gaucho and his donkey mate win them the jackpot for the race. And yet, the beast displays its wings and thus its own and the Gaucho's winning trick by flirting effeminately with a bird high on a pole.

The third packaged trip opens into a dancing book of "magic realism" manned, as it were, by Joe Carioca, who invites Donald to Bahia, black capital of Brazil. However, Joe's throbbing book's Bahia is not Afro-Brazilian as it should be, but a red blob of white paired items—ranging from palm trees, to love birds, to boats, to a candy-selling, swaying woman (Miranda complete with a modest turban—*sîm frutas*—and make-up that makes her look like Annette Funicello in the *Mickey Mouse Club*) accompanied by minstreling chorus boys (looking like Franco-American gay-hip gondolieri in straw hats, striped T-shirts, and tight toreador pants). Evidently Brazilian humanity is too much for a mere secondhand view of the scene through cartoons or a single country.

The multinational Brazilian loving, music, and dancing are thick as molasses and transparent as a transgendered message. Joe seduces Donald into a slow samba. The tropic neither separates the boys from the girls, nor does it unite them, but it rather hyperfeminizes and hypermasculinizes seemingly at random. Dangerously (en)gendered superwomen/fruits like Carmen and supermen/birds, like the speeded-up araquan bird, succeed in derailing the samba and the train trips to the hot heart of Bahia. The former does it by Carmenizing, that is, transgendering, everyone in sight to her canned-samba beat; the latter, by literally drawing away the rail lines (again in a so-so Disney proto-sample of "magic realism" and a novel view of the commercial Latino Boom). Eventually Brazil drowns us in a testoteroned travesty of sisterhood (under the aegis of male imitations of the image of Carmen many times multiplied). This leads Donald to have a hot and humid dream lubricated by Joe Carioca's and his own Carmen impersonations.

Once again, the transient softening effect of the feminized tropics is counteracted by the equally transient hardening of Latino men dancing/fighting as cocks engaged in *capoeira*, the Afro-Brazilian martial art. The transnational, transgendered, even transsexual, phantasy book finally closes on them, even though Joe manages to pull Donald away by his tail. Donald has been squashed into a little sailor hat with legs (which mimics the dreamy siesta under the sombrero), but he manages to erect himself back into full-blooded American duckhood. At this point he has an image crisis: the animated film has him splitting into a kaleidoscope of amigo, and less than amigo, personae.

The fourth voyage comes packaged in an enormous box that yields a three-cornered piñata and eventually a tour of Mexico guided by Panchito, dressed as a *charro* cock who sweeps the other birds into a magic serape trip/trick. Donald remains a somewhat frustrated voyeur of what is given as Mexico's main sights—all of them mestizo feasts with a colonial bias: native beaches, dances, Christmas traditions, and nightlife. Mexicans, rendered as kitschy divas, do their coquettish folklore, backed by pusillanimous male accompaniment.

The American hero gets into the act only as he circles Acapulco, armed with a retractable telescope that bristles at the sight of a seductively pale bunch of sun-screened señoritas. He dives into the scene and plays along with the Mexicanas' sadomasochistic game, until the señoritas run away. The "wolf in duck's clothing," proclaimed by the film, is challenged by a woman daring him, in untranslated Mexican-accented Spanish: "*¡ándale, patito, ven!*" (dare, *patito*—sissy?—come!). In the Caribbean and elswhere "pato" implies "gay" and/or "sissy."

Finally Mexico offers him the romantically threatening female heads of star flowers and all sorts of love-me/love-me-not petals scattered at his feet and ready to make him slip—as if these petals were the peels of Carmen's bananas, or the wrappers of homemade candies sold on the pulsating streets of Bahia. Donald eventually becomes one of the flowers and tries to kiss, in lesbian fury, one of the real ladies' corollas, to no avail. The flowers transform themselves into female cacti, whose lead is a *charra* (echo of Panchito). Panchita, as I have come to call her, whips Donald into final submission.[22] And he likes it. Donald then plays the bull—a paper bull at that—in an improvised corrida where Joe Carioca and Panchito take turns playing the killing *matador* and the pricking *banderillero*. Donald gets it from both ends, and again he likes it—after all, Uncle Walt is looking over his shoulder, and ours.

As observed by Julianne Burton-Carvajal, Donald's bullfighting scene represents a kind of outpouring of traditional macho behavior aimed to counteract any lingering interpretation of his amigo bonding as amorous advances.[23] What I would consider Donald's hypermacho "homosexual panic" is counteracted by Panchito's "ironic voice-over," to the tune of: "like brother to brother / we're all for each other."[24] This slogan contrasts with the earlier climax of the gay caballero's song: " . . . friends though we may be/When some Latin baby / Says yes, no or maybe / Each man is for himself."[25] In the Pan-American pursuit of a "united states of being" Donald has thrown all caution to the wind; he has become one of/with us Latin birds, perhaps a subversive *pájaro* in his own right.

Salve Columbus

In fact Donald Duck did discover América, an America written and pronounced with a specific diacritical mark and pronounced with some sort of an accent, a subversively gendered and sexed accent. Through a series of well-packaged voyages, the magic of Disney presents us like children to a childlike world of unity and progress in which men are less than men and women are more than women. The packaging of the voyages is clever: it almost fooled me into believing that I was among the Latinos who had contributed something to the continental mass of the forever-new New World. I am referring to the packages sent by my fellow birds to that plastic duck of the North, which contained—as you might recall:

(1) A tiny box from which emerges rhythmically improvised Latino ingenuity which lends an improvisatory hand to Donald's film equipment, and through which we witness a penguin version of a cold-blooded land South of the Border.

(2) A medium-sized box from which emerges a mythical Pegasus/Europa's bull, folklorized, updated, and rendered into a shrew, that is, a flying donkey whose gaucho partner hides his wings.

(3) The next-size-up box that turns out to be a three-dimensional book complete with a crooning Brazilian parrot with a proto-Speedy González as a sidekick, and that contains a song-and-dance Brazilian tour.

(4) The biggest of the boxes reveals a three-cornered piñata which breaks to reveal a Pandora's box of seaside beauties, religious folklore, flowering paradises, and electrified Latino performances.

The seduction of the gifts eventually threatens the gender and sexual core of the ducking voyager with "United States" in mind. The four Columbian voyages of discovery retold by Disney transform Donald. Such gift-wrapped voyages, like Columbus's own, might confuse an audience of children and naïve buyers but challenge an adult audience with a desire for transatlantic exchanges. In the first trip the duck plays the hot bird to the cold-blooded penguins at the edge of "progress." In the second, he learns a new Latino trick in male bonding and love of animals at the Euro-mythical edge of the pampas. In the third, Donald dances with a "wolf" or two in parrot clothing, succumbing to the transgendered word and world of the Brazilian wild. By the end of the fourth and final trip, the caballeros gaily impersonate Pan-American unity.

The film ends with an orgasmic Pan-American night of fireworks, enjoyed in unison by the bird trio. Joe the parrot and Panchito the cock cozy up to the middle man, Donald the Duck, who is dressed up as a madonna in a serape. Disney's pietá is superficially convincing and profoundly pitiful, but a faithful representation of the transgendering effects of mixing apples and oranges, Latinos/as and Americano/as, in a Christian communion of commercial proportions and surprising gender disruption and libidinal eruption. Indeed, Donald has survived a Pan-American war of gender, sex, and fireworks, nothing quite comparable to World War II or, for that matter, World War III.

Banana Boat Song

Oh no, Donald, don't do *that*!
—Joe Carioca, in *The Three Caballeros*, after receiving a warm
abrazo and kiss on the cheek.

Mister, don't eat the bananas.
—Lyrics of a Cuban-American song composed and sung by
Chirino.

Besides Christopher Columbus's New World voyages aboard the Niña, the Pinta, and the Santa María, I retain Walt's twentieth-century voyages of discovery aboard *The Three Caballeros* as a controversial model of my own exile and critical "arrival" on the US academic scene. The very impurity and injustices of these voyages provide motivation and justification, but also consolation and compromise, for my own modestly transcultural, transgendered, and transexual "revenge" on the Western discourse and made-in-the-US macho image, both of which I am marginally a part. What I hope with my critical "banana boat song" is not necessarily to prevent—or, for that matter, to encourage—any Mister's touching of my people's bananas (elaborating on Chirino's lyrics in the epigraph), but to use to Latin American advantage whatever Donald did, unconsciously or wickedly, in the name of a US brand of liberation. I could even add to Donald's own US-manipulated hope for us my own discreet postcolonial traces of libidinal freedom. I wish Donald's and my own literary "nephews" would listen, pick up, and open up the subliminal meaning of a true Pan-American union and relative freedom for all. Perhaps the reading public should take their own cruise of discovery in that most unusual of love boats:

> I shall leave this letter on a twig, hoping that it will be seen and picked up by some passing riverboat. Now I shall beat my way out of here across the swamps and brush. Nothing will stop me till I reach civilization. . . . Goodbye. (I am running out of berry juice),
> Your Uncle Donald[26]

11

Cultural Contagion:
On Disney's Health Education Films for
Latin America

Lisa Cartwright and Brian Goldfarb

Between 1941 and 1943, Walt Disney, his wife, and a group of Disney
Studio animators made three highly publicized trips to Latin America
under the auspices of the US government. On the basis of material collected during these trips, the Disney Studio produced nearly two dozen
films in Spanish, Portuguese, and English versions, a majority of which
(fifteen, to be exact) are educational shorts produced for Latin American
audiences on the subject of health and sanitation. In an essay in this
volume, Julianne Burton-Carvajal focuses on three popular films in the
travelogue genre that were also produced out of this tour: *South of the
Border With Disney* (1942), *Saludos Amigos* (1943), and *The Three Caballeros* (1945). Burton-Carvajal argues that this trilogy constitutes "a totalizing account of [Disney's] cross-cultural journey."[1] Essentially travel films,
these works successfully shift from didactic documentary to a more complex narrative style—a progression in which, in Burton-Carvajal's words,
"personality assumes precedence over geography and literal depictions
of place give way to more mythic geographies animated by imagination
and desire."[2] As Burton-Carvajal shows, the mythic geographies constructed in Disney's trilogy are largely (neo)colonialist fantasies of conquest and spectacle; desire is chiefly that of Disney and his patrons for
the land, fauna, and female bodies that comprise the phantasmatic Latin
American culture they have created on film.

South of the Border's narrator explains that the studio's Latin American
tour was conducted to "gather a store of material" on Latin America.
However, focusing exclusively on forms of popular culture, including
dance, music, tourist sites, and above all on "natural" beauty, the trilogy
seems to indicate that the tour completely bypassed "material gathering"
in such areas as Latin American subjectivity, community and domestic

culture, labor, industry, or health care. However, these issues are at the core of Disney's fifteen health care films. If the trilogy Burton-Carvajal analyzes functions as a document of Disney's "cross-cultural journey," we would argue that the health education films document a different, and equally important, facet of Disney's involvement in US-Latin American affairs: his role as pedagogue. Not, as Burton-Carvajal claims, mere "by-products" of this journey, the Disney educationals were part of a joint effort by Disney studios and the US government to, in the words of a studio report, "[teach] the fundamentals of social science free from religious or political influence."[3]

Produced for Latin American audiences in response to the US government's interest in educating about personal and household diet, grooming, and sanitation, these films fix intently on the private bodies and domestic lives of the subjects so strikingly absent in the trilogy Burton-Carvajal analyzes. However, far from giving voice to Latin American subjectivities, these films constitute a different set of colonialist imaginings and desires.

Characterized as innately lazy and/or ignorant, the Latin American subjects and families created in the animated health shorts are held individually responsible for their own states of disease and poverty. The most personal aspects of bodily care, from eating to coughing to defecating, become the subject of a repetitive and paternalistic discourse. The pedagogical strategy used in these films is to didactically associate illness and poverty with particular bodily "customs," and health and prosperity with Western scientific standards of hygiene.

If *The Three Caballeros* is an articulation of Disney's (and the US's) erotic desire for its own spectacularized image of Latin America, the fifteen health films are attempts to control and regulate the bodies and lives of Latin American workers and peasants at the most intimate level. (Disney would not get so intimate with US audiences until a bit later in the decade, with, for example, his 1947 production for women viewers, *Story of Menstruation,* made under contract with the Kimberly-Clark Corporation.) The health films for Latin America mark a broader cultural fascination and revulsion toward Latin America cultures. The specter of disease and contagion portrayed so menacingly in these films was, for US audiences, emblematic of a more generalized danger posed by contact with foreign, and particularly "primitive," cultures—an anxiety heightened by the increasing US contact with South America and the Caribbean through corporate expansion by companies like United Fruit and Goodyear Tire Company, Roosevelt's strategical reassertion of the Good Neighbor policy (a program originally outlined in 1933, the year of *Flying Down to Rio*'s release), and the global crisis in markets and alliances brought on by the war. This anxiety expressed itself, in part, through a national public health discourse that repeatedly collapsed together the agendas of personal defense against disease and national defense against invasion. The health films' obsessive attention to bodily habits reflects a broader obsession with the threat of "contamination" of the national body with Latin American cultures through the colonialist "cross-cultural" agendas of government and corporate programs.

The program of "cultural exchange" promoted by Roosevelt in his advocacy of a "hemispheric partnership" saw its cultural expression not only through government-sponsored venues such as *South of the Border With Disney,* but earlier, in Hollywood productions like *Rio's Road to Hell* (1932) or *Only Angels Have Wings* (1939). It is important to note that, by the twenties, film already was being used by US corporations in Latin America. In the words of video producer Joel Katz, film was the "pen" used by US corporations to promote to US audiences their takeover of Latin American land, natural resources, and labor. In his documentary *Corporation With a Movie Camera,* Katz notes that United Fruit used the same footage to produce films for three distinct sets of viewers. *About Bananas, Banana Land,* and *The Banana Industry* were respectively aimed at educational, public, and industrial audiences. Clearly, Disney's tour was a part of a larger shift involving many uses of cinema to serve corporate and government interests. In order to understand the Disney films in this colonialist matrix, it is necessary to situate them in the broader context of corporate and government agendas in Latin America.

The Intersection of Cultural Production, Corporate Expansion, and Government Interests

Two figures were chiefly responsible for the selection of Disney as cultural emissary to Latin America: Nelson A. Rockefeller and John Hay Whitney. A brief account of their careers should illustrate the degree to which corporate interests, government agendas, and cultural production intersected to support US presence in Latin America at the start of World War II.

As head of the foreign department of the Chase Manhattan Bank, and with major business interests in Latin American-based corporations such as the Creole Petroleum Company, Rockefeller was deeply invested in the fate of Latin American-United States relations. He was also well known for his work on Latin American public health initiatives through the Rockefeller Foundation, and cultural affairs were closely linked to his corporate activities. Indeed, the value of culture did not escape him: Rockefeller's first trip to Latin America (in 1935) was to visit a Venezuelan museum of art,[4] and throughout subsequent travels, he invested in art and artifact, amassing a valuable collection on the basis of which he founded in New York the Museum of Primitive Art (a collection of indigenous art from the Americas, Africa, Oceania, and Early Asia and Europe).[5]

Not just a corporate businessman and art collector, Rockefeller also had close personal connections high up in the US government. The degree of his pull there is evident from the following: disturbed by Nazi presence in Argentina witnessed during a 1939 business trip there, Rockefeller wrote to then-president Franklin Delano Roosevelt to express his "deep concern over Nazi influence and penetration" in Latin America. Interestingly, Rockefeller posits both public relations and public health and welfare intervention as measures to eradicate Nazi presence: he recommends that FDR institute a US program in cooperation with "nations of the Western Hemisphere . . . to achieve better relations among those nations and *to help raise their standards of living.*"[6]

The president followed Rockefeller's advice within a year. He invited him to head a new federal Office of the Coordinator of Inter-American Affairs (CIAA), where he could carry out the initiatives described in his letter. Rockefeller accepted the position—after divesting his interests in Creole Petroleum. He also resigned from a position that constituted a different kind of conflict of interest, this one in the area of art and culture: He gave up his post as president of the board of directors of the New York Museum of Modern Art.

Rockefeller's position at MOMA was filled immediately by his close associate John Hay Whitney, whom Rockefeller would shortly hire to direct his new federal office's Motion Picture Section. Whitney facilitated a contract between the office of the CIAA and the MOMA Film Library through which the latter would act as institutional intermediary for film producers who contracted with the government, as well as processing, dubbing, and editing documentary and non-theatrical productions for Latin American audiences.[7] Though objections apparently were raised regarding the spending of museum funds on government projects and Whitney's and Rockefeller's continued financial interests in the museum, they were met with circular and contradictory (but apparently accepted) rationales.[8]

The intersection of corporate, government, and cultural interests in Rockefeller's office alone indicates the degree to which empire-building takes place through a dense network of overlapping and seemingly contradictory affiliations and agendas. The involvement of Disney in this matrix is similarly rife with contradiction and overdetermination. Through Rockefeller's office, entertainment, newsreel, industrial, and educational films were all part of a multivalent strategy in which communications and corporate interests figured centrally.

Communications Media in the CIAA Agenda

In the US project of establishing familiar, "neighborly" relations with Latin American countries, communications media played an absolutely critical role. This was most evident in the case of telephone and telegraph communications. By the early forties, Germany had ownership and/or control over telephone systems in northern Argentina, Ecuador, Uruguay, Paraguay, southern Chile, and Mexico. The US government saw Nazi ownership of Latin American communications systems as a direct threat to defense efforts. In 1941, the office of the CIAA conducted an extensive study of inter-American communications facilities, producing a proposal that sheds light on the Good Neighbor policy.

In the words of FDR, the US was interested in not only "divesting enemy nationals of their present financial control of communications systems," but also "improving such facilities for the use of the governments of all the American republics."[9] Initiating US-based inter-American communications systems was not a new idea: to monitor its far-ranging locations, United Fruit set up a US-Central American radio communications system that, in 1913, became its subsidiary, the Tropical Radio and Telegraph Company. The CIAA had in mind a similarly US-centered model. Its "Recommendations of Policy and Program of Action" suggests not only the transfer of Latin American telephone and telegraph network ownerships from Axis to "hemispheric" corporate interests, but US administration and censorship of the region's Transradio Consortium.[10] FDR explicitly outlined a plan for the US Board of Economic Warfare's administration of a "corporation or corporations" to administer communications in conjunction with State, War, and Navy Departments communications programs. In short, an "inter-American" system would be US-centered; "hemispheric" control was a euphemism for US control.

The cinema was another component of the CIAA's communications-based strategies. In a report of the office, Whitney argues that "moving pictures constitute one of the best mediums to foster understanding and more friendly relations between peoples."[11] In keeping with this view, the CIAA facilitated—and, in some cases, literally subsidized—the export of US industry films (both entertainment and educational); film personalities (like Disney, Orson Welles, and Claudette Colbert);[12] and film equipment (the office provided the Mexican national film industry with needed production equipment, gratis).[13] Evidence of the desire to establish "more friendly relations" (and a more secure export market) extended to the CIAA's allotment of forty thousand dollars to Darryl F. Zanuck for the reshooting of portions of his *Down Argentine Way* that were offensive to Argentinian viewers.[14] In taking up Disney as a chief cultural emissary, not only did the CIAA want to help secure Latin American markets for US exports (including films) in place of the closed European markets (although they certainly did foster this goal);[15] they wanted primarily to cultivate a "safe" and welcoming environment for US corporate and governmental presence. This agenda entailed the cultivation of the US as cultural authority in Latin America—a project that the CIAA believed to be particularly well suited to both animation and the pedagogical address of educational media.

The CIAA saw in Disney the perfect foil in this project of engendering US authority. For Whitney, Disney's role as producer of benign children's entertainment placed him outside the range of suspicion of involvement in governmental matters. Rockefeller's office sent Disney and his entourage to Brazil, Argentina, and other countries with the idea that his presence would win over everyone from the general public to the highest public officials. A CIAA staff member affirms the choice: "The cultural and scientific big names alike have accepted [Disney] and we had the right thought that he was the one representative we might send who above all others was outside the range of criticism." As evidence, he notes the enthusiastic response of the Rio public to Disney and to *Fantasia*—a screening of which, he explains, was the first occasion on which the "president of Brazil" (probably meaning the premier, dictator Getulio Vargas) made an appearance in a public movie theater.[16] The significance of this staff member's perceptions cannot be underestimated in light of Brazil's previous rejection of US alliance, and Vargas's previous enthusiasm for Nazi powers.[17]

Implicit in the CIAA's marketing of Disney was the idea that Latin Americans generally were particularly susceptible to animation's mode of address—an address that, during this period in the US, increasingly was directed at audiences of children. As Eric Smoodin has shown, Disney's US-government-funded shorts promoting new income tax laws directed at working-class citizens during this period were regarded by some audiences as patronizing and paternalistic.[18] This same paternalistic agenda marked the CIAA's interest in Disney films. It is no coincidence that, in Rockefeller's Museum of Primitive Art, contemporary Latin American art was presented with art of early Europe and Asia—as if Latin American art reflected a "less evolved" stage of cultural development. Imperialism's scientific scales of human development and human evolution conveniently collapse into one convenient term, primitivism. Thus the CIAA selected what increasingly was being regarded as a children's medium, animation, for its paternalistic endeavor. Articulating this belief in Latin American audiences' naïve regard for US authority, a CIAA staff member insisted that, in addition to Disney animation, footage of US overseas defense efforts also should be shown to the Brazilian public, for "no exaggeration [of US military power] would surpass the hopes and *expectations* of these people and no exaggeration will be banned or even cut" by Brazilian theaters. Perhaps more than Uncle Sam, Disney personified the benevolent and protective paternal figure that the US wanted Latin America to embrace in a familial display of "hemispheric unity." While the entertainment film was regarded as an important part of winning the attention of popular audiences, newsreels and educationals were a more overt means of controlling and conforming political views, as well as individual and community cultural practices, across Latin American cultures.

Disney and the Corporate Agenda

The participation of Disney in the CIAA project does not necessarily imply that he actively supported its agendas. Disney, and the film industry in general, also stood to benefit directly from a presence in Latin America at exactly this point in time. As Smoodin has shown, with the start of the war and resultant shifts in the global market, Europe and Mexico effectively closed their doors to Hollywood film distribution and exhibition.[19] To the studios, Latin America held potential new markets, as well as potential new studio sites—locations that would, it was presumed, bring more lax regulations and cheaper labor. At the time that Disney toured Latin America, his own studio was in the midst of a labor dispute.[20] The chance to tour Latin America provided Disney with an opportunity not only to escape the heat of this conflict, but to contemplate escape from US labor laws.

While Disney himself did not set up a corporate outpost in South America in the forties, he did gain a new audience for future marketing ventures that would include film exhibition, comic book distribution, and television broadcasting. However, in a trend that has escalated throughout the century, many other corporations had already established themselves in South America by the early decades of the century. United Fruit was incorporated in 1899 in Central America, earning the nickname "the Octopus" through its rapid takeover of sites in South America and the Caribbean. Disney's public health films provided for multinationals a source of cultural indoctrination and regulation of the workers they hired. As companies like United Fruit set up plants, they also instituted communications, sanitation, and other public services for the entire communities of residents they imported. Disney's public health and education films were, in part, attempts to provide models for domestic life for the local workers these companies hired, to be administered as "teaching aids" by managers, many of whom could not speak Spanish or Portuguese well enough to communicate with their employees.[21]

In order to understand this pedagogical agenda, it is necessary to consider to which audiences specific Disney films addressed themselves. While *The Three Caballeros* and its companion films were shown in Latin America as well as in the US, *South of the Border* especially directs a pedagogical address to US viewers. The film relays data on aspects of culture that would be well known to local cultures (about local flora, for example). The narrator's stated desire to accumulate "color" to take home to Hollywood suggests that, whether Disney and the CIAA intended it or not, this film, at least, is addressed primarily to US viewers as potential "students" (or tourists) of Latin American countries.[22] Rockefeller stated repeatedly that Disney's three-reel record of his popular tour should "have a special appeal in the other American Republics."[23] Carl Mora holds that this goal was achieved in *The Three Caballeros,* in which "in the persons of "Donald, José, and Panchito, the United States, Brazil, and Mexico were pals, none more equal than the others." He attributes the film's success in part to Disney's attention to cultural specificity ("no *chinas poblanas* dancing flamenco or gauchos doing rhumbas").[24]

While the entertainment films may have successfully addressed Latin American audiences with respect, they simultaneously addressed a different audience with different interests. Rockefeller's agenda of fostering respect for, and knowledge about, Latin American cultures among the US public was a critical part of his agenda of acquiring resources in Latin America for US consumption.[25] "Training" in the cultures of Latin America was requisite to the work of "exported" corporate supervisors and their families.

While the Disney travelogue/entertainment films for Latin America may have had multiple uses, there is no ambiguity about the didactic address of the Disney health films. These fifteen shorts were aimed directly at Latin American workers and peasants. In the Disney Studio survey for the CIAA on the subject of literacy in Latin America (cited in note 3), film is recommended as a pedagogical tool, specifically for the teaching of "social science." The document proposes the production of twenty key films on the astonishingly general theme of "Man." In *Lectura para las Americas,* a series whose intended audience and mode of address is made evident in its very title, it is clear that "social science" is a euphemism for personal hygiene, and "man" a euphemism for the individual physical body. The series uses drill phrases on health, diet, and hygiene to replace the typical Dick-and-Jane rhetoric of the US reader. *La historia de José* (1944) phonetically breaks down the phrase *José es un joven sano* (José is a healthy boy); this is followed by *José come bien* (*José Eats Well*). *La storia de Ramon* (1944), in which Ramon drinks contaminated water, is followed by *Ramon esta enferma* (*Ramon is Sick*), in which Ramon purifies his drinking water by boiling it. In these films, minimal animation and repetitive, didactic voice-overs function to drill viewers not only in reading, but in the "proper" measures of bodily care.

In *Cleanliness Brings Health* (1944), a somewhat more complex animation whose explicit agenda is health education, a male voice-over introduces viewers to two households, designated "the careless family and the clean family." Johnny, the child of the careless family, writhes in pain inside his family's broken-down house. The narrator takes the viewer through a sequence of events through which dysentery passes throughout Johnny's household. Sick to his stomach, Johnny goes to the cornfield to defecate. "The cornfield was where everybody went," explains the narrator. "It was the custom. But it was a very bad custom." We then follow Johnny's father as he works with his hands in the contaminated soil, eats a meal without washing the soil from his hands, and subsequently suffers from dysentery. The "clean" family, we are told, uses an outhouse, covers its food with mosquito netting, and cooks on a fire that is raised above the ground to keep it away from contamination.

Cleanliness Brings Health promotes the idea that health is a matter of "custom," and is readily available to anyone who is not lazy. Health is presented as the reward of sheer labor and proper use of the environment. Illness is represented as the product of a bad life-style choice.

While films like *Cleanliness Brings Health* suggest that the US was eager to share knowledge about sanitation and hygiene, they avoid the main issue surrounding dysentery and other intestinal diseases: that is, the fact that the very methods of industrial and community development practiced by corporations since the turn of the century have instituted major crises in public health that previously had not existed—crises such as the displacement of communities, the creation of highly concentrated living situations without the establishment of adequate infrastructure, and the resultant taxing and polluting of water supplies. As in nineteenth-century England and the US, the creation of the company town in many cases fostered close living conditions without the institution of proper water supplies, sewage, and ventilation, causing contamination of local water supplies and the spread of disease.

By following intestinal dysentery as it works its way through a single family unit, *Cleanliness Brings Health* elides the most critical environmental condition through which dysentery has continued to be endemic in rural areas of Latin America: lack of management of water resources and sewage. Even in the past twenty-five years, one in fourteen deaths in Latin America can be attributed to waterborne intestinal infections such as dysentery. Disney promotes health as a merit system (health rewards labor, illness is punishment for laziness) in regions where, in fact, US development was primarily responsible for placing the health of communities in crisis.[26]

Water contamination is the subject of *Water: Friend or Enemy* (1943). But here water itself is anthropomorphized as the public enemy responsible for disease transmission. Serving as narrator, a drop of water declares ambiguously that "Man has forced me to these murders." As in *Cleanliness Brings Health,* responsibility for clean water is placed with the individual. Starting with an image of well water imprinted with a skull and crossbones, the film instructs in methods of sealing a well and housing a spring for home use.

Saneamiento del ambiente (1945) (*Environmental Health*) shifts the locus of health concern from the single family unit to the larger community. Opening with a pan of a clean and prosperous urban area, the film's narrative takes us back through its history to show how prosperity is linked to the institution of sanitary measures like sewage and water systems. Here, as in *Cleanliness Brings Health,* disease transmission is associated with individual negligence. The intestinal infection of one resident who lives by a stream at the edge of town is passed to the entire community through the water supply, a stream which the resident uses for sewage. Here community labor, rather than public facilities, combats disease: neighbors help the resident to build a proper outhouse.

While *Saneamiento del ambiente* does invoke civic responsibility for health concerns, it fails to address corporate culpability for urban sewage and sanitation needs, not to mention the political and governmental mechanisms through which these systems are constructed. Through animation, centralized refuse disposal, fresh water systems, and sewage lines virtually construct themselves. Animation stands in as the image of industry, which is itself strikingly absent from the urban center portrayed in the film. As in *Cleanliness Brings Health,* economic prosperity comes about in this town through "healthy living" itself. The factor of US corporate development, implied through the work of the animator, is at once present and absent, allowing for the ruse of an autonomous community unaffected by corporate growth.

Repeated throughout Disney's fifteen CIAA health films is the idea that contagion is caused by individual negligence. In *La enfermedad se propoga* (1944) (*How Disease is Transmitted*), Juan infects his entire community when he defecates in his fields; Tomas infects his whole family by coughing without covering his mouth; smallpox is transmitted by careless contact. Ultimately, the message of these films as a whole is that poverty and sickness are brought on by "custom" or life-style (a cultural choice), and not through corporate or governmental policies regarding environment, economy, and politics. This point is driven home most dramatically in *The Winged Scourge* (1943), the most lavish of Disney's CIAA health educationals.

Although grouped with the productions that were addressed unambiguously to Latin American audiences, it is likely that *The Winged Scourge* was produced for US audiences. Unlike the other rural-based films, in which ownership of property is never addressed, this film identifies a character as owner of the vast farm he surveys from the porch rocker of his large, Colonial-style farmhouse. Breaking with the conventions of the simply drawn and didactic health educationals, *The Winged Scourge* uses more detailed animation, stars popular Disney characters (the seven dwarves), and employs a sound track that is much more reminiscent of a newsreel. A dramatic musical score opens the film as an urgent male voice-over identifies as "Public Enemy Number 1" the anopheles mosquito ("alias malaria mosquito"), an insect that is described as a bloodthirsty female vampire, "thief and killer." A map of the world shows the hot spots of malaria, a set of areas that includes the southern border states of the US, as well as areas throughout Latin America. This map shot, though brief, is significant, because it suggests an important cultural subtext of the film: that transmission of disease occurs across national borders from south to north, from tropics to temperate zones, from "careless" and poor to clean and prosperous households. If Latin American audiences are not the primary target of this film, the Latin American is nonetheless the absent embodiment of disease in the film's general xenophobic discourse on protection from invasion by disease.

The film's contagion narrative begins with the image of a prosperous farm. Anopheles, having fed on a malaria-ridden victim, sinks her stinger into the farm's owner. This cuts to a dismal rendering of the whole estate in a shambles, ruined because its owner was unable to work and protect his land, all because he didn't protect himself against the vampire mosquito. "Multiply this man's tragedy by numbers of cases," the narrator warns, "and we have millions of dollars lost." The voice-over abruptly switches into the direct-address discourse of national defense. Over a shot of a movie theater, he calls out to the audience for volunteers to "help us combat this evil." The seven dwarves step forward from their seats to conduct an antimosquito campaign.

Once again, the thesis is that personal negligence leads to disease, and poverty is punishment for poor personal hygiene. But here, in this film made for US audiences, the fear of contagion that is a subtext in the Latin American films is made overt. *"Defense Against Invasion,"* to quote from the title of another Disney health film produced for US audiences during the same year, is the recommended mode of protection against the transnational "infection" incumbent on cultural and economic relations with Latin America. In the "mythic geography" constructed by the Disney Studio in its health care films, individual Latin American bodies, as well as Latin American geography, are viewed as vectors of contagion that threaten to invade US borders through a proximity that is geographical, cultural, and physical. But what is completely disavowed in this xenophobic narrative is the role of US empire-building in the development of the very conditions that foster disease transmission.

If the Disney entertainment/travelogue films supported by the CIAA are animated by a colonialist desire that fixes itself on potential objects of conquest (*Women and Flowers,* for example, to borrow from the title of a recent documentary on the Colombian flower industry), the Disney/ CIAA public health films for Latin American audiences are animated by an opposite desire to contain Latin American bodily processes within bodies and national borders. These educationals at once deny the responsibility of US corporations for the spread of disease within Latin American communities, while protecting against the perceived threat of flow of these same diseases (through rivers, insects, or travel) across the border. In the Disney/CIAA production *Defense Against Invasion,* four boys waiting for vaccinations at the doctor's office are told that the body is like a city. While the defenseless body is overwhelmed by germs, a vaccinated body provides munitions to counter invasion. The health films for Latin America were, in a sense, a cultural "vaccine" qualified with the stamp of social science, ostensibly protecting Latin Americans against contagion while effectively protecting the US public from knowledge of the role of US corporations in Latin American "development."

12

Images of Empire:
Tokyo Disneyland and Japanese
Cultural Imperialism

Mitsuhiro Yoshimoto

Global Culture: Image, Information, and Commodity

In the last ten years or so, postmodernism has become such a widely accepted notion that there are now literally hundreds of books and articles on this topic in the fields of literary studies, art, architecture, film studies, women's studies, history, geography, sociology, political science, and so on. And there are also a number of other works which deal with postmodern issues without explicitly using this catchword. As the field of postmodern studies expands by cutting across the disciplinary boundaries, we can observe a new development of interest in the discussion on postmodernism. Rather than examined exclusively from a purely philosophical perspective of the West, postmodernism has also become a subproblem of the larger question of how transnational capitalism is transforming the cultural interactions between nation-states and in the networks of economic blocks on the global scale. This shift of interest from postmodernism as a Western phenomenon to the worldwide interactions of various modes of cultural production reflects a radical transformation of world geopolitics brought about by the collapse of the Cold-War structure and the emergence of a still uncertain "New World Order."

This transformation of the world order has had an effect on the disciplines of humanities and social sciences in such a way that, firstly, the disciplinary boundaries have relatively speaking become less absolute, and secondly, the identities of some disciplines are now in the process of disappearing. In the humanities, for instance, we can see the effect of geopolitical change in the so-called Paul de Man affair. For a foreigner like myself working in American academia, what is so fascinating about this incident is the surprised reactions of both deconstructionists and antideconstructionists, as if they suddenly realized that what literature professors do at universities is connected to outside nonacademic affairs. For me, coming from a country where the issue of war responsibilities of intellectuals dominated the post-World War II discursive space, it is rather perplexing to see a belated fiasco over de Man's early writings. What is at stake in the de Man affair is not so much his alleged collaboration with Nazis but the fundamental structure of literary studies, which was taken by surprise by the sudden intrusion of the raw facts of politics. The reception of de Man's early writings simply shows that the New Critical paradigm, which, created at the height of the Cold War, brackets politics and other nontextual facts, continued to dominate literary studies until the end of the 1980s despite the onslaught of Continental critical theories on American academia. If there is anything like the "lesson of Paul de Man," it is to remind us that the participation in such a seemingly innocent activity as an academic study of literature is always inseparable from outside sociopolitical forces. And it is important to realize that the discovery of de Man's early writings and its aftermath in the late 1980s are more than coincidental with the crumbling of the Cold-War structure.[1]

In social sciences, the problem of new world geopolitics has been taken up by theorists of the world-system. Despite social sciences' traditional indifference to the issue of culture in the development of the capitalist world-system, the world-system theorists like Immanuel Wallerstein or the social theorist Anthony Giddens now try to incorporate a cultural dimension into their theories, thus challenging postmodern theorists with humanities backgrounds. For instance, in his essay "The National and the Universal: Can There Be Such a Thing as World Culture?" Wallerstein speculates on the possibility of creating a truly universal, world culture. Yet he deals with the issue of cultural globalization from the age-old perspective of the particularity/universality dichotomy, so that no insight on the specific nature of the current process of cultural globalization is presented. Wallerstein's inability to understand the problematic of cultural globalization can be observed in the following remark:

> We face the very bizarre situation today of a major debate within US universities between, on the one side, those who advocate a universe of cultures via the promotion of Black studies or women's studies or the extension (if not the elimination) of the so-called canons in literature and, on the other side, those who advocate a universal culture via the promotion of courses in Western civilization. Truly the world is upside down. One arrives, it seems to be argued by both sides, at the universal via the particular (although they differ as to which particular).[2]

I will not here go into his complete misrepresentation of the objectives of multiculturalism, but only point out that the relation between particularity and universality is far more complex than Wallerstein argues. As Slavoj Zizek forcefully states, particularity can never be completely subsumed under universality, and the "universal" becomes possible only when we stop reifying the universal law and start respecting the excess of the particular:

> What confers . . . the dignity of a "person" is not any universal-symbolic feature but precisely what is "absolutely particular" about him [*sic*], his fantasy, that part of him that we can be sure we can never share. To use Kant's terms: we do not respect the other on account of the universal moral law inhabiting every one of us, but on account of his utmost "pathological" kernel, on account of the absolutely particular way every one of us "dreams his world," organizes his enjoyment.[3]

Zizek continues:

> Fantasy as a "make-believe" masking a flaw, an inconsistency in the symbolic order, is always particular—its particularity is absolute, it resists "mediation," it cannot be made part of a larger, universal, symbolic medium. For this reason, we can acquire a sense of the dignity of another's fantasy only by assuming a kind of distance toward our own, by experiencing the ultimate contingency of fantasy as such, by apprehending it as the way everyone, in a manner proper to each, conceals the impasse of his desire. The dignity of a fantasy consists in its very "illusionary," fragile, helpless character.[4]

Thus, Wallerstein's misdirected obsession with world culture is precisely a product of illogic Wallerstein himself criticizes. Similarly, Julia Kristeva's recent embrace of universally common features of humanity, which she thinks were first upheld in the wake of the French Revolution, merely equates French nationalism (particularity) with the fundamental principles of humanity (universalism). Along with the Habermasian critique of postmodernism, Kristeva's celebration of the Enlightenment idea of universality can be understood as a last-ditch effort to preserve the hegemony of Western Europe in world geopolitics, or as an ideological support for unified Europe as a superstate.

What is lacking in the analysis of global culture from the perspective based on the universal/particular dichotomy is the discussion of concrete, distinctive features of contemporary global culture. For instance, what are the dominant vehicles of global culture? As Paul Virilio argues, one of them can be observed in the field of military technology, which is becoming evermore sophisticated as a result of high-tech development. The focal point of modern military technology has been the ability to see without being seen by the enemy. But because of the enormous destructive power of high-tech weapons, this technology of surveillance is no longer a sufficient condition for the success of a war. The instantaneous transformation of the landscape of the battleground makes any map of that area immediately obsolete. To assess a new situation and plan a next strategic move, military intelligence has to have a sophisticated apparatus of observation which makes it possible to remap as quickly as possible the constantly changing surface of strategic battlefields in multiple locations. To win a postmodern war, one has to be able to simulate images through which the invisible becomes visible. In postmodern warfare, we are not dealing with the image as the analog representation of reality but with the digitally processed image. Therefore, on the one hand, it is more appropriate to see the postmodern image not as sign but as part of information networks, and on the other, because of its uncanny ability to simulate reality, the postmodern image contributes to the creation of another or virtual reality.

If there is any meaning in such a notion as global culture, it can be understood only as a result of the tripartite expansion of image, information, and commodity networks on the global scale. But the key word here is the image.[5] For among the latter three, it is the image that plays the pivotal role of connecting them to each other. Yet in various examinations of global culture, this crucial role of the image is often neglected. As Benedict Anderson focuses on what he calls "print capitalism" to explore the origins of nationalism and nation-states, to comprehend the current globalization of culture we need to examine seriously what I would like to call "image capitalism."

In the development of global culture and image capitalism, the crucial questions are the following: who has a new technology of the image; for instance, the technology of high-definition television (HDTV) whose compositing power is completely transforming the relationship between the image and reality? And who owns the software or image archive which can be used as image capital? Both of these questions obviously have enormous implications for the formation of the post-Cold War system. The recent uproar in Washington over Shintaro Ishihara and Akio Morita's book *Japan That Can Say No* simply indicates the enormous stake in the development of high-tech industry with regard to military, and more importantly, economic national security.[6] We can understand in the same context the Americans' reaction against Sony's purchase of Columbia Pictures and Matsushita's takeover of MCA/Universal. We can add to this list the sensational reporting of the eighties of a Japanese paying millions of dollars to purchase van Gogh's paintings. Aside from its real impact on the art market and the world of the art museum, Japanese purchase of van Gogh's paintings had more of a symbolic impact on Western consciousness.

Globalization of culture is therefore inseparable from the expansion of Japanese capital into the global image market. But in spite of the phenomenal success of the Nintendo video games that have fundamentally changed the lives of American kids, it does not mean that the image now flows only from Japan to the US. In fact, the contrary is the case. The Japanese electronics giants took over Hollywood studios precisely because of a triumph of Hollywood images on the global market. At the same time, however, the relative decline of the US in the world economy is also hard to deny. How should we interpret, then, these seemingly contradictory phenomena, the triumph of American popular culture and the decline of American economic power on the global scale? How can we explain the fact that the more the Japanese acquire global economic power, the more they seem to be Americanizing, instead of Japanizing, themselves?

This contradiction between culture and economy is perhaps nowhere more accurately present than in the case of Tokyo Disneyland, arguably the most famous or infamous imitation of the product of American popular culture in Japan. Having already been appalled by Disneyland in California, many Japanese and Western intellectuals are stunned by the appearance of this modern utopia—or according to them, dystopia—in the vicinity of Tokyo. For instance, they ask: Why is there this Japanese fascination with things American? What has happened to Japanese tradition? Yet in the end, what is disturbing is not the construction of a Disneyland in Tokyo, and its enormous commercial success; instead, what is truly amazing is the existence of intellectuals who still do not realize that their clichéd response is as banal as the object of their criticism, Disneyland itself. In the rest of this essay, I would like to discuss Tokyo Disneyland, by rephrasing Zizek, as the "utmost pathological kernel of postmodern Japan," the "absolutely particular way the Japanese dream their world, organize their enjoyment." This pathological kernel has something to do with the way the Japanese situate themselves in the new global order emerging simultaneously with the erosion of the Cold-War system, and also the way the Japanese imagine themselves as members of a homogeneous nation.

The Economy of Tokyo Disneyland

The opening of Disneyland in Anaheim, California in 1955 was facilitated by two factors: the restructuring of the amusement park industry, and the restructuring or transformation of the film industry.[7] One of the major differences between a theme park like Disneyland and the mere amusement park lies in their relationships to the outside environment. Unlike the amusement park, the theme park tries to create an autonomous, utopian space cut off from the rest of society. To create a space of fantasy, any elements which remind visitors of their daily life and the outside world are carefully excluded. For instance, Disneyland has only one main entrance, and architectural structures and landscape are arranged in such a way that, once inside, the visitors cannot see anything beyond the boundary of the theme park. The paradox of this fantasy is that the more successful Disneyland is in its creation of a fantasy space, the less conscious visitors are of its fantastic nature. Fantasy succeeds only when it is not perceived as such. And the self-enclosure and the imposition of strict rules maintaining the coherence of theming guarantee that there is nothing overtly fantastic about Disneyland.

Besides physically blocking the visitors' view of what lies immediately outside the park, there is another powerful method of creating a self-enclosed totality. As David M. Johnson describes, most of the attractions in Disneyland are structured around particular themes, whose coherence is guaranteed by the linear narrative of an opening, a development, and a resolution.

> As an extension of the packaged tour idea, the Disney people have created what can be called "packaged history," and their treatment of history, fantasy and the future leads to the blending together of these themes and treatments until they are all in effect the same thing. For their films, and so for most of their amusements, the Disney creators have taken the raw material from history, fantasy and other sources and packaged it into units, each with a discrete beginning, middle and end. They have in effect added conventional *plots* to inherently plotless materials.[8]

To make sure that the visitors do not construct their own versions of a narrative, in each attraction they are not allowed to walk freely from one point to another; instead, the flow and pace of their movements are carefully controlled by a ride which, by following a prescribed route at a steady pace, automatically carries them from the entrance to the exit. According to Susan Willis, the thematic coherence of Disneyland as an aggregate of these micronarratives is maintained by its overall structure regulating the visitors' movement:

> Commentators have remarked on the importance of movement in Disneyland both as a consequence of having to get forty thousand people a day through the park and as a symptom of Los Angeles itself, where daily life is conducted behind the wheel of a car. . . .

But I would argue that the significance of movement goes beyond the necessary and symptomatic and resides finally in the way theming is constituted through movement, as a narrative.[9]

Thus, by providing the visitors with a single interpretive context in which they make sense out of their narrative experience, Disneyland creates the illusion of being a self-sufficient, autonomous space in which the reality of fantasy is ingeniously concealed.

Disneyland constructs an autonomous, self-enclosed space, and moreover, carefully controls and manipulates visitors' experience by narrativizing that space. In other words, rather than as a mere upscale version of the amusement park, Disneyland should be understood as an extension of the cinema. In this gigantic movie theater, the spectator sees not the two-dimensional image reflected on the distant screen but a three-dimensional image that actively interacts with the spectator. Three-dimensional images are produced not only by various mechanical attractions and "Audio-Animatronics," but also by all the employees—in Disney's euphemism, cast members—who work in the visible surface of the park. And even the ordinarily boring experience of waiting in line for a ride or an attraction becomes part of the interactive entertainment performed by Mickey Mouse and the stable of other Disney characters.

But let us not lose our perspective. Visitors do not interactively participate in the construction of narrative for its own sake. The ultimate purpose of narrativizing experience is to naturalize consumption activities, so that visitors consume without being aware of it. In a successful theme park like Disneyland, spending money which is successfully incorporated into the narrative flow, becomes part of the attraction itself. The physical layout of Disneyland carefully disperses shopping areas as if they are attention-drawing scenes appearing every ten minutes in a popular Hollywood movie. Besides food and soft drinks, the majority of goods sold at shops are Disney's character merchandise. Spending money, however, may not necessarily be seen by the visitors as the acquisition of those goods but as becoming part of Disney narratives in which those characters are imbedded. The narrativized space of Disneyland feeds the visitors with those preexisting narratives, in which Disney characters are naturally integrated as characters, not as commodities. The ingenuity of Disney magic lies in its attempt to integrate shopping as part of attractions without destroying the autonomy of the latter; that is, shopping areas are located at strategic points in Disneyland without interrupting the narrative flow created by the park's spatial organization. The sense of imposition or manipulation is carefully eliminated, so that the visitors do not feel any pressure to spend money at the shopping areas. Instead, the visitors "voluntarily" transform themselves into avid consumers who try to reexperience or reinforce the pleasure given to them by various attractions. Shopping becomes a way to reenact repeatedly the active participation in the construction of narratives, which in turn diverts the consumers' attention away from the act of spending money and the commodityness of character merchandise. And as the technique of narrativizing shopping experience perfected by Disney has become a model for the retail industry, it is increasingly becoming difficult to distinguish shopping malls from theme parks (compare the West Edmonton Mall in Canada).

Thus, the basic characteristics of Disneyland can be summarized as follows:

> (1) it is an exclusionary space;
> (2) visitors—or in Disney vocabulary, "guests"—participate in the interactive game of narrativization;
> (3) that process of narrativization is subsumed under the comprehensive commodification of visitors' experiences.

In other words, Disneyland is a total entertainment/consumption system utilizing not only perception but also tactile senses. Because of these characteristics, it can be argued that Disneyland is a realization of *Gesamtkunstwerk* dreamed by Adorno's Wagner and various other artists.[10] For instance, Eisenstein developed his theory of montage from his experience in theater, circus, and amusement parks. For Eisenstein, film as an exponentially radicalized combination of these precinematic institutions was the most effective means to agitate and mobilize the masses for the revolutionary cause. And Eisenstein's theory seemed to be substantiated when the cinema became the most dominant form of mass entertainment, and its genealogical predecessors, the circus and amusement park, gradually lost their mass appeal. But in 1950s America, even the cinema began to be eclipsed by new commodity culture and leisure activities exemplified by television and automobiles. And it was Walt Disney who, like Eisenstein, noticed the fundamental connection between the amusement park and the cinema, and, contrary to Eisenstein, revitalized the former by feeding back to it the structural principles of the latter.

The rise of Disneyland and other theme parks is inseparable from the inadequacy of the cinema as the image apparatus fulfilling the demand of newly emerging consumer audiences. In the age of high consumerism, the image is transformed into the commodity-image, which is not merely the object of perception but that of tactile experiences. The consumption of the commodity-image is realized not just by passively seeing it but by actively participating in the interactive play of perception and consumption. And in the age of transnational capitalism and economic blocks in which we now live, this desire to simulate the fantasy as the object of comprehensive experience is culminating in the construction of theme parks based on the technology of virtual reality.

The connections between high consumerism and theme parks are also present in the case of Tokyo Disneyland. To understand these connections, we need to examine first what it means for the Japanese to go to Tokyo Disneyland. In 1958, the "Disneyland" show, which had originally been broadcast on ABC in the US, began to air on Japanese television. The glitter of commodity-image and Disney's sanitized world of fantasy made the show enormously popular among both children and their parents. The broadcasting of the "Disneyland" show lasted until 1967, and this period between 1958 and 1967 more or less coincided with the age of the so-called high economic growth characterized by the annual average of more than eleven percent increase in GNP. In the 1960s, this television show made Disneyland one of the most powerful symbols of the affluent society for which the Japanese were earnestly striving. Thus, the opening of Tokyo Disneyland in 1983 gave a generation of Japanese a sense of completion or achievement, which is concomitant with the ideological construction of 1945 as the absolute breaking point in modern Japanese history and the reification of the notion of *sengo,* that is, the "postwar."

In Disneyland, every mundane experience is transformed into entertainment enticing the visitors into shopping. Another related aspect of the Magic Kingdom is the absolute separation of leisure from work.[11] Any menial work, which is necessary for maintaining the proper functioning of Disneyland, is carefully hidden from the visible surface of the park. Disneyland is constructed in such a way that the "backstage" would never be exposed to the visitors' eyes. As a consequence, Disneyland succeeds in creating the impression of a utopian space of leisure, from which any trace of work is diligently erased. And perhaps this partly explains why Tokyo Disneyland has been so popular among the Japanese: the work-weary Japanese, who, even in their "leisure" activities—playing golf, going on a group tour, and so on—cannot get away from the world of work, have finally found a space in which they can momentarily forget about their everyday work.

Another important aspect of Tokyo Disneyland is its location, Tokyo, the expansion and transformation of which into a global financial capital symbolize the 1980s "bubble economy," a kind of "Casino Capitalism" (Keynes) based on speculative investment.[12] Nonfinancial institutions—trading companies, the manufacturing industry—and private citizens with little knowledge of stocks and money markets eagerly took part in the dangerous game of *zaiteku* or financial wizardry based on new information technology. Surplus capital generated by speculation has overflowed into the rest of Japan and abroad. And wherever Tokyo capital is exported, we witness the soaring of land prices. In the metropolitan area of Tokyo, even a small house barely big enough for a family of four has become simply out of reach for an average white-collar worker. Although the Japanese middle class in Tokyo do not have enough money to buy their own houses, thanks to the steady growth of the high-tech economy they do have more than sufficient savings to buy durable goods and luxuries, or to indulge themselves in conspicuous consumption. Rather than expending the income for their own houses, which is impossible to do anyway because of the skyrocketing real estate prices, the middle class in Tokyo have begun to spend money outside their homes. A myriad of trendy shops and expensive restaurants have mushroomed, and both banal and fascinating postmodern buildings are constantly constructed, destroyed, and deconstructed. For many Japanese, Tokyo is no longer a place to move to in order to find jobs and get ahead in the world;[13] instead, Tokyo has become the largest theme park, visited by people from all over Japan for enjoyment, to have fun. Thus, the phrase "Tokyo Disneyland" needs to be understood in its double sense: a Disneyland in Tokyo and Tokyo as a Disneyland.[14]

Tokyo Disneyland and Japanese Nationalism

Even though Tokyo itself has become a gigantic theme park, the eeriness of Tokyo Disneyland still stands out. Nearly a carbon copy of the "original" Disneyland in Anaheim, Tokyo Disneyland gives the visitors the "authentic" American flavor.[15] Then, along with MacDonalds and Kentucky Fried Chicken, is Tokyo Disneyland a sign of American cultural imperialism? Although it is tempting to answer "yes" outright, before jumping to this conclusion let us try to clarify first what cultural imperialism is.

The most prevalent image of cultural imperialism is that of a hegemonic power, such as the United States, trying to indoctrinate and brainwash the population of periphery regions. The onslaught of American popular culture on Latin America was seen, for instance, as a means to naturalize the overwhelming presence of the US as a hegemonic power and the subordinate positions occupied by Latin American nations in that hegemonic system. The question is what kind of relationship exists between culture and imperialism? Is it possible to discuss cultural imperialism separate from economic imperialism? What are the differences among the imposition, influence, and exchange of foreign cultures? What are the necessary conditions which make cultural imperialism a workable critical notion?

Culture by definition cannot be confined within a national boundary, and it can exist only in the network of constant exchange and traffic, so that the mere infusion of a foreign culture does not constitute cultural imperialism destroying a native culture. On the contrary, the idea of "native" itself would not occur unless there is that infusion in the first place. For the discourse of cultural imperialism to become meaningful, first the world needs to be reconfigured, so that a specifically modern type of imagined community, that is, the nation-state, emerges, along with the newly invented images of native culture and unbroken national history.

If culture can thrive only when there is constant traffic and exchange, mere cultural domination is an impossible idea to accept. Any culture exists only in constant flux and transformation, so that culture by itself cannot be dominating or dominated. The traffic of culture becomes cultural imperialism only when that traffic is accompanied by imperialism in a conventional sense, the relationship of economic domination between imperial powers and their colonies. Moreover, as the example of American cultural imperialism in Latin America shows, the popular culture of a hegemonic power is imbued with the latter's national imaginary. On the people in Latin America, this discourse of American nationalism has an effect of naturalizing the hegemony of the US as the most advanced state in the world. Domestically, Americans see the popularity of their culture abroad as a sign of their popularity and superiority; moreover, that popularity makes Americans believe that every foreigner potentially wants to become an American. Here, we can see a perverse inversion of logic reinforcing the imaginary identity of nationhood: the desire to dominate others is pathologically transformed into the openness of Americans welcoming others as potential new Americans. Thus, the idea of cultural imperialism becomes meaningful when the following two conditions are satisfied: (1) the basic unit of world politics is a nation-state constantly trying to reinforce its imaginary identity; and (2) imperialism or the economic domination of the periphery by the metropolitan states precedes or simultaneously occurs with the unidirectional overflow of foreign culture from the latter to the former.

These two basic conditions of cultural imperialism make the case of postmodern Japan particularly interesting and complicated, especially when we find an emblematic image of American cultural imperialism, a Disneyland, in the land of a non-Western global economic superpower. To say that Japan as an economic superpower belongs to the First World, but culturally is still part of the Third World because of a Japanese obsession with Western culture, is a very unsatisfactory explanation. This kind of statement is ultimately unacceptable because it too easily accepts the putative identity of Japan as a nation-state, and also creates a false impression that once it happens, the domination of the world by the Western powers would never change. Does the case of Japan fundamentally discredit the discourse of cultural imperialism? Or is Japan only an exceptional case? I think the further examination of Tokyo Disneyland would help us to break this impasse created by the paradox of postmodern Japan.

Although it is almost an exact copy of Disneyland in Anaheim, Tokyo Disneyland is also adjusted to suit the specific needs of its predominantly Japanese visitors.[16] Among various adjustments, the most important ones are definitely modifications of Main Street USA, which constitutes the ideological backbone of the original Disneyland in California. As Stephen F. Mills claims:

> Main Street USA is a monument to an "era of good feeling", a born-again belief in the squeaky clean virtues of front-porch USA, and nostalgia for a supposedly uncomplicated, decent, hard-working, crime-free, rise up and salute the flag way of life that is the stuff of middle America's dreams, an ersatz image of the past imposed within the here and now. The image is composite, deriving as much from 1850s Missouri as from the suburban-small town of the 1950s (glimpsed in the movie *Back to the Future*).[17]

To simulate the center of a small middle-American town and to call it "Main Street USA" has little to do with caprice or with Walt Disney's biographical background. Instead, as Mills's description suggests, Main Street USA is the essential part of Disneyland as an apparatus of nationalism reproducing America as an imagined community of the nation-state. However, the significance of Main Street USA can be understood only when it is put in the simultaneous process of narrativization and commodification which goes beyond the physical boundary of Disneyland and extends into the discursive space of the United States as a whole. When Disneyland opened in 1955, America was in the golden age of consumer capitalism. High consumerism, characterized by new kinds of daily experiences and patterns of behavior, was made possible by the victory in World War II and by the pursuit of the Cold-War policy. The ideological objective of Disneyland is to equate the commodification of daily life with the narrativization of American nationalism as a world hegemonic power. The kernel of this articulation is Main Street USA, which is simultaneously a recreation of a mythic small-town America, and a collection of various gift shops and restaurants; the imaginary sense of nationhood is reinforced (narrativization) whenever visitors buy Disney goods and souvenirs (commodification).

In Tokyo Disneyland, two important changes are made with regard to Main Street USA. First, to protect the visitors from bad weather—compared to California or Florida, there is a lot more rain and occasional snow in Tokyo—the arcade covers the entire area of Main Street USA.

This addition of the arcade transforms this space into a semi-indoor amusement facility, which gives the visitors the feeling of being inside a gigantic shopping mall. Second, the name itself is fittingly changed from "Main Street USA" to "World Bazaar." This change of name not only makes the objective of Tokyo Disneyland much more explicit, but also erases any trace of American nationalism which might not be palatable to the Japanese masses. (It is interesting to note that there is a Main Street USA in Euro Disney.)

This careful elimination of any images which could remind the Japanese of American nationalism is a key to understanding what in the end Tokyo Disneyland is. The success of Tokyo Disneyland is dependent on the precarious balance between the accommodation of the behavioral patterns and needs of Japanese consumers and the preservation of "Americanness." If it were an exact carbon copy of Disneyland in the US, it would be possible to say that Tokyo Disneyland is a symbol of American cultural imperialism. Even if somebody objects and points out that unlike Euro Disney, Tokyo Disneyland is locally owned by Japanese, we could still say that those Japanese owners merely play a role of intermediary, with a mentality of colonized natives. Yet, the slight differences between the "original" Disneyland and Tokyo Disneyland, no matter how minor they might be, make the traditional discourse of cultural imperialism inadequate for explaining the specificity of Tokyo Disneyland.

In the wake of Tokyo Disneyland's success, many other theme parks have been built since the mid-1980s. What is unique about these recently built Japanese theme parks is that many of them are recreations of foreign monuments, villages, cities, or simply landscapes. They are called *ikoku-mura* or *gaikoku-mura* ("foreign villages"), in which life-sized images of Europe and the US are carefully simulated. Does this proliferation of Euro-American "extraterritorial areas" mean that Japan is increasingly Westernized? Why are so many theme parks simulating Euro-American architecture and landscapes? Before hastily concluding that "foreign villages" are another sign of Japan's Westernization, we need to remind ourselves that the products of American mass culture or any other foreign culture are by themselves nothing more than material objects. And nothing can be understood just by pointing out the conspicuous presence of Western landscapes and commodity goods in Japan. The analysis must go beyond the surface observation and examine the way in which those objects are consumed by the Japanese.

The majority of these "foreign villages" are located in places away from Tokyo, such as the northern island of Hokkaido and the southern island of Kyushu. Conceived as showcases for advanced technology and newly acquired wealth in the age of the "bubble economy," the "foreign villages" are constructed to attract the tourists from neighboring prefectures and sometimes from all over Japan to boost the local economy and, no matter how strange it might sound, to reestablish the specificity of regional culture. As Tokyo has become the information city in which Japanese politics, business, and culture are all concentrated, economically, politically, and culturally speaking, the relative autonomy of the rest of Japan is increasingly eroding. The degree of erosion and the dominance of Tokyo are so extensive that, for instance, any attempt to revitalize the local economy cannot but be dependent on Tokyo capital and corporate culture, which are responsible for the demise of regional autonomy in the first place. To the extent that the overflowing of capital from Tokyo to other parts of Japan is mainly responsible for a theme park construction boom, the "foreign villages" and the transformation of imaginary geography need to be understood not as a sign of mere Westernization of Japan, but of an imperial expansion of Tokyo's hegemonic culture.

In postmodern Japan, commodification has exponentially accelerated and extended into daily life, so that it is no longer the question of commodities in the world but that of the world as a commodity. The following description of the West Edmonton Mall in Canada can easily be read as that of the imaginary landscape of postmodern Japan:

> Inside, the mall presents a dizzying spectacle of attractions and diversions: a replica of Columbus's *Santa Maria* floats in an artificial lagoon, where real submarines move through an impossible seascape of imported coral and plastic seaweed inhabited by live penguins and electronically controlled rubber sharks; fiberglass columns crumble in simulated decay beneath a spanking new Victorian iron bridge; performing dolphins leap in front of Leather World and Kinney's Shoes; fake waves, real Siberian tigers, Ching-dynasty vases, and mechanical jazz bands are juxtaposed in an endless sequence of skylit courts. Mirrored columns and walls further fragment the scene, shattering the mall into a kaleidoscope of ultimately unreadable images. Confusion proliferates at every level; past and future collapse meaninglessly into the present; barriers between real and fake, near and far, dissolve as history, nature, technology, are indifferently processed by the mall's fantasy machine.
>
> *Yet this implausible, seemingly random, collection of images has been assembled with an explicit purpose: to support the mall's claim to contain the entire world within its walls* [emphasis mine].[18]

What is common to this largest shopping mall in the world and postmodern Japan is a desire for totality, a will to contain the world within itself as a postmodern monad.

In postmodern Japan, everything is commodified, including the sense of nationhood. America is, therefore, just another brand name, like Chanel, Armani, and so on. We can, of course, read a sign of colonial mentality in the Japanese craving for "America" as a brand name; however, we can also cynically say that it is only part of the system of differences which needs to be reproduced perpetually for the survival of the Japanese capitalist economy. And what the selective appropriation of Western cultures ultimately indicates is not colonial mentality, but the postmodern cynicism of contemporary Japan. For instance, the constellations of commodity goods are skillfully marketed and consumed as marks of various types of American life-styles: the life-styles of New York yuppies, California surfers, Oregon naturalists, and so on. Yet American automobiles, which once epitomized the American way of life, are unpopular among the Japanese because, compared to certain Japanese cars, they are not American enough. Or we can also think of many Japanese tourists travelling in Europe, who discover that the real Europe is not as real as they thought. As the proliferation of foreign villages suggests, some of these tourists apparently must have come to a conclusion: why not create a cleaner, safer, and more comfortable Europe inside Japan? If "[f]or millions of visitors, Disneyland is just like the world, only better,"[19] postmodern Japan is also just like the world, only better.

Donna Haraway, after studying Japanese primatology, makes an interesting observation on the complex interplay among the notions of "nature," "native," and "origin:"

> Nature as "wild" does not concern the Japanese in the way it does Euro-Americans, but nature as "native" is a matter of great concern. Focus on *specificity* in all its layers of meaning—individual personality, collective culture, habitat, troop identity, kin lineage—is an operation for building primate mirrors for a people preoccupied not with the colonial "other," but with the problem of establishing its uniqueness in the context of a history of extraordinary cultural importations and reinventions, from Buddhism to Darwinism.[20]

> For the Japanese, the issue, echoing in primate studies as in other cultural practices, seems to be less the *origin* of language, the boundary between animal and human, than the *uniqueness* of one's own language, the boundary between native and stranger, the subtle play between conservation and change.[21]

Haraway's observation has two important implications for our study. First, the concept of "nature" in Japan does not so much establish the opposition between nature and culture (that is, the colonial "Other" as "subhuman primitive"). Rather, it has more to do with the construction of native Japanese uniqueness in relation to the foreign "Other." Second, in the discursive space of modern Japan, "nature" is always already contaminated by culture, so that the interest in "nature" has little to do with the search for origins. By themselves, there is nothing extraordinary about these two implications; however, when they are taken together, it becomes clearer how complex, for instance, the relationship between native and foreign is. As Haraway argues, the Japanese are obsessed with the idea of Japanese uniqueness, which, many of them believe, cannot be comprehended by non-Japanese. Yet at the same time, there is no interest in the origin either; that is, for the Japanese, it is not particularly important whether a certain cultural artifact or practice is originally from a small Japanese village, a Chinese capital, or European countryside. Then how are these seemingly contradictory principles of cultural production—the obsession with native uniqueness and the indifference to origins—reconciled with each other?

Many Japanese theorists argue that Japanese culture has always been a hybrid of various foreign cultures. One of the most well-known proponents of this view is the literary critic Kato Shuichi, who, in *Hybrid Culture: Japan's Small Hope,* argues that any attempt to isolate pure, native elements in Japanese culture is bound to fail.[22] According to Kato, the Japanese desire for purification can be manifested in two diametrically opposite forms: modernism and nationalism. Modernists think that there is a single evolutionary path of human history, and that the West is far more advanced according to this universal scale of human development. For modernists, then, modernization necessarily means Westernization, and modernization of Japan is identical to Westernization of Japan. According to the modernists' way of thinking, feudal Japanese traditions must be eliminated as quickly and completely as possible, and how successfully they are eliminated becomes a means of measuring how modern Japan is. And it is obviously as a reaction against this compulsive desire for Westernization that nationalist sentiment emerges. However, this opposition between modernists and nationalists is not really an opposition, since what motivates modernists in the first place is their desire to catch up with the West in order to avoid Western colonization, and later on, to transform Japan into an imperial power in its own way. In other words, to the extent that the impulse to modernize and Westernize Japan is inseparable from a strong nationalistic sentiment, what first appear to be two opposite manifestations of Japanese obsession with purity are only two different modes of Japanese nationalism. Moreover, the alternative advocated by Kato, that is, the positive affirmation of the hybridity of Japanese culture, can also easily degenerate into a form of both sophisticated and vulgar nationalism: the Kyoto ideologues celebrating the world-historical mission of Japan overcoming the modern in the early 1940s, the notion of the Great East Asian Co-Prosperity Sphere as an ideological justification of Japanese imperialism, Japan as the dialectical unification of the East and the West, and so on.

The hybridity of Japanese culture, which Kato positively affirms, is in the end quite different from the genuine hybridity of, for instance, Donna Haraway's notion of the cyborg.[23] For as Maruyama Masao points out, in Japan, we do not necessarily observe the hybridization but rather the coexistence of different cultures, which are not mixed and transformed into a new culture, but exist side by side without interfering in each other's business. Instead of hybridity, it is dehistoricization or decontextualization that is at work in the Japanese discursive space.[24] If the genuine hybridity invokes the image of the cyborg, it is because true hybridization would be impossible without simultaneously transforming the subject of hybridization. In contrast, the selective hybridity of the Japanese merely dehistoricizes foreign cultures, and the identity and purity of the body as a receptor of foreign cultures are never questioned. Instead of debunking the idea of pure Japaneseness once and for all, the Japanese ability to accommodate, appropriate, domesticate, and eclectically refine disparately diverse foreign cultures simply reinforces the sense of native uniqueness.

Put in the context of Japanese eclecticism without negativity, Tokyo Disneyland can no longer be understood as a mere neutralized version of the "original" Disneyland in America. To the extent that it perfectly fits in with the nativist discourse valorizing the selective hybridity of Japanese culture, Tokyo Disneyland is in fact one of the most powerful manifestations of contemporary Japanese nationalism. Since there is nothing overtly Japanese about Tokyo Disneyland in particular or the popular culture of postmodern Japan in general, they can be exported to Asia and other parts of the world without arousing nationalistic protest movements in those areas. Far from being a manifestation of American cultural imperialism, Tokyo Disneyland epitomizes the ingenious mechanism of neocultural imperialism of Japan. The commodified West as the image works as a proxy, which internally strengthens a hold of national imaginary over the Japanese, and externally enables Japanese economic expansion without directly provoking local nationalistic reactions.

Japan's Small Hope

Tokyo Disneyland teaches an important lesson to those of us interested in US-Japan comparative studies since it puts into question facile stereotypes of American and Japanese society. Because of Disney's preoccupation with cleanliness and quality control in the service area, and attentiveness to minute details in the area of management, Disneyland is arguably the most Japanese institution in the United States. Similarly the Japanese obsession with perfectionism and cleanliness makes Japan the best market for Disney enterprise, the epitome of American popular culture. Yet more importantly, we can glimpse the logic of a global culture in Tokyo Disneyland, which epitomizes the contradiction of the new global economy in the age of the post-Cold-War system. Contrary to Wallerstein's claim, in the economy of global culture, the particular and the universal, or the national and the global, are not antithetical to each other. Moreover, Tokyo Disneyland makes us see that the increasing irrelevance of national boundaries in the global flow of capital and the consolidation of the sense of nationhood can be interdependent and mutually reinforce each other.

In Japan, this new logic of postmodern nationalism—or what Fredric Jameson refers to as neo-ethnicity—is euphemistically called *kokusaika* or internationalization. While domestically it means the presence of more imported goods and image-information, externally it refers to the phenomenon of more Japanese going abroad (tourists, businessmen/women, students, and so on). What *kokusaika* does not include is precisely one of the most fundamental ways of internationalizing Japan: the genuine acceptance of foreigners and those Japanese who are too "contaminated" by foreign cultures. To the extent that, by using images, it creates an invisible empire, *kokusaika* can best be understood as an ideology of Japanese neo-imperialism in the post-Cold-War era.

Yet in spite of the subtle manipulation of image, information, and commodity networks, the insularity of the Japanese nation is gradually eroding, so that there is a possibility for the ingenious mechanism of Japanese image capitalism to malfunction. For instance, while Tokyo Disneyland is welcoming the guests at its main entrance gates, another group of "guests" are trying to go through a different kind of gate controlled by the more powerful authority. Every day, a number of foreign visitors are arriving at the New Tokyo International Airport in Narita, and many of those who successfully go through customs are staying in Japan as illegal "guest" workers. For many Filipinos, Thais, Pakistanis, and Iranians, Japan is a Magic Kingdom where they can earn their lifetime income in just a few years. However, they immediately learn that they are not allowed to enter this Magic Kingdom through the main entrance as guests; instead, they find themselves in the underground tunnels and maintenance facilities hidden from the real guests. Their fantasy about Japan, a Magic Kingdom, is shattered to pieces once they successfully go through customs, start working in small-scale factories owned often by subcontractors, and face the reality of Japanese image capitalism. While the Japanese government is reluctant to open the labor market to foreign workers, the presence of those illegal foreign workers all over Japan suggests that the Japanese economy cannot do without them. Unlike "America" or "France," these are not images but real people; they are not the Other but others who have no obligation to cooperate with the collective narcissism of the Japanese; and unlike images, they cannot be quickly "consumed" and "discarded." The Japanese, who are so caught up in their postmodern fantasy, need to take seriously foreign workers' fantasies about Japan in order to distance themselves from their own. And this might be one of the few options left for Japan not to make the same historical mistake again.

Reception

13

The Mickey in Macy's Window: Childhood, Consumerism, and Disney Animation

Richard deCordova

Walt Disney's Mickey Mouse films emerged against the backdrop of a complex set of debates about children's leisure and the role of the cinema in children's lives. During the late 1920s and early 1930s the cinema's address to children was contested ground and a matter of frenzied concern. Reformers denounced the movies' influence on children and mounted well-organized efforts across the country to regulate and control this aspect of children's leisure. One particularly important aspect of these efforts involved the creation and supervision of a canon of films for children. Reformers asked whether a given film addressed the young moviegoer as a "true" and "proper" child.

Disney's films entered and achieved a privileged position in this canon of films for children. In Mickey Mouse, the cultural interests of children, the business interests of the film industry, and the political and cultural interests of reformers seemingly merged. And today, something like a sacred connection exists between Mickey Mouse and idealized childhood. However, as the occasional early references to Mickey's vulgarity attest, that connection was by no means natural or unproblematic. It was the result of a particular historical work, a work that I want to begin to examine in this essay.

My focus here is not so much on the films themselves as it is on the marketing and merchandising strategies that "sold" the cartoons (and the characters) to children and assured reform-minded adults that this was a healthful purchase. It is at this level that we see the most explicit and emphatic attempts to assure Disney animation's uncontested address to children.

My title's reference to Charles Eckert's famous article, "The Carole Lombard in Macy's Window," gives an indication of the direction of my argument. In that article, Eckert describes a significant transformation in the American film industry. From the late 1920s to the middle 1930s there was an intensification and rationalization of the process through which films were linked to consumer goods. Such organizations as Hollywood Fashion Associates and the Modern Merchandising Bureau emerged to coordinate the display of fashions in Hollywood films and fan magazines with the subsequent production and marketing of those fashions to the public. And the studio exploitation departments systematically began to conceive of story ideas and scripts as opportunities for a wide range of lucrative product tie-ins. For Eckert these developments consolidated the cinema's role as a force in the rise of American consumerism.[1]

The period Eckert discusses coincides with the period of Mickey Mouse's ascendance as a commodified cultural icon. Although Eckert does not mention Disney, it is well known that the Disney Company was at the forefront of these innovations in the early 1930s. Much popular writing on Disney has described the merchandising of Mickey Mouse, or at least described the results of that merchandising—a vast array of dolls, toys, clothing, and novelty items produced from 1930 on, and sold to an appreciative and generally young public. Unfortunately, to my knowledge, none of this work has attempted to place Disney's efforts in the context of the industry's broader efforts; nor has it related those efforts to issues of spectatorship or consumerism.

Several scholarly works, by contrast, have followed from Eckert to produce compelling arguments about the relations between film and consumerism in the first decades of the century. This work however, like Eckert's, has ignored Disney, in large part, no doubt, because it has concerned itself with consumers other than children. The situation beyond film studies, in the fields of social and cultural history, is much the same: a body of knowledge about the rise of consumerism but very little on children's participation in that process.[2] In short, a kind of gap exists in the research, a gap that prevents us from thinking as clearly as we might about Disney animation's address to children and particularly its address through the mechanisms of consumerism.

We should begin by distinguishing between two different registers of consumption that tied the child to the cinema.

First, the child was a consumer of films, someone who paid a certain amount to see a show. Second, the child was a consumer of products displayed through films. The system of merchandising and promotion employed by Disney and the other studios in the early 1930s worked by creating elaborate networks of mutual reference between these two registers of consumption.

Particularly elaborate networks formed around Mickey Mouse. In Cecil Muncie's account, the beginnings of Mickey Mouse merchandising can be traced to three events. In late 1929, Walt Disney sold the rights to use Mickey on school tablets to a New York company. In January 1930, Charlotte Clark began the small-scale production of Mickey Mouse dolls in a house rented by the Disney Company. And finally, and most importantly, in February 1930, Disney signed a contract with the George Borgfeldt Company for the international licensing, production, and distribution of Mickey Mouse merchandise.[3] Although the Disney Company was never satisfied with Borgfeldt's efforts, the merchandising of Mickey Mouse was soon astoundingly successful. By the beginning of 1932 there were twenty-one licensees in the United States alone, most producing a number of different Mickey Mouse products. Children could, with enough money, have the image of the mouse on almost all of their possessions—their underwear, pajamas, neckties, handkerchiefs, and jewelry; their toothbrushes, hot water bottles, and bathroom accessories; their silverware and china; their toys and games; and their school supplies.[4]

The Disney Company was interested in the publicity value of these items as much as the substantial royalties they would generate. As Roy Disney noted in a letter to Borgfeldt, "The sale of a doll to any member of a household is a daily advertisement in that household for our cartoons and keeps them all 'Mickey Mouse Minded.'"[5] When Borgfeldt's Carl Sollmann expressed his concern that business would be hurt by the saturation of the market with Disney toys, Roy Disney replied, "we feel that we should publicize our character from every angle and accept every opportunity."[6] Sollmann looked at the toy business as a producer; Disney looked at it more as an advertiser. The more publicity the better.

In this sense, Disney and Borgfeldt's interests were complementary more than convergent. They were each interested in consolidating half of the circuit between the two forms of consumption noted above. For Disney, the consumption of the toy would lead to the consumption of the movie; for Borgfeldt, the consumption of the movie would lead to the consumption of the toy. At the local level at which consumption actually took place, this network might better be described as a path, a path that connected the worlds of film exhibition and retailing, and therefore led (in its ideal form at least) from the movie theater to the department store and back. The activities in these two spaces were, as we shall see, strategically linked.

In 1931 and 1932, Mickey Mouse became a fixture in department stores across the country. Mickey Mouse items began to be grouped together in toy departments, and given their own separate displays.[7] And Mickey Mouse became the prominent figure in store windows targeted at the young consumer. The toy trade press of these years reproduced numerous store windows built around Mickey and Minnie Mouse, windows at Gimbel Brothers' in Philadelphia, Kresge's in Newark, Nugent's in St. Louis,

Bullock's in Los Angeles, Stearn's in Cleveland and Bloomingdale's, Lord and Taylor's, Stern Brothers' and the Grand Central Toy Shop in New York.[8] The following description, from 1932, gives some sense of the spectacular nature of these windows:

> For stopping crowds, O'Connor-Moffatt certainly took the prize for the early trade. The wonderful Mickey Mouse show with Minnie Mouse at the piano, and a world of little Mickey's and other animals about, caught and held constant crowds. Meanwhile a talking machine mechanism, attached by a vibrating mechanism to the windows, gave out a cheerful mousey melody to the bystanders on either side of the corner.[9]

Mickey Mouse became a kind of star of the toy department, around which could be assembled a large supporting cast of other dolls and toys. This is particularly evident in the description of the Christmas festivities for children at Kresge's in 1932. Mickey Mouse passed out presents and acted as "master of ceremonies" for a show in the Mickey Mouse Barn on the fifth floor. And on the sixth floor, Mickey introduced Santa and Mrs. Claus, who were placed on thrones in the rear of the toy department's Mickey Mouse section.

Borgfeldt helped organize a certain amount of this publicity for its products. It built a Mickey Mouse booth at Bloomingdale's, provided large fake cheeses for Mickey Mouse window displays, and had Charlotte Clark make costumes so that Mickey and Minnie could appear "live" at stores. But it seems that much of the impetus for these extravagant promotions came from the stores themselves.

The stores' enthusiasm for Mickey Mouse is not difficult to understand given the popularity of the films and the early signs of the toys' success. One less obvious source of this enthusiasm should be stressed, however. The toy industry's greatest problem during this period was that it was too much of a seasonal business; the majority of purchases took place in the month before Christmas and the rest of the year was comparatively slow. The trade struggled to find ways to overcome this problem. For the toy industry to flourish, the child's consumption patterns had to be modernized, wrested from the stranglehold of the yearly ritual and connected to other rituals and, particularly, to the flux of everyday life. The movies played an important role in most stores' efforts for year-round sales. One Kansas store explained its success in this regard by pointing to its windows that tied in with movies at the local theaters. *Playthings,* a trade paper for the toy industry, explained the extra stock dividends that Lord and Taylor paid by noting the store's unique window displays and including, as an example, a Mickey Mouse window.[10] By tying toys to movies, stores tied the consumption of toys to the everyday rituals of moviegoing, and a different kind of temporality. Mickey Mouse, as a regularly recurring character, was especially suited for this strategy.

Mickey Mouse was also important in the toy industry's efforts to generate other yearly rituals, notably Children's Day in June and Mickey Mouse's birthday in October. *Playthings,* in fact, urged stores to arrange Mickey Mouse birthday parties as a way of livening up a dull season. It specifically encouraged stores to cooperate with local movie theaters and to offer to dress up their lobbies with a display of Mickey Mouse toys. Here the theater became quite explicitly an extension of the department store.[11]

If the department stores' activities served as an elaborate advertisement for Mickey Mouse films, the theater's activities served as an equally elaborate advertisement for the department stores and particularly for Mickey Mouse toys. The films themselves, of course, popular as they were, served as such an advertisement. But to these films we must add another set of practices, the display and giveaway of Mickey Mouse toys at the theaters. By 1931, at least, theaters across the country had begun to receive a stream of Mickey Mouse dolls and toys for display and giveaways. These were occasionally supplied by Disney, Borgfeldt, or Columbia, the studio that distributed Disney films, or bought by the theater itself, but, in what seems to have been the standard formula, they were also supplied by individual department stores.[12] Stores got involved through the most elegant scheme of Mickey Mouse merchandising of the period, the Mickey Mouse Clubs.

The principal elements of the Mickey Mouse Club scheme were outlined in a general campaign booklet published in 1930 by the Disney Company. According to the plan, exhibitors would arrange a series of Saturday matinees for children, organizing the audience for these matinees into a club built around the character of Mickey Mouse. Each matinee, or "meeting" of the club would consist of a Mickey Mouse cartoon, followed by the introduction of the club's officers, the recitation of the Mickey Mouse Club Creed, the singing of "America," a stage show and/or contest, the Mickey Mouse Club Yell, the Mickey Mouse Club Song and then, finally, the films featured for the day.[13]

The club programs were not designed simply to appeal to children, but to incorporate as fully as possible the cultural activities of children within a community. Children enrolled in local music, dance, and dramatic schools, for instance, found themselves drawn or directed to the Mickey Mouse Clubs, because the stage shows were used as showcases for their talent. Marble shooting contests, doll dressing contests, model airplane making contests, ice-cream eating contests, Easter egg hunts, and dog parades functioned similarly, taking interests and activities unrelated to moviegoing and incorporating them into the flow of the matinee. Some clubs even tried to bring outdoor activities, which were seen as the greatest threat to children's attendance on Saturdays, within their orbit by sponsoring baseball teams or summer picnics.

The clubs extended their reach in another way, by forming networks of tie-ins with local businesses that catered to children. Department stores, dairies, candy stores, banks, newspapers, and sporting goods stores—all businesses that served as points of contact between children and the world of commerce—became potential sponsors. Sponsors split the cost of running the clubs, and in return received advertising at club meetings and the right to use the image of Mickey Mouse in their store windows and newspaper ads.

Tie-ins with department stores were the most common. Those tie-ins linked the club's activities with the selling of toys quite effectively. To join the club, children had to go to the department store's toy department for an application. At club meetings, the department store's sponsorship would be noted, and the latest Mickey Mouse toys would be given away in contests to a handful of very lucky children. The rest of the children would then covet the toys and, ideally, figure out a way to return to the store to buy one.

The growth of the Mickey Mouse Clubs was impressive. By the end of 1930, a hundred and fifty theaters across the country had clubs and, according to Disney's estimates, there were a hundred and fifty to two hundred thousand members.[14] By 1932, *Photoplay* magazine claimed that the clubs had one million members.[15] Although these figures may exaggerate actual membership, they are credible. Between 1930 and 1932, local papers, the national trade press, and the semimonthly "Official Bulletin of the Mickey Mouse Club" chronicled the successes of the clubs in every part of the country. Milwaukee alone had ten clubs and twenty thousand members. Chicago had at least twenty-five clubs. Los Angeles had still more.[16] In 1932, new club chapters were being formed at the rate of about thirty per month. A writer in the *Motion Picture Herald* claimed that the membership of the Mickey Mouse Club approximated "that of the Boy Scouts of America and the Girl Scouts combined."[17]

The idea of a children's cinema club was not an original one. The *Film Daily Yearbook* had recommended juvenile booster clubs in its *Exploitation Guides* in the three years prior to 1930, so it is very likely that exhibitors had been experimenting with the idea for some time. In fact, in 1927, the *Exhibitor's Herald* devoted an article to an "Our Gang" Matinee Club that had been organized by a Chicago exhibitor. That club, and perhaps others like it, existed as a precedent for a children's club based on the characters in a short subject film series.[18]

The Mickey Mouse Club was not, in any case, the only children's cinema club operating between 1930 and 1933. The Loew's and Warner Bros. theater circuits had kiddie clubs during these years, and dozens, if not hundreds, of individual theater managers devised their own clubs. The Capitol Theater Booster Club, the Indians are Coming Club, the Do Right Club, the Young-Timers and the Ancient Order of the Tom Cats are among many mentioned in the trades.[19]

All of the clubs worked to consolidate around the moviegoing experience what Daniel Boorstin has called consumption communities.[20] What set the Mickey Mouse Clubs apart from these other clubs was the extent to which they organized these communities not only around the consumption of movies but also around the consumption of toys. It is significant that the toy press during these years was encouraging toy departments to organize children's' clubs to promote year-round sales. Mickey Mouse clubs, designed by Disney and run by theater managers, provided them an ideal, ready-made vehicle to achieve these goals.[21]

The picture I have drawn is far from complete, but it does give some sense of the elaborate ways that the child was interpellated as consumer through the merchandising of Mickey Mouse. At this point it is possible to return to the question of address, and ask what if any relationship existed between this merchandising, the broad debates about the movies and children, and the canonization of Mickey Mouse.

Let me begin by merely noting that the merchandising of Mickey Mouse toys to children seems to have proceeded in the early 1930s without any criticism from reformers. I would like to suggest that this is more perplexing than it may, on its surface, seem. The Mickey Mouse films, after all, elicited at least scattered signs of resistance. And the values of consumerism were contested from a variety of fronts during the period. Daniel Horowitz has traced the history of moral arguments against consumerism, arguments which, in the 1920s and 1930s, centered on the middle class's susceptibility and conformity to standardized culture.[22] And Roland Marchand has described the ambivalence that even advertisers felt when contemplating the logic of waste and extravagance that characterized consumerism.[23] Today, of course, activists reflexively bring these kinds of arguments to the merchandising of cartoon character toys. They did not, however, bring such arguments to the merchandising of Mickey Mouse in the early 1930s; nor do they generally bring those arguments to Mickey today. It is important to ask: Why not?

It would be misleading to say that issues of consumerism did not enter into the debates over the cinema and children during this period. In fact, most reformist discourse in the first decades of the century related fairly directly to the child's new status as a consumer of films. The movies were part of a new marketplace of culture to which children had unprecedented access. Their freedom of choice as consumers blurred traditional distinctions between child and adult culture, and placed the authority that parents and teachers had normally had in the socialization of children in crisis. The numerous studies done of children's movie attendance and movie preferences reveal a fundamental concern with the effects of consumerism. Some studies, moreover, called critical attention to the ability of movies to prompt desires for the products they picture, especially products such as cigarettes and clothing.[24]

But it is clear that ancillary products relating to Mickey Mouse were not an issue. In fact, it can be argued that these products played an important role in naturalizing Disney animation's address to children, consolidating the sacred bond I mentioned earlier. I would like to offer two broad and brief explanations for this, explanations for the ways in which the reading of toys worked to consolidate Disney animation's address to children.

The first has to do with the new valuation of play in the first decades of the century. Both the film industry and the toy industry were singled out in the 1920s and 1930s as arenas of reform. There are, in fact, some interesting parallels between reform activity in the two industries. Reformers in both arenas stressed character education, criticized the glorification of gunplay, and produced elaborate age-grading schemes to guide children's consumption. However, there is a particularly striking difference between the voices of reform in the two industries. The vision of the toy reformers is obviously a much more affirmative one. Very few specific toys are criticized, and though the distinction between educational and noneducational toys is frequently made, the former category was quite large and its boundaries not well defined. The rhetoric of toy reform was informed by the idea that play itself, in itself, was valuable for the child.[25]

A 1931 article in *Toys and Novelties* reveals for us the ways that the interests of reform and the dictates of consumerism could so unproblematically converge around toys:

> We are continually purchasing new toys for our kiddies because we believe it is one of the finest investments we could possibly make toward their proper growth and development. It is up to you to sell the same idea to every home in America.[26]

A similarly general statement during this period about "continually sending the child to the movies" would have sounded ludicrous. In 1934, Mickey Mouse Doll houses, playhouses, pencil sets, paint sets, dial phones, and chime sets were put forward as evidence that Mickey had turned educator.[27] In fact, not all of these toys are obviously educational. But, according to the rhetoric of the day, toys generally were educational. For this reason, the toys offered more solid ground on which to assure the sacredness of Mickey Mouse's address to children than did the films.

A second explanation centers on the ideology implicit in the iconography of toys, an iconography shared by animation. Mary Ann Doane has examined the intertwining of identification and object choice—being and having—in the female spectator's simultaneous address by the movies and consumerism.[28] Although the comparison holds some dangers, it is clear that a similar sort of intertwining occurs in children's address by Mickey Mouse films and toys. This is illustrated most vividly in the widespread popularity of Mickey Mouse playsuits, which allowed children to dress up as Mickey or Minnie Mouse. Photos of Mickey Mouse Club activities typically show the officers dressed in such costumes. Members, in fact, were instructed to greet one another by saying "Hi Mickey!" or "Hi Minnie!" What does it mean for a child to "be" a mouse? And what does it mean for a child to "have" a mouse? During the early decades of the century, as today, there was an enormous cultural investment in the association of childhood with animality. The most lauded forms of children's culture—toys, zoos, circuses, children's literature—were built on that investment, and the structured set of fantasies it offered.

The animalization of the juvenile world arguably had a very specific and powerful function in relation to the changing historical construction of childhood in the nineteenth and early twentieth centuries. This might be explained broadly through reference to the increasing currency of Romanticism, which linked the child with nature. Jackson Lears has identified two strains in the new construction of childhood that follow from links Romanticism made between childhood and nature. In the first, nature was a way of establishing children's innocence, their distance from the corrupting influence of social life. In the second, nature was a way of establishing children's vitality, their distance from the stultifying elements of social life. The child's relationship with nature and its association with innocence on the one hand and primitivist vitality on the other could be effectively concretized through symbolic procedures that linked the child to animals.[29]

The fantasy positions laid out (for both children and adults) in the association of children with animals circulated around and conflated two paradigmatic distinctions, that between child and adult and that between animal and human. Reformers were interested in conserving the set of traditional distinctions between child and adult, which the cinema presumably blurred. One way of bringing those distinctions back into focus was to superimpose them on the more culturally stable distinction between animals and humans. That is what the association of animals and children worked to do.[30]

We may look to the work of G. Stanley Hall for a more specific sense of the context in which the connection between animals and children gained its significance. Hall's writing at the turn of the century melded Romantic notions of childhood with theories about evolution and psychological development. As a founder of the Child Studies Movement in this country, Hall was an instrumental force in articulating and carrying forward central tendencies in the discourses of reform. His theories held that the various stages of the child's development recapitulated, through a genetically inscribed memory, the history of the race. Therefore, childhood recapitulated the social and instinctual impulses of the so-called Age of Savagery, while adolescence similarly recapitulated the Age of Chivalry. Proper parental and educational guidance avoided the "omnipresent dangers of precocity" by guiding the child through each stage of its development and by encouraging, at each stage, the proper exercise of the tendencies of the race's past. The child that did not fully live out its savage impulses would be scarred in its development and therefore unable to function properly as an adult in the modern world.[31]

This paleopsychic theory gave animals a very special place in the consideration of childhood, for it held that at the earliest stages of the race's development, humans were very close to animals. Therefore, Hall could argue, "children . . . in their incomplete stage of development are nearer the animals in some respects than they are to adults."[32] The tendency to anthropomorphize animals is established as a particular result of the child's ancestral link with animals.

> To the young child, there is no gap between his soul and the soul of animals. They think, feel, act much as he does. They love, hate, fear, learn, sleep, make toilets, sympathize and have nearly all of the basal psychic qualities that the child has.[33]

Hall's description of the paleopsychic connection between children and animals becomes the basis for his argument for the centrality of animals in education. As Hall puts it,

> Just as man's development would have been very different without animals and the fishing, hunting and pastoral stages, so childhood is maimed if long robbed of its due measure of influences from this comprehensive arsenal of educational material. Instead, I can almost believe that, if pedagogy is ever to become adequate to the needs of the soul the time will come when animals will play a far larger educational role than has as yet been conceived, that they will be curricularized, will require a new and higher humanistic or culture value in the future comparable with their utility in the past.[34]

Hall therefore pleads for "menageries . . . in every public park, pets, familiarity with stables, for school museums of stuffed specimens," and for "instruction in every school concerning insects, birds and animals. . . ."[35] He might as well have called for Mickey Mouse. Although Hall's chapter gives some clues about the ways that animals can serve the needs of scientific, psychological, and moral education, it is clear that he is concerned not with ends so much as means, that is, with the contact that is established and maintained between the child and the world of animals.

What is particularly important to note here is that animals tended to link children to a different time. Johannes Fabian has argued that the West has constituted the other as occupying not simply a different space (conceived geographically, hierarchically, or taxonomically) but a different time. Such distinctions as nature/culture, traditional/modern, and child/adult (and we might add animal/human) are central to Western society as temporalizing strategies.

The world of toys was built around this primitivist impulse. It was a world of animals, racial others, and figures from the near or distant past. The playsuits available during the period—the Indian, Cowboy, Scout, and Mickey Mouse suits—all depend on this impulse. Yet we must admit that the Mickey Mouse films and the Mickey character itself were in many ways aggressively modern. In fact, children during this period were in many ways on the very cutting edge of modernity. Reformers were disturbed about the movies in large part because the cultural construction of childhood had traditionally depended so much on the child's association with the past. Generally, for them, the more modern a film, the less suitable it was for children. Mickey's association with animality and particularly with the iconography of toys worked to counterbalance his modernity and place him more on the side of traditional childhood.

In *The World of Goods,* Mary Douglas and Baron Isherwood have argued that the primary function of goods is to make "visible" and stable the categories of culture."[36] Film reformers acknowledged this view in their refusal to demonize consumerism and oppose it to notions of traditional childhood. These reformers were preoccupied with the cinema's address to children because the cinema mixed adults and children and called into question the hallowed distinction between the two. They were particularly concerned with adolescence because that was where the distinction became particularly problematic. If, as I have argued, the merchandising of Mickey Mouse toys was important in making sacred Disney's address to children, it is because that merchandising worked more assuredly than the movies to push the image of the child back into traditional categories of childhood.

14

Fantasia:
Cultural Constructions of
Disney's "Masterpiece"

Moya Luckett

Recent work in film and television studies focusing on the issue of reception has led to an increased emphasis on the specific social and historical context(s) in which a text is released and understood. As these contexts change each time a film is seen, any interpretation or reading will be shaped by a combination of the text and the context of its exhibition, by questions of gender, audience interests, foreknowledge and expectations, and by the social and cultural place of the reader. Reception studies examines how various social and cultural backgrounds affect audience evaluations, critical judgments, and interpretative strategies. In *Interpreting Films,* Janet Staiger's approach to reception studies emphasizes how contexts mold interpretations, how responses from controlling cultural forces attempt to shape a "normative" reading of a text, and how "marginal" responses rework texts in the service of a personal or social agenda.[1] Such interpretations of films can offer the analyst traces of how texts are positioned in larger cultural debates. A study of public interpretations and judgments of films (such as publicity and reviews) can also help establish what audience expectations might have been. While it is impossible to access each spectator's biases and prior knowledge, reviews survive as a marker of various culturally determined evaluations of films and can give a sense of the variety of publicly circulating readings.

Reviewers not only construct their own subject positions vis-à-vis a text, they also offer possible subject positions that other viewers might wish to adopt. The historical-materialist approach to reception studies advocated by Staiger places these findings within a broader social and historical context, acknowledging the writer's own position within the reception of the film. Staiger writes:

> The reception studies I seek would be historical, would recognize the
> dialectics of evidence and theory, and would take up a critical distance
> on the relations between spectators and texts. It would not interpret
> texts but would attempt a historical explanation of the event of interpre-
> ting a text.[2]

Staiger's approach to reception studies involves tracing both dominant
and marginal interpretive strategies in order to analyze how readers take
up subject positions with regard to a text. As reception studies is concerned
with the plurality of audiences and the variety of their readings and
interpretations of films within various historical, social, and regional
contexts, it does not attempt to flatten out differences or debates under
an ideal or dominant reader/viewer. Rather, reception studies involves
studying the strategies audiences use to make sense of a text, and considers
how any interpretation reorients and reworks textual material in the viewers' (or critics') attempts to understand a film. This issue of "making
sense" is foregrounded in the case of a "difficult" or unconventional film.
If a spectator's viewing history does not provide relevant or sufficient
foreknowledge for adequate comprehension, (s)he is probably more likely
to rely on judgments and interpretations offered by critics and reviewers.

Walt Disney's *Fantasia* fell into this category when first released in
1940. The film presents eight pieces of classical music, each segment
introduced and interpreted by musicologist Deems Taylor. Disney intended *Fantasia* to be an open text, featuring both narrative and nonnarra-
tive "visualizations" of music, with the initial intention that these sequences could be reorganized and other sequences would be added.[3] To
aid audience comprehension of his film, Disney produced a thirty-two-
page program, which the studio distributed to audiences during the film's
1940 to 41 release. This program discussed the ideas behind the production
of *Fantasia* and provided background knowledge on each musical selection. Publicity for the film even tutored viewers on when and how to
attend the film. As advertisements warned:

> It is important that all attending *Fantasia* be seated before curtain
> time. . . . *Fantasia* does not start in the conventional manner. . . .
> There are no titles on the screen. The opening is a delightful surprise.
> We urge you to be seated before curtain time to enjoy it to the fullest.[4]

The first release of *Fantasia* not only met with a great deal of critical
attention, designed to guide the audience's viewing, but stimulated a
debate on its status as an interpretation and adaptation of classical music.
The controversy over the film can be located within discourses of "cultural

authority"—in particular surrounding the status of film as "art." While film critics almost unanimously praised the film as "important,"[5] music critics despised the way it diluted the classics. The force of these arguments indicates how even such a "quality" film was regarded as part of a despised popular culture by representatives of "high" culture.

In this essay, I shall be examining reviews, publicity, marketing, and critical evaluations of *Fantasia* in the context of both its original release and two later reissues (1954 and 1991). I have chosen this strategy in order to see how changing cultural contexts helped to shape the different ways in which the film was received across time. Given that *Fantasia* was the subject of an intense cultural debate during its first release, I have chosen to focus on the 1940 to 41 period to examine how the film figured in the ongoing discourses around popular culture and high art. I then examine the reissues from 1954 and 1991 to investigate the (re)circulation of these terms in later periods. In each incarnation, *Fantasia* has been associated with issues of quality and (film) "art" as well as the application of new technologies (such as stereo, widescreen, and home video/laser discs). The reception of *Fantasia* has also raised questions of how cultural definitions of the popular and the "lowbrow" are related to mass distribution. Given the cultural climate of 1940, Disney's initial restricted release of *Fantasia* suggests that the studio was trying to place the film as an elite work of "art." However, changes in definitions of art and popular culture eventually allowed *Fantasia* to become both the best-selling video of all time and an undisputed masterpiece by 1991.[6]

Fantasia premiered at New York's Broadway Theatre on Wednesday, November 13, 1940. Unlike other Walt Disney productions, which were distributed through RKO, *Fantasia* was handled exclusively by Disney on its initial release as a road show in large urban theaters (road showing was reserved for prestige pictures during the classical Hollywood era; the producer would take charge of the film's distribution and exhibition on a theater-by-theater basis, showcasing the movie in the best theaters and restricting its release to key urban markets).

One reason for this treatment was the need for theaters to close for about one week in order to install "Fantasound," the new stereophonic sound system developed by Disney in association with RCA for *Fantasia*.[7] However, Disney's plans for the exhibition of *Fantasia* also suggest that the concept of a restricted release, coupled with the opportunities for individual treatment offered by road-showing, would help construct *Fantasia* as an artistic and cultural event. As Leonard Maltin notes, Disney had initially intended *Fantasia* to be "treat[ed] . . . as a concert, instead of a film (there was even talk, for a time, of opening it in concert halls instead of conventional theaters)."[8] Since *Fantasia* premiered in New York rather than Los Angeles, it attracted the attention of representatives of "high" culture rather than just movie reviewers, with leading music critics invited to attend the film's premiere.[9] *Fantasia* would not open in Los Angeles until three months later, revealing Disney's desire for the film to be an event associated with East Coast culture and tradition rather than Hollywood glitter and frivolity.

Yet, as I shall discuss below, much of the controversy surrounding *Fantasia*'s first release was precisely the result of this critical construction of the film on the boundaries of high art and popular culture. Although representatives of "high" culture, most notably music critics, did pay attention to *Fantasia,* they generally maligned the film, protesting that it bastardized and destroyed the pleasures and dignity of the music. Debates surrounding *Fantasia* were as much the result of the film establishment's praise of the film as the music critics' disapprobation. The resultant controversy placed *Fantasia* within contemporary debates about cinematic "art," and larger hierarchies of art, in particular (quality) music versus (popular) film. Following the success of *Gone With the Wind* in 1939, Hollywood made a prominent move towards quality and "art" in early 1940s cinema. "Prestige" pictures—high budget, class A productions— were usually adaptations of best-selling novels or literary classics.

According to Tino Balio, quality films were the leading production trend of the 1930s, differentiated from other releases not just by budget, but through the practice of road-showing.[10] This individualized distribution and exhibition treatment highlighted a film as different, as a unique cultural product, rather than as just another part of a studio's output. Stress on the individual, "prestige" film accompanied exhibitor's calls for an end to block booking, a practice which forced theater owners to accept a seemingly endless string of "inferior" pictures. In 1940, *Variety* reported that Sam Goldwyn advocated a reduction in the number of films produced, both to maximize profits and to give the public what they wanted: quality films.[11] The front-page headline from *Variety,* 21 August 1940, asked "Why they Don't Go To Pix?" and gave the principle reason as "not enough good pictures." Based on a nationwide survey conducted by George Gallup for *Variety,* the article revealed that:

> [com]plaint about the quality of Hollywood product far surpasses in frequency any other reason for shunning film theaters. . . . Significant in the squawks about the quality of films is that virtually no complainant states that there are no good pictures, but all maintain "there are not enough good pictures." In other words, there appears to be a growing recognition of Hollywood's efforts to turn out better films, which is encouraging. With *Gone With the Wind* and *Rebecca* leading the mentions, there's less of the slam-bang condemnation of all films, which used to characterize critics of Hollywood.[12]

Variety stressed that one consequence of audience demand for quality pictures was that long runs for prestige films were becoming increasingly commonplace.[13] *Variety*'s correspondent claimed that this resulted in audiences actually *creating* a production and exhibition trend by favoring prestige pictures at the expense of lower-budget movies. Within this climate of critical and audience attention focused on the quality film, it is not surprising to find Disney promoting *Fantasia* as an ultraprestigious picture.

By 1940, Disney's reputation as a producer of quality films was fully established, especially after the two feature films, *Snow White and the Seven Dwarfs* and *Pinocchio,* had been widely acclaimed by the critics. Trading on this reputation, Disney advertised in March 1940 that *The Ugly Duckling* had won an Academy Award for Short Subject (animated cartoon), and stressed that this was "Number Six in the parade of Disney shorts to win the Academy Award for six consecutive years!"[14] Prior publicity for *Fantasia* emphasized Disney's genius, as established by these earlier successes, and thus helped bridge the cultural gap between animated cartoons and "high art." For example, just prior to *Fantasia*'s premiere in November 1940, the *New York Times Magazine* reported that "the Disney who brought fairy-book folk alive here has freed music from the stage and made it flow and surge through the auditorium, has given it a new dimension and a new richness."[15] The cost, ambition, and technical innovation of *Fantasia* (and the attendant Fantasound) also helped contribute to the construction of Disney as a genius who was about to ascend to new heights. On the day of *Fantasia*'s world premiere in New York City, Douglas W. Churchill of the *New York Times* reported that:

> An event of considerable cinematic importance will take place tonight with the world premiere of *Fantasia,* the Walt Disney musical cartoon feature, at the Broadway Theatre. . . . *Fantasia* cost approximately $2,200,000 and has been in production for more than two years.[16]

While Disney's earlier animated features had been well received, they were seen as works of genius within the unpretentious and childlike sphere of fairy tales rather than within the arena of "high art." The employment of Disney's "genius" in the advance publicity for *Fantasia* thus ascribed to him a connoisseur's knowledge of music, and associated him closely with his collaborators—conductor Leopold Stokowski and commentator/ musicologist Deems Taylor—as a fellow custodian of "high" culture. Pictures in the *New York Times* show Disney, Stokowski, and Taylor conferring on *Fantasia,*[17] while publicity articles for the film stress Stravinsky's admission that "That is what I must have meant by my music."[18] Advance press for *Fantasia* also emphasized the artistic merit of Disney's previous cartoons, with the *New York Times* reporting that *Steamboat Willie* had been "preserved for posterity in the archives of the Film Library of the Museum of Modern Art."[19] Indeed, the film critic for the tabloid *New York Daily Mirror* expressed some doubt as to whether he should even attend the film's premiere by poking fun at the invited audience:

> research disclosed that the entire house for tonight's opening at the Broadway Theatre has been taken over by the British War Relief Society at a $10 top and that the list of ticket holders looks something like the Social Register and Burke's Peerage combined.[20]

Although the marketing of *Fantasia* appeared to target a highbrow audience, it is important to note that both the *New York Times* and the "lowbrow" *New York Daily Mirror* carried daily advertisements for *Fantasia* throughout November 1940. Advance publicity of this kind clearly attempted to rework the cultural position of Disney, but rather than placing Disney in the position of disseminating high art in the guise of mass culture, this publicity seemed to position *Fantasia* as a product worthy of the elite. Efforts to build Disney's cultural capital indicated that *Fantasia* would be of interest to an audience new to Disney (who needed to be informed about the film). The Disney name alone acted as a sufficient draw for mass audiences, as prior successes indicated that they would come to *Fantasia* anyway.

Advance publicity almost certainly shaped the critical reception of *Fantasia*, especially the emphasis placed on Walt Disney's musical expertise. This same publicity probably helped the controversy over the film's merits. It is not surprising that music critics were angered by the film. They had been led to expect "the first full-length concert of classical music in the history of the movies,"[21] but may have felt they received instead "an irreconcilable conflict between domineering screen image and domineering music."[22] Olin Downes, music critic for the *New York Times* complained that "in more than one instance those who went to the picture as a picture, or variously specialize in that field, declare that the spectacle itself was so engrossing that they forgot the music!"[23] Meanwhile, Edward Downes, music critic for the *Boston Evening Transcript*, returned to see *Fantasia* a second time when it premiered in Boston only because he was so blinded by anger during the New York premiere.

> The 'Pastoral' Symphony à la Disney made me so angry that I began to wonder whether it had colored all my other impressions of *Fantasia*. So *in a masochistic desire to be impartial and objective* I returned to the Majestic Theater this week to see and hear *Fantasia* for a second time. (my emphasis)[24]

The music critics' objections to *Fantasia* centered around the mixing of music and cinema. These critics argued that the music was generally drowned by the images, or that the images themselves anchored the music too much, restricting its associative powers. This debate foregrounds how issues of audience knowledge and perspective are central to a film's reception. In this instance, the debate involved prior knowledge (and interpretations) of the music selections featured in the film, a knowledge which itself indicated the degree of cultural capital possessed by the viewer. Indeed, the question of pleasure in interpreting the music was central to the music critics' objections to the film. Edward Barry, music critic of the *Chicago Daily Tribune,* foregrounded this issue in his review:

> Whatever objections one may have to the rest of the production must be based principally not on any old fogy notions of reverence towards the classics but on a selfish, practical desire to extract from such a piece as Beethoven's Sixth Symphony every possible ounce of exhilaration and delight. When some of the composer's most incredibly lovely ideas are drowned out by audience laughter at the antics of centaurs one does not need to be an old fogy to cry "Hold! Enough!"[25]

Barry's comments are telling, in that the pleasure he takes from the music is opposed to the laughter of the crowd. Such criticism, like the above comment from Edward Downes, reveals that issues of pleasure and taste form an integral part of the critical aversion towards *Fantasia,* and signal different modes and conventions of reception in "high art" and popular culture as perceived by these representatives of "high" culture.

Part of the issue here, therefore, involves the music critics' devaluation and even erasure of cinematic forms of pleasure. Their experience of reviewing concerts called on forms of knowledge and questions of taste different from those required for reviewing films. One consequence was that the different conventions and knowledge required for music reviewing led to critical frustration, producing reviews which foregrounded prejudices against the cinema itself. However, it would be a mistake to assume that these attacks on *Fantasia* formed one homogeneous set. Music critics articulated their objections in three principal ways. These objections concerned the fusion of classical music and film, the issue of appropriate interpretations and translation of music, and, finally, the question of the cultural status of this hybrid of music and film.

One group of music critics were totally against this mixing of forms. This type of objection took two forms: critics like Edward Downes of the *Boston Evening Transcript* not only believed that film and classical music were fundamentally formally incompatible, but argued that music could not be mixed with *any* media:

> Great music always tends to dominate no matter what combination of the arts. That was proved in Richard Wagner's music-dreams, where not the drama, but the music is the deciding factor, and was shown again in the evolution of the Russian ballet. And the greater the music, the more irresistibly it dominates. On the other hand, it is a fundamental law of the film that a moving image on a screen dominates everything else, dialogue, music and sound effects. *Therefore, unless the film does violence to its own nature and retires, so to speak, into the background, it will do violence to any truly great music.* (my emphasis)[26]

Another group, exemplified by the *Chicago Daily Tribune*'s Mae Tinee and Edward Barry, cited differences and incompatibilities in the forms of reception demanded by the two media as the root of the problem. For these critics, the pleasures of watching film were grounded in distraction, whereas classical music demanded contemplation and introspection. A great part of the problem of *Fantasia*, therefore, lay in the way the images drowned and dominated the subtle contemplation required to appreciate good music. Edward Barry summed up this problem:

> For a fidgety generation that cannot read a book without having the radio turned on, Walt Disney's *Fantasia* is an undoubted boon. It offers a full length program of good music well performed by the Philadelphia orchestra and beautifully recorded by sound technicians. Yet because of what goes on on the screen it is never necessary—indeed it is seldom possible—to concentrate on the music.[27]

Similarly, *film* critic Mae Tinee complained:

> how in heaven's name can one appreciate great music while the mind is distracted by the cavortings of gargoyles, dinosaurs, flying horses . . . and the like? Granted that music and dreams always go together. BUT—every listener wants to dream his own little dreams.[28]

For Barry, the "distractions" of cinema involved color and movement, two of its fundamental characteristics, whereas Tinee specified that it was the types of images that caused her to be distracted. By positing cinema itself as the distraction, Barry creates a hierarchy favoring music, the form that involves concentration and which provides the substance of the program. Furthermore, Barry's radio analogy implies that popular culture is the real problem, promoting distraction above the forms of contemplation demanded by the "high arts" (such as literature and classical music).

Distraction and contemplation are terms embedded in a modernist ontology of perception, and such intellectual connotations helped to reinforce the hierarchies and boundaries of "high art" and popular culture. Because distraction and contemplation were opposed as modes of perception within these reviews, critics concluded that *Fantasia* could not be a success. They believed that there was either a formal incompatibility present, or claimed that the mode of reception demanded by music and film made their combination unsuccessful. In each case, critics attempted to define an essential property of each form in order to explain the film's failure.

Another charge levied against *Fantasia* centered on the question of its translation and interpretation of music. Again, this objection takes two forms. First, critics objected to the images chosen by Disney, most notably those illustrating Beethoven's "Pastoral Symphony" and Stravinsky's "Rite of Spring." Olin Downes described the visualization of the "Pastoral Symphony" in the following manner;

> If Beethoven's idea is too dull then let it be. But for heaven's sake!— to inject into this simple and wonderfully beautiful musical evocation of the country-side groups of "Centaurettes," roughing for encounters with manly centaurs who looked like a cross between a prize fighter, a bartender and a horse's buttocks, and then set these to billing and cooing together, the while a red-nosed and bulbous caricature of Bacchus burlesques the show! This, to my mind, is as witless, as utterly inapropos of Beethoven's music as any invention could be— really terrible![29]

Critics frequently linked these issues of image appropriateness to the audience's foreknowledge of the music and the composer's own intentions behind each piece. As a result, critics' judgments of "inappropriate visualization" were concerned with the effect that the film would have on "lowbrow" audiences:

> it may be said that *Fantasia* will give the unwary the idea that the core of musical experience may be approached by the Disney route and that the ecstasy and exaltation which the art offers have something to do with visual images. This danger is especially serious since the picture bears, by implication at least, the seal of approval of such respected musicians as Stravinsky, Stokowski, and Taylor.[30]

Music critics thus positioned themselves as cultural custodians possessing more authority than even the composer, conductor, and musicologist.

The second objection regarding *Fantasia*'s interpretation of the classics concerned the way Disney adapted the selections according to the tripartite division of music discussed by Deems Taylor at the beginning of *Fantasia:*

There are three kinds of music on this *Fantasia* program. First, there's the kind that tells a definite story. Then, there's the kind that while ⁺ has no specific plot, does paint a series of more or less definite pictures. Then there's the third kind, music that exists absolutely for its own sake . . . absolute music.

Of course, the music most favored by each music critic fell into the realm of "absolute music," hence rendering its visualization impossible. For example, Olin Downes of the *New York Times* argued that Stravinsky's "Rite of Spring" was pure music, and consequently was unsuitable for translation into any other medium:

at the basis the "Sacré" is not music for spectacle at all, but pure music—perhaps the purest Stravinsky ever wrote, in the sense of music which *obeys laws peculiar to itself and has very little to do with an outside medium or idea* save—perhaps—the general idea represented by its title: the performance of rite of spring by a primitive people. To impose upon this music a children's lesson in geology, sociology and bacteriology is to us a far cry indeed from the quality of Stravinsky. (my emphasis)[31]

This issue of absolute formal purity relates the question of translation or adaptation to the first series of criticisms based on the formal characteristics of each medium. Critics used the concept of "pure music" as a means of denying *Fantasia*'s claims to "art" by maintaining a gulf between the two media.

These critics share with Walter Benjamin the idea that

Translatability is an essential quality of certain works, which is not to say that it is essential that they be translated; it means rather that a specific significance inherent in the original manifests itself in its translatability.[32]

Fantasia is different from the linguistic translations discussed by Benjamin, not just because it is a translation from music to film, but also because the original is present. Disney explicitly voiced *Fantasia*'s project as "seeing music and hearing pictures," articulating the role of these images in terms of a translation of the music.[33] According to Benjamin, a translation does not just involve the transmission of a message, but the expression of something other, something ineffable within the original. However, because music critics saw their favorite music as pure and untranslatable, this ineffable other could not be transmitted through images, being absolutely bound to the form of music itself.

Finally, some music critics objected to *Fantasia* explicitly on the grounds that it destroyed cultural hierarchies, diluting the music by accompanying it with images in order to make it palatable to "lower-brow" audiences. Edward Downes stated that *Fantasia* worked best when it was interpreting lesser, or insignificant, pieces of music, while Edward Barry (cited above) expressed his distaste at audience laughter. Interestingly, it was not only the music critics who disliked *Fantasia*'s mixture of high art and popular culture. Mae Tinee, film critic for the *Chicago Daily Tribune,* disliked *Fantasia* precisely because she felt that the pleasures of animation and classical music should be kept separate. Tinee expressed nostalgia for Disney's earlier works, and claimed that she could not understand *Fantasia*: "Certainly only genius could concoct such an anomaly and I am of the opinion that only genius could understand it. . . . I'm only a low brow trying to get along—and I couldn't seem to get along with *Fantasia*."[34] As Tinee's comments show, the desire to keep "art" and popular culture separate was not only expressed by representatives of "high" culture.

Interestingly, none of the music critics objected to the film on the grounds that the music itself was chopped up and rearranged. Their dominant concerns were with the music being combined with images, demonstrating how the issue of adaptation can affect reception. For the music critic, this newer, popular art form was ultimately bastardizing the music of the masters (and as *Fantasia* is, after all, an animated cartoon, connotations of an address to children also come into play).

For the film critic, however, other "frames" may have had more relevance. By 1940, Disney had not only acquired his reputation as a genius, but his association with classical music had been established through the history of the *Silly Symphonies* cartoon series. While *Fantasia* was a daring experiment as an expensive, feature-length project, the idea of Disney working with classical music had been somewhat naturalized for these critics through the *Silly Symphonies*. Furthermore, Disney's reputation as a daring innovator was also foregrounded by the elaborate Fantasound system, which was widely praised for the quality of music reproduction by film and music critics alike. The film critics' praise for *Fantasia* must also be read within the context of the attack on Disney (and, by implication, the cinema itself) by the music establishment. Within this context, it might even appear disloyal to one's profession to give *Fantasia* a bad review. Other than Mae Tinee, all the film reviewers I found point to *Fantasia* as a masterpiece. Most reviews discuss each segment of the film, some even ranking them in order of their success.

Interestingly, the music and film critics generally agree about the respective merits of each segment. My sample of fourteen critics unanimously agreed that "The Sorcerer's Apprentice" and "The Nutcracker Suite" were successful adaptations, with only four critics registering praise for "The

Pastoral Symphony." This points to the critics' desire to defend the form that they loved, particularly in the face of a (perceived) attack. Thus, music critics generally chastised *Fantasia,* whereas film critics praised it as a great innovation and as wonderful entertainment. This bias may account in part for the different overall tone of film and music reviews— although they share opinions on the merits of individual segments. Ulti- mately, for the music critics, *Fantasia* was a threat from a popular culture that did not only not know its place, but which threatened to destroy the boundaries between the arts, and between "art" and popular culture. It is thus not surprising that these critics singled out for praise only the most Disneyesque segments of *Fantasia,* revealing that they wanted him to do what he was good at and to stay away from "high art," particularly classical (or "absolute") music.

Given the tone of the music critic's reviews and the extent of the controversy, it might appear that *Fantasia* incurred this wrath because it was an unusual, or unprecedented, combination of high art and popular culture. Yet *Fantasia* was not an isolated example of the blurring bound- aries dividing cultural hierarchies, and should be seen as part of the widespread dissemination of "high art" during this period. The populariza- tion of classical music through mass-media technologies had begun in the teens, and had led to the celebrity of musicians such as Walter Dam- rosch and Leopold Stokowski. Stokowski was a popular figure, who had gained fame for his habit of conducting without a baton, and had even appeared in the 1937 Deanna Durbin film, *One Hundred Men and a Girl.* In the 1940 *Fantasia* ceremonial program, Stokowski discusses the importance of disseminating classical music to a mass audience:

> The beauty and inspiration of music must not be restricted to a privi- leged few but made available to every man, woman and child. That is why great music associated with motion pictures is so important, because motion pictures reach millions all over the world.[35]

Deems Taylor, Disney's collaborator and the music commentator featured within *Fantasia,* was a radio personality and a "popular musicologist whose reputation for making music meaningful to American audiences (notably on New York Philharmonic radio broadcasts) made him a logical candidate for inclusion in this project."[36] *Variety*'s review of *Fantasia* commented on the popularity of such classical music broadcasts:

> Affinity of music and the screen has been a long established partner- ship. *Fantasia* best can be described as a successful experiment *to lift the relationship from the planes of popular, mass entertainment to the higher strata of appeal to lovers of classical music.* The boost

isn't so far from general taste as might be imagined, in the light of the proselyting [*sic*] which radio, with the help of Toscanini, Damrosch and others, has been carrying on in millions of American homes for some years. (my emphasis)[37]

Fantasia's melange of popular culture and high art was thus related to the radio industry's project of popularizing classical music, and consequently was linked to other "middlebrow" fusions of high art and popular culture, such as the Book-of-the-Month Club.

Forms of mass distribution, such as broadcast radio, Hollywood cinema, and modern methods of merchandising (such as mail order), threatened the privileged status of "art" and its singular identity. Mass distribution helped to define the status of a cultural product as popular culture, as it provided easy access to all classes, often at a nominal cost. In contrast, the work of art was defined as rare and only accessible to an elite group— whether this access was provided by location (by proximity to a cultural center, such as Carnegie Hall or the Museum of Modern Art), cost (theater tickets were expensive, whereas movie tickets were relatively cheap), or by an understanding that only a certain type of education could provide (the kind of knowledge that the music critics tended to draw upon in their discussions of *Fantasia*). According to Walter Benjamin, a work of art not only has an original identity, but this identity and its authenticity can be physically tested. It is this property—the "aura"—that is eliminated once works of art are mass-produced and distributed. With the loss of the aura, mass-produced "art" loses its distance from everyday life, and its function is transformed from ritual to political.[38] The destruction of these cultural boundaries, which helped create the much maligned domain of the "middlebrow," was well in place by the time *Fantasia* premiered, and the debates centering around the film drew upon the terms of high-culture paranoia that were already in circulation. In her analysis of the Book-of-the-Month Club, Janice Radway discusses how, fourteen years prior to *Fantasia,* this commodification of literary classics generated a similar controversy:

> In wedding cultural production to mass distribution, and more particularly to mass consumption, [Book-of-the-Month Club founder, Harry] Scherman was challenging some of his culture's most fundamental ideological assumptions about the character of culture, education, literature, art, and criticism.[39]

Yet, unlike the Book-of-the-Month Club, *Fantasia* was not just a marketing scheme, but a film produced by Walt Disney, who had acquired the reputation of a genius within his field. However, as in the case of

Harry Scherman, critics charged Disney with cheapening high art. As Radway notes, these disputes stemmed from contemporary debates about "the exercise of cultural authority."[40] With similar charges being leveled at a book-retailing scheme and a prestige film, we can ascertain that even "quality" cinema had a lowly place in the artistic hierarchy of cultural custodians during the early 1940s.

One of the most important issues here in distinguishing high art and popular culture, as they were perceived in 1940, was the concept of *standardization*. In their discussion of the "culture industry," Theodor Adorno and Max Horkheimer blame the standardization of mass culture (including radio and cinema) for creating a society of passive, obedient consumers and a variety of totally homogeneous mass cultural products.[41] As Radway states:

> Standardization, in fact, was a code word for mass production, mass distribution, and mass consumption. It was portrayed repeatedly as an evil specter spreading its cloak of uniformity over a once vitally differentiated population, producing as a consequence uniform automatons open to coercion by others.[42]

As a mass-produced and mass distributed work, *Fantasia* threatened classical music's artistic exclusivity by providing it with widespread access. However, *Fantasia* also posed a potential threat in offering a standardization of *interpretation*. Rather than allowing audiences to make their own interpretations, the critics feared that the power of Disney's images would anchor the music, so that, for example, "We shall never again be able to hear the piece ['The Sorcerer's Apprentice'] without visualizing Mickey Mouse as the apprentice."[43] This might not only threaten the elite status of classical music, but might even render the music critics redundant. There would be no need for their comments and interpretations on music, because they would be replaced by Disney's animation.

Because of the expenses and difficulties of Fantasound installation as well as Disney's plans to road-show *Fantasia,* the full version of the film never had widespread distribution, only playing in fourteen American cities in its complete form.[44] Further road-showing was hindered, in part, by government orders for radio apparatus for defense purposes, which resulted in RCA delaying the production of further Fantasound installations.[45] The expense of each Fantasound installation, at around thirty thousand dollars, combined with the need for theaters to close for around one week for installation, further insured the film of an extremely limited release.[46] Given that widespread distribution is key in defining popular culture, such restricted distribution indicated that Disney wanted *Fantasia* to be seen as something special.

The construction of *Fantasia* as a cultural event took two major forms, both of which worked against concepts of standardization. First of all, *Fantasia* was only shown in large cities. Advertisements for the film in local papers proclaimed that very few places would have the opportunity to exhibit *Fantasia*. For example, advertisements run in Chicago, where *Fantasia* opened on February 19, 1941, announced that "Chicago has been selected as one of the few cities in the world that will see *FANTA-SIA*,"[47] and warned the reader that "Because of Special Fantasound Equipment *FANTASIA CANNOT BE SHOWN IN ANY OTHER THEATER WITHIN 85 MILES OF CHICAGO*."[48] Advertisements in the local press for every city where *Fantasia* played broadcast similar notices. Advertisements in the *New York Times* stated that "Because of special equipment necessary for its presentation, *FANTASIA* will be shown only at the Broadway, and no other theatre in N.Y."[49] Because *Fantasia* was not easily seen by mass audiences living in other cities, "community parties" were organized, so that people could travel to see the film. *Variety* reported that this new form of promotion was used during *Fantasia*'s Boston run. It involved attracting business from New England, with

> One or more patrons from a community [being] . . . invited to head a local movement to form a special party to *Fantasia*. Two railroads (Boston & Maine and Boston & Albany) are cooperating in the promotion by offering a 25% reduction in round trips for the parties.[50]

As *Fantasia* had a limited run, audiences had to make more of an effort to see the film, helping to construct its exhibition as a special event. Likewise, the film's publicity helped to manipulate public perception of the rarity of the film's exhibition. Although *Fantasia* set a contemporary record for the forty-nine-week duration of its run in New York,[51] the end of its run was advertised as early as May 1941, five months before it left the Broadway Theater.[52] Similar publicity helped to boost *Fantasia*'s box office near the end of its Philadelphia run, with *Variety* observing that the film was "getting the benefit of 'last-chance-to-see-it' advertising."[53] Again, the nature of this publicity was to shape the exhibition of *Fantasia* as an uncommon cultural event. Rather than promising easy access to the film, the publicity emphasized that its exhibition was to be short-lived, restricted to a few places for short periods of time. Although a version of *Fantasia* was widely distributed by RKO in 1941, it was shown without Fantasound, and was cut from 120 minutes to eighty-eight, making it a different and less prestigious film.[54]

Disney's plans for *Fantasia* also worked against the standardization expected from popular culture, in that he planned to *change* the order and content of the segments across time. Unlike other films, whose reels can only follow one order if they are to make sense, *Fantasia*'s reels were designed to be somewhat interchangeable. The 1940 *Fantasia* Souvenir Booklet features a program for the film and informs the viewer that "From time to time the order and selection of compositions on this program may be changed."[55] Because Disney planned *Fantasia* as a concert, he wanted to allow for variations in the screenings of the film and the opportunity to change selections. Although, at one level, this might be seen as working *against* the integrity of a "real" work of art, such variation was intended to associate the film with "artistic" performances, such as a concert, opera, or live theater, which are always different, always unique. This strategy was planned to increase box office by attracting repeat customers, as well as to allow the selections to be chosen to suit the region, or the types of audiences at each theater.[56] Neither plan was fulfilled, but had they been, *Fantasia* would not have addressed audiences as a mass, but would have been tailored to those audiences' perceived tastes.

Both the marketing strategies for *Fantasia* and the critical controversy that it engendered reveal that the film's reception in the early 1940s posed a problem for critics and audiences alike. Although *Fantasia* had grossed $1,300,000 on its first eleven engagements by the end of April 1941,[57] the film's production costs, as well as the costs of Fantasound installation, meant that *Fantasia* did not return a profit on its initial release. The expense of the film, as well as its restricted release, made *Fantasia* a prime candidate for reissue, a strategy that Disney has frequently used to maximize its profits. Although *Fantasia* was reissued during the 1940s, I wish to turn briefly to the 1953 to 1954 rerelease of the film, and finally to the 1991 to 1992 video rerelease, to examine the patterns of marketing and reception of the film across these later periods. I have chosen this strategy to see how changes in social and cultural attitudes shape changes in the reception of a single film, and to examine how these different evaluations of a text are themselves a marker of cultural change.

Marketing and Critical Reception of 'Fantasia': 1954 and 1991

Just as the 1940 to 1941 initial release of *Fantasia* can be seen in the context of the production trend towards "quality" pictures, the film's 1953 to 1954 reissue followed the trend towards the "Big Picture." With Hollywood seeking to differentiate its product from television, 1953 saw the development of 3-D and various wide-screen processes. Like Fantasound, the CinemaScope process offered stereophonic sound, thus enhancing all dimensions of the moviegoing experience. However, the development of various wide-screen (and depth) processes helped to contribute to a shortage of films, with producers uncertain about which systems would succeed. As a result, a variety of old films were rereleased during 1953 to 1954 to make up for the dearth of new product.[58] Although many films, such as *Gone With the Wind,* were rereleased successfully during this time, it is important to look at postwar production trends to understand why Disney felt that *Fantasia* would be well received.

As Janet Staiger and Susan Ohmer have discussed, Hollywood turned increasingly to market research in the 1940s and 1950s in order to address various audience tastes more precisely.[59] Staiger observes that "Demographics provided by ARI and Handel's firm indicated to the majors that by 1950 young people were at the movies more than older individuals," that "persons in higher socio-economic brackets attend[ed] more frequently than those in lower levels," and that the better educated people were, the more likely they were to see films."[60] Given that the 1950s film audience was generally younger and better educated than the general public, it is quite likely that Disney saw this as an appropriate time to rerelease *Fantasia,* as a youthful audience would possibly be less conservative and, thus, more open to Disney's innovations. As film audiences were also well educated, it is likely that they would be judged to be more open to watching a film centered around eight pieces of classical music.

Indeed, *Variety* reports that the Disney organization believed their 1953 to 1954 scheduled rerelease would be a success because the film was both artistically and technically advanced: "[*Fantasia*] was 'before its time' when originally released in 1940. Film was equipped with stereophonic sound which now goes hand in hand with 3-D and wide-screen."[61] In 1953, stereophonic sound would be neither the problem nor the novelty that it was in 1940, so the film could be handled through more widespread channels of distribution. However, while this also implies that *Fantasia* would be less innovative, the idea that the film was "before its time" preserved its status on the cutting edge of technology. Furthermore, Disney also announced plans to follow the trend towards wide-screen production by adapting *Fantasia* for wide-screen (SuperScope). Therefore, like other Big Pictures, *Fantasia* entered the 1950s fully equipped with Technicolor, stereophonic sound, and wide-screen. Consequently, certain similarities can be seen between the 1940 to 1941 and 1953 to 1954 releases of *Fantasia,* in that the film was associated with the latest technological innovations, and formed part of a production trend favoring high-budget, prestige pictures. Although *Fantasia*'s status as "art" was initially constructed in part through its restricted release, the 1954 reissue was justified in terms of the film's "timeless" qualities. As *Fantasia* was a "masterpiece" that had been seen by only a few people, frequent reissues would counter this problem by making the film available to a larger public. Consequently, the film's status as "art" justified its more widespread distribution.[62] Thus the connotations of high art married to technology were carried over into the reissue, while those of "rarity" did not survive.

The widely advertised 1991 to 1992 video rerelease of *Fantasia* contrasts with the 1953 to 1954 reissue, which was not extensively publicized. Yet this video release followed many of the marketing strategies adopted for the film's initial release, and like both the 1940 to 41 and 1953 to 1954 releases, Disney adopted the latest forms of technology for *Fantasia* in order to maximize its profitability. Disney offered four forms of video release of *Fantasia:* a sell-through (low-priced) video cassette listing at $24.99; a deluxe souvenir video boxed set, priced at $99.99, featuring a sixteen-page commemorative program, a documentary on the making of *Fantasia,* two CDs of the sound track, and a limited edition lithograph of Mickey Mouse as the Sorcerer's Apprentice; a $39.99 extended play laser disc; and a boxed set of standard play laser discs, featuring a thirty two-page commemorative program, the lithograph of Mickey and the *Fantasia* documentary, also priced at $99.99.

In November 1991, *Variety*'s Stuart Miller reported that "Old Vids Are New Again With Special Packages," citing the examples of commemorative boxed set video releases of *It's a Wonderful Life* (forty-fifth anniversary edition), and the fiftieth anniversary rereleases of *Gone With the Wind, Citizen Kane,* and *Fantasia.* Miller observed that the supplementary materials offered in the deluxe editions of each film (such as documentaries, posters, booklets, trailers, programs, and the like) offered extra profit to distributors at a minimal cost. Miller quoted Steve Chamberlain, Executive Vice President at Turner Home Entertainment, who placed this phenomenon at the cutting edge of video retailing: "It's part of the gradual evolution of the video business, from rental to sell-through to this."[63] The strategy of marketing collector's editions of these videos also encouraged viewers to *buy* rather than rent. As Michelle Hilmes noted;

> Most VCR owners still prefer to rent than to buy. . . . However, the studios net no profit from these rentals; the "first sale" doctrine embodied in existing copyright law, hotly contested by the studios in 1982–3, prevents them from sharing in profit subsequent to the first sale of a cassette.[64]

By offering tapes at low prices, studios can often show more profit, as consumers will generally buy the film. However, studios usually only choose to market certain films on sell-through, such as children's films, exercise tapes, selected blockbusters such as *E.T., Pretty Woman,* and *Home Alone,* or reissues of recent hits or classical Hollywood films.[65] However, a collector's edition, priced between fifty and a hundred dollars, cannot only stimulate sales but also maximize studio profits. Furthermore, the market for such deluxe editions reveals the stratified cultural capital now available within popular culture. By offering *Fantasia* at two price tiers, Disney could benefit from an address to both the sell-through and collectors markets.

The two forms of the film thus start to accrue multiple and often contradictory connotations. Whereas a sell-through video might be bought for family use, and thus acquire the reputation of (quality) children's entertainment, the high-cost collector's edition tapes and laser discs acquire the aura of art, especially as they are limited editions which include lithographs and, in the case of the video set, two CDs of classical music. Furthermore, all four versions of the film were available to retailers for only fifty days—again constructing the film as a rare object, and enhancing its status as a work of art. This strategy was also successful in stimulating sales. As *Variety*'s Stuart Miller observed, "One successful tactic is limiting the availability of the product: Disney's *Fantasia* is available to retailers for 50 days only. In addition to 9 million-plus regular copies, the 200,000 deluxe sets with CDs, an extra video and a lithograph have sold out."[66] Indeed, by January 1992, *Fantasia* had become the biggest selling video of all time, notching up sales of 14,169,148 cassettes. This figure did not even include "direct-mail or club sales or laserdisc sales. . . . It includes only sales of standard and deluxe edition videocassette sales into the retail marketplace in North America. The deluxe edition, priced at $99.99 suggested retail, accounted for 280,000 of the total."[67] Two weeks later, *Variety* reported on its front page that this "Vid of 52-year-old pic [had] deliver[ed] as much to Disney's first-quarter earnings as its theme parks worldwide."[68]

The video reissue of *Fantasia* also conformed to two other related production and exhibition trends of the 1990s. First of all, the video market overtook the theatrical exhibition market, leading to the "home theater" trend. In March 1992, *Variety* reported that a Harris Poll showed more Americans were choosing to stay at home for their entertainment. While noting that the number of Americans who subscribed to cable and who owned VCRs had increased, the poll found that the number of tapes that each household rented had remained constant at around twenty-one to twenty-two per year.[69] By the early 1990s, video rentals not only exceeded theatrical box office revenues, but according to *Variety*, "For the first time ever, sell-through revenues were greater than revenues from rental releases in 1990," indicating that people were now taking home video so seriously that they were building video libraries.[70] The trend towards home theater not only boosted video cassette sale, but also stimulated the innovation of new technologies. In June 1991, *Variety* reported that the home theater trend had led to more sales of consumer gadgets, and had put the spotlight on new technological innovations, such as laser disc players.[71] By releasing *Fantasia* in laser disc form, Disney maintained the film's association with new technologies and packaged the film as an important commodity, given that the laser disc's superior sound and image reproduction has led to its reputation as the connoisseurs' choice. The status of *Fantasia* as a collectible film and as a masterpiece was reinforced by the film's success on laser disc; according to *Variety,* it sold "an industry record of 190,000 copies."[72] According to *Entertainment Weekly,* people were even "snatching up the disc (the film is available on both tape and disc for only 50 business days) before buying the equipment to play it."[73]

The success of *Fantasia*'s video rerelease resulted, in part, from following production and exhibition trends, and from the marketing of the film. Press and magazine advertisements and television commercials stressed that *Fantasia* would only be available for a short time, and then it would never appear again. The advertising slogan—"The *final* release of the original masterpiece"—was even printed on stickers adhering to the shrink-wrap covering the videos. Widespread (mis)reporting, as in the *Entertainment Weekly* item above, suggested to many consumers that the film would only be in the stores for a short time, thus stimulating the video's sales. Although the video was released in November 1991 for the Christmas market, there were still copies available in the stores as late as July 1992. Buena Vista, Disney's distribution company, further tried to enhance the frenzy over *Fantasia* by announcing in early November, 1991, that "it had run out of *Fantasia* videocassettes and has suspended orders indefinitely."[74] Although Buena Vista stressed that "it has been our experience that to artificially restrict supply just limits the success of the release,"[75] this marketing strategy made it appear that videos of the film were a rare commodity, thus preserving the film's status and value, while creating widespread consumer demand for, and interest in, the film. This demand was further enhanced by advertising and publicity claims that this was the *last* time that the original *Fantasia* would ever be available. Disney also announced plans to add more musical selections to the film, thus following the plans for the *original* concept of the film, which were dropped in 1941 after its first release. Publicity for the planned *Fantasia Continued* included a *Premiere* magazine poll (not sponsored by Disney), where readers wrote in their suggestions for musical selections. Interestingly, the readers' second-ranked selection was Debussy's "Clair de Lune," which had been scheduled for the original release of *Fantasia,* and then for the first planned update of the film. *Premiere*'s columnist observed that, "Few wanted to rock the Mouse—old Leopold and Walt can rest in peace," indicating that fans did not mind the film being updated, especially in accordance with the original plans, but that they wanted it to conform to the initial idea of a concert of classical music.[76]

This strategy of updating the film constructed the rerelease, then, as a moment of nostalgia. Television commercials for the video emphasized childhood memories, featuring a father talking to his infant son about why he bought the tape of *Fantasia*—in the process revealing that the purchase was for the father, not the son. As the father was too young to have seen the original *Fantasia,* the commercial also played upon memories of reissues which were shorter than this "original" version of the "masterpiece" now available on video. Plans to update the film were likewise imbued with nostalgia, since this would conform to Walt's original desires for the film. At the same time, the advertisements stressed that the original *Fantasia* would be "gone forever," creating a romance around this "original" version of the film. Paradoxically, this strategy helped establish *Fantasia*'s scarcity, even as it became the top-selling video of all time. The television commercial also established a new, 1990s form of address for *Fantasia* centered around the family, which might be seen, more specifically, as an address to different generations of children—the grown-up child and the small child. Mae Tinee warned the prospective 1941 audience that *Fantasia* was unsuitable for children because " 'Night on Bald Mountain' [is] . . . a dash to frighten all your little children out of their senses! (And to think I should ever have to say that of a Disney movie!) . . . *Fantasia* is NOT for children."[77] Similarly, the *Christian Science Monitor* recommended the first release of the film for "adults and *mature* young people," (my emphasis).[78] But the 1991 commercial shows a young child watching the video with his father.

This commercial signals some of the social and cultural changes that affect the different receptions of *Fantasia* in 1940 and 1991. Given that childhood is itself a cultural construction, a culture's ideas about what constitutes appropriate childhood entertainment can provide clues about a society and its ideology.[79] As new technologies have become more commonplace and domesticated, children have shown more mastery over programming VCRs and playing computer games than adults. With the mass marketing of children's video cassettes at sell-through prices, video technology has become increasingly associated with children's culture. Given that Disney has always associated *Fantasia* with the latest technological developments—from stereophonic sound to laser disc players—it is not surprising that children form a significant part of the (perceived) audience for the film in 1991. While the critical establishment of the 1940s found Disney's adaptation of Beethoven's "Pastoral Symphony" "an unscrupulous perversion of a great work of art,"[80] the critics of the 1990s did not consider any segments of the film distasteful, as it had fully acquired the reputation of "an acknowledged masterpiece."[81] Indeed, it is quite possible that the images that horrified the critics in the 1940s have become naturalized for the audience of the 1990s through the resemblances between Disney's centaurettes and pastel unicorns and the iconography of children's toys, most notably the successful "My Little Pony" line, which includes similarly colorful unicorns and winged horses. What appeared as sacrilege to the critics of the 1940s now appears to be a sequence particularly suited to child audiences. The only debate over this segment to occur in 1991 concerned the removal of four shots, and the cropped framing of several others to remove racist images of black centaurettes. The cropped images are only noticeable on close examination of the video due to lack of definition, increased grain, and, in one frame, problems with color registration. However, a group of fans protested Disney's tampering with the film, and the company's refusal to acknowledge that this had been done. According to *Entertainment Weekly:*

> some animation buffs are riled by the studio's unilateral decision to permanently alter an acknowledged masterpiece. "This is a movie supposedly protected as a national treasure by the US Government," says Jim Korkis . . . "But because the original creator can tamper, Disney is allowed to release this on video without a warning label about the changes."[82]

There is a definite similarity between the "animation buffs' " position on *Fantasia* and the 1940s music critics' opinions on the classical music selections, inasmuch as both groups are against changes being made to their preferred works of art. By 1991, *Fantasia* was considered as much a masterpiece as the music it visualizes. This highlights the most fundamental change in the film's reception from 1940 to 1991, which is closely related to important changes in the status of film as a cultural object. Yet the discourses on *Fantasia* from 1940 and 1991 structure the experience of viewing the film in a remarkably similar manner. The film's association with modern forms of technology persists through its success on home video, particularly in the laser disc market. In addition, the 1940 to 41 and 1991 to 92 advertising campaigns both stress the uncommon opportunity to see *Fantasia,* one that should be taken up immediately. Although in 1941 this might have meant that one had to travel to a key city and pay high prices to see the film, in 1992 one could watch the film at home. Ironically, the 1991 to 92 advertising and marketing campaigns successfully preserved the original connotations of art, which were rooted in the concept that viewing *Fantasia* was a rare experience, while allowing for the widespread distribution of the video. *Fantasia* can now be heralded as an unquestioned "work of art," which signals an important change in late-twentieth-century culture. Mass-produced or distributed objects are no longer deemed to be necessarily "low" on the cultural hierarchy. Furthermore, critical accusations that *Fantasia* is an offensive and hybrid work that inappropriately mixes music with images are no longer culturally relevant, given the rise of music videos and MTV. Indeed, when *Fantasia* is seen in the context of music videos, its combination of classical music and Disney animation only underscores its status as a "work of art" for its new defenders from the "high culture" establishment.

Notes

Introduction: How to Read Walt Disney

1. Funicello appeared with Tesh on *At One With* on September 13, 1991. In Washington, D.C., the program was carried by the NBC affiliate.

2. The syndicated program on which Smith appeared was called *Memories . . . Then and Now,* and was shown in Washington, D.C. (in its repeat broadcast) in June 1992 on the NBC affiliate.

3. For an analysis of Disney's relationship with the FBI in particular, and the federal government in general, see ch. 5 of my book, *Animating Culture: Hollywood Cartoons From the Sound Era* (New Brunswick: Rutgers University Press, 1993).

4. Max Apple, *The Propheteers* (New York: Harper and Row, 1987).

5. Thomas P. Hughes, *American Genesis: A Century of Invention and Technological Enthusiasm* (New York: Penguin Books, 1989), p. 3.

6. Richard Schickel, *The Disney Version: The Life, Times, Art and Commerce of Walt Disney* (New York: Avon, 1968); Robert D. Feild, *The Art of Walt Disney* (New York: Macmillan Company, 1942).

7. Ariel Dorfman and Armand Mattelart, *Paro leer al Pato Donald (Valparaiso: Ediciones Universitarias, 1971); How to Read Donald Duck: Imperialist Ideology in the Disney Comic,* David Kunzle, trans. (New York: International General, 1975).

8. Louis Marin, "Disneyland: A Degenerate Utopia," *Glyph,* 1 (1977), pp. 50–66.

9. See, for example, Susan Willis, "Learning From Mickey: The Evolution of the Logo," in *A Primer for Daily Life* (New York: Routledge, 1991), pp. 54–61; Willis, "Fantasia: Walt Disney's Los Angeles Suite," *Diacritics,* vol. 17 (Summer 1987), pp. 83–96; Steve Rugare, "The Advent of America at EPCOT Center," in *Cartographies: Structuralism and the Mapping of Bodies and Spaces,* Rosalyn Diprose and Robyn Ferrell, eds. (North Sydney, Australia: Allen & Unwin, 1991), pp. 103–112; Alexander Wilson, "The Managed Landscape: The Organization of Disney World," *Impulse* (Summer 1985), pp. 22–25; Steve Nelson, "Reel Life Performance: The Disney-MGM Studios," *The Drama Review,* 34, No. 4 (Winter 1990), pp. 60–78.

10. Charles Krauthammer, "Disney World: A Vision of Japan in America," *Washington Post* (January 24, 1992), A23; George Will, "In Europe, Mickey Mouse," *Washington Post* (April 16, 1992), A23.

11. The statistic about the Disney navy is taken from *Disney World: 20 Years of Magic: A Yearlong Birthday Party*, a special edition published by *Newsweek* (Fall/Winter 1991), p. 8.

12. *Good Morning America*, broadcast on ABC on September 30, 1991.

13. See *Animating Culture*, ch. 5.

14. *Grand Opening of Euro Disney*, CBS, 1992.

15. *20/20*, ABC (November 18, 1991).

16. Stephen Kern, *The Culture of Time and Space: 1880–1918* (Cambridge: Harvard University Press, 1983).

17. Carolyn Marvin, *When Old Technologies Were New: Thinking About Electric Communication in the Late Nineteenth Century* (New York: Oxford University Press, 1988).

18. "The Mighty Mouse," *Time* (October 25, 1948), p. 96.

19. For a description of the tour, see Richard Shale, *Donald Duck Joins Up: The Walt Disney Studio During World War II* (Ann Arbor: UMI Research Press, 1976), pp. 40–49; see also Smoodin, *Animating Culture*, ch. 5.

20. *Disney World: 20 Years of Magic*, p. 13.

21. *Ibid.*, p. 15.

22. *Ibid.*, 47.

23. See *Animating Culture*, ch. 5.

24. Between 1933 and 1935, the Macmillan Company published a number of the Payne Fund studies, with such titles as *Movies and Conduct, Motion Pictures and Standards of Morality*, and *Movies, Delinquency, and Crime*. The Middletown project was first published in 1929; an updated version appeared in 1937. For a discussion, see Garth Jowett, *Film: The Democratic Art* (Boston: Little, Brown and Company, 1976), particularly pp. 142–143, 262–263.

25. Susan Ohmer, "Measuring Desire: George Gallup and Audience Research in Hollywood," *Journal of Film and Video*, 43, Nos. 1–2 (Spring–Summer 1991), p. 6.

26. "Boy Meets Facts," *Time* (July 21, 1941), pp. 73–74.

27. Susan Ohmer, paper delivered at the Society for Animation Studies Conference, Rochester, New York, October 1991.

28. "The Testimony of Walter E. Disney Before the House Committee on Un-American Activities," in *The American Animated Cartoon: A Critical Anthology*, Gerald Peary and Danny Peary, eds. (New York: E.P Dutton, 1980), pp. 92–98.

5. Disney's Business History: A Reinterpretation

1. For information regarding Disney, I began my research at the Disney Archives in Burbank and the National Archives in Washington, D.C. Then I moved to a close reading of *Business Week, Film Journal, Forbes, Fortune, Motion Picture Herald, Variety*, and the *Wall Street Journal*. The following books also helped: Leonard H. Goldenson, *Beating the Odds* (New York: Charles Scribner's Sons, 1991); Ron Grover, *The Disney Touch* (Homewood, IL: Business One Irwin, 1991); Joe Flower,

Prince of the Magic Kingdom (New York: John Wiley, 1991); and John Taylor, *Storming the Magic Kingdom* (New York: Knopf, 1987).

2. In 1936 Mary Pickford took charge of United Artists. Her first major duty was to renegotiate a renewal of the Disney contract. Roy and Walt Disney sought better terms, including future television rights. Mary Pickford balked. RKO stepped in and topped United Artists' offer on all counts.

3. The *Disneyland* television series later would be retitled *Walt Disney Presents, Walt Disney's Wonderful World of Color, The Wonderful World of Disney,* and finally *Disney's Wonderful World.*

4. Bass grew ever richer on his Disney investment. According to a January, 1991 Disney proxy statement Bass's half-a-billion-dollar investment had swelled to nearly three billion dollars.

5. *101 Dalmations* had been rereleased before (in 1969, 1979, and 1985), and had accumulated a box office gross of ninety million dollars, placing it behind the cumulative total of *Snow White and the Seven Dwarfs* (more than $140 million total), *The Jungle Book* ($130 million), *Bambi* ($110 million), and *Lady and the Tramp* (ninety million dollars).

6. It should be noted that at the end of March 1992, Disney announced that it had agreed to sell its Los Angeles television station, KCAL, to Pinelands, Inc.

6. Disney After Disney: Family Business and the Business of Family

1. Here and throughout this essay, the term "new Disney" refers to the company after September 22, 1984, when Michael Eisner became CEO and Frank Wells signed on as President.

2. Jeannie Kasendorf citing Katzenberg in "Mickey Mouse Time at Disney," *New York,* vol. 24, No. 39 (1991), p. 40.

3. Peter J. Boyer, "Katzenberg's Seven Year Itch," *Vanity Fair,* vol. 54, No. 1 (1991), p. 146.

4. Aljean Harmetz, "Glory and Humiliation in the Screen Trade: A $1,000,000 Insult Beats a $300,000 Insult Any Day," *Esquire,* vol. 116, No. 1 (1991), p. 81.

5. John Gregory Dunne, "Truth, Illusion and Very Good Insurance: I'd Like to Thank the Members of the Academy . . . " *Esquire,* vol. 116, No. 1 (1991), p. 91.

6. Ron Grover, *The Disney Touch: How a Daring Management Team Revived an Entertainment Empire* (New York: Richard Irwin, 1991), p. 54.

7. Kasendorf, p. 36.

8. Grover, pp. 253–254.

9. *Ibid.,* p. 253.

10. Christopher Knowlton, "How Disney Keeps the Magic Going," *Fortune,* vol. 120, No. 8 (1989), p. 128.

11. Grover, p. 90.

12. Knowlton, p. 132.

13. John Taylor, *Storming the Magic Kingdom: Wall Street, the Raiders and the Battle for Disney* (New York: Ballantine, 1987).

14. The details of the Walt Disney/ABC deal were as follows: ABC invested five hundred thousand dollars and also guaranteed a $14.5 million loan and received 34.5 percent of Disneyland and Walt's commitment to produce a weekly Disney television show.

15. To be fair, of the $33.4 million in losses posted by the film unit, $28.3 million could be attributed to start-up costs for the Disney (cable television) Channel.

16. The chronology and story line laid out in this section is derived primarily from one source: John Taylor's excellent *Storming the Magic Kingdom*.

17. Taylor, p. 70.

18. Taylor, p. 89 (*Business Week* softened Gold's remarks to read: "Disney needs Arvida's twenty-thousand acres like a hole in the head).

19. The version depicting Jacobs outmaneuvered by Bass is told by Taylor, pp. 236–239. Bass' response/alternative version is told by Grover, pp. 37–45.

20. Grover, p. 154.

21. I would like to acknowledge a generous grant from the College of Liberal Arts, Oregon State University. Their support is, as always, much appreciated.

7. Painting a Plausible World: Disney's Color Prototypes

1. The film stock was itself black and white; it was the filtering prism in the camera which allowed each strip to record only blue, green, or red portions of the spectrum. In the lab the color matrices were struck from these black-and-white negatives via Technicolor's exclusive process. For more on the process, see Bordwell, Staiger, Thompson, *The Classical Hollywood Cinema* (New York: Columbia University Press, 1985), pp. 353–357.

2. *Variety* (December 17, 1930), p. 11.

3. "What? Color in the Movies Again?" *Fortune* (October 1934), p. 96.

4. For more on Technicolor and Disney's early collaboration, see my "A Studio Built of Bricks: Disney and Technicolor," *Film Reader*, 6 (1985), pp. 33–40.

5. It should be noted that, unlike Technicolor's live-action cameras, Disney's color animation camera contained only one strip of film, but for each image three sequential, rather than simultaneous, frames were exposed on the film stock. The red, green, and blue filters rotated in the camera and the lab separated them into the three required matrices.

6. Herbert Kalmus, "Technicolor Adventures in Cinemaland," *Journal of the Society of Motion Picture Engineers* (December 1938), p. 578.

7. *Ibid.*, p. 578.

8. Bordwell, Staiger, Thompson, *Classical Hollywood Cinema*, p. 353.

9. Roger Noake, *Animation: A Guide to Animated Film Techniques* (London: McDonald, 1988), p. 12.

10. Frank Thomas and Ollie Johnston, *Disney Animation* (New York: Abbeville Press, 1981), p. 248.

11. Robert Boynton, "Color in Contour and Object Perception," *Handbook on Perception* vol. 8, Edward C. Carterette and Morton P. Friedman, eds. (New York: Academic Press, 1978), p. 196.

12. David Bordwell, *Narration in the Cinema* (Madison: University of Wisconsin Press, 1985), p. 101.

13. Louis Cheskin, *Notation on a Color System* (Chicago: Color Research Institute of America, 1949), p. 38.

14. Interestingly, it was not until 1939 that Technicolor got a Special Academy Award for its "contribution in successfully bringing three-color feature production to the screen."

15. *New York Times* (March 17, 1935).

16. Eric Rideout, *The American Film* (London: Mitre Press, 1937), pp. 101, 106.

17. Bordwell, Staiger, Thompson, *Classical Hollywood Cinema,* pp. 243–244.

18. Brian Coe, *The History of Movie Photography* (Westfield, NJ: Eastview Editions, 1981), p. 133.

19. Christian Metz, *Film Language* (New York: Oxford University Press, 1974), p. 239.

20. See my "Exercising Color Restraint: Technicolor and Hollywood," *Postscript,* 10, 1 (Fall 1990), pp. 21–29.

21. Natalie Kalmus, "Color Consciousness," *Journal of the Society of Motion Picture Engineers* (August 1935), p. 141.

22. Bordwell, Staiger, Thompson, *Classical Hollywood Cinema,* p. 356.

23. Thomas and Johnston, *Disney Animation,* p. 69.

24. *Variety* (July 28, 1937), p. 14.

25. *Variety* (December 1, 1937), p. 14.

26. *Variety* (August 22, 1933), p. 18.

27. See Ron Magid, "Fantasia-stein," *American Cinematographer,* 72, 10 (October, 1991), p. 88.

28. Tino Balio, *United Artists: The Company Built By the Stars* (Madison: University of Wisconsin Press, 1976), pp. 137–138.

29. *Variety* (April 28, 1937), p. 16.

30. RKO's distribution wing had lobbied local theater owners hard to get uniform ticket prices and suspend separate "kiddie discounts" for this one feature. Thus, in some towns, like Denver, Pittsburgh, and San Francisco, which did suspend or reduce the discounts, *Snow White* did break box office records, while in others, like Cincinnati, which retained children's prices, attendance records only were surpassed.

31. *Variety* (February 16, 1938), p. 8.

32. *Ibid.,* 11.

33. *Variety* (June 16, 1937), p. 5.

34. "What? Color in the Movies Again?" p. 97.

8. The Betrayal of the Future: Walt Disney's EPCOT Center

1. This essay originally appeared in *Socialist Review,* 15, No. 6 (November–December 1985), pp. 40–54. It is adapted from *The Culture of Nature: North American Landscape from Disney to the Exxon Valdez* (Cambridge, Mass: Blackwell Publishers, 1992).

2. Quoted in Barbara Smalley, "EPCOT: Disney's Dream Come True," *Express* (April 1983), p. 41.

3. These hotels were entirely prefabricated in a factory built by US Steel at Disney World. Each module was wired, plumbed, and furnished before being slid like a drawer into a steel structure. All rooms come with dimmer-controlled moonlight. Three more hotels are planned at this writing: Thai, Venetian, and Persian.

4. On this last point, see the periodicals *Processed World, Reset, Terminal 19/84,* and the *Journal of Community Communications.* See as well as my own "Information, Technology and Democracy: An Introduction," *Fuse* (April 1983).

5. Louis Marin, "Disneyland, a Degenerate Utopia," *Glymph,* 1 (1977), pp. 50–66. On Disneyland, see also David M. Johnson, "Disney World as Structure and Symbol: Re-Creation of the American Experience," *Journal of Popular Culture,* 15, No. 1 (Summer 1981).

6. Marin, "Disneyland," p. 61.

7. See Robert Venturi, Denise Scott Brown, and Steven Izenour, *Learning from Las Vegas* (Cambridge, MA: MIT Press, 1977).

8. On Andrew Jackson Downing see Giorgio Ciucci, *et al., The American City: From the Civil War to the New Deal* (Cambridge, MA: MIT Press, 1971). On Olmsted, the collection *Civilizing American Cities: Frederick Law Olmsted's Writings on City Landscape,* S.B. Sutton, ed. (Cambridge, MA: MIT Press, 1971) is good. See also Albert Fein, *Frederick Law Olmsted and the American Environmental Tradition* (New York: George Braziller, 1972).

9. "Surprise Package": Looking Southward with Disney

1. In the 1941 feature film of the same name, a *comedia ranchera* (ranch comedy) directed by Joselito Fernandez, it fell to the lusty-voiced Jorge Negrete to belt out the title song. His performance established his fame—not only in Mexico but through-out Latin America—as "the quintessential singing *charro* (cowboy) and the prototype of Mexican masculinity." See Carl J. Mora, *Mexican Cinema: Reflections of a Society, 1896–1988* (Berkeley: University of California Press, 1982, revised edition 1989), p. 56.

2. This essay is adapted from "Don (Juanito) Duck and the Imperial-Patriarchal Uncon-scious: Disney Studios, The Good Neighbor Policy, and the Packaging of Latin America" in Andrew Parker, Mary Russo, Doris Somner, and Patricia Yaeger, eds. *Nationalisms and Sexualities* (New York: Routledge, 1992), 21–41. Versions of the original talk were presented at Michigan State University, the University of New Mexico, and the University of California at Santa Cruz. The oral presentation includes nearly a half hour of film clips. It would be an understatement to say that the clips are half the fun; without them, the arguments lose immediacy and impact. And no amount of supplementary verbiage can convey the intricate, hyperstimulated exuberance of the Disney images which provoked the essay. So, if *The Three Caballe-ros* is not very fresh in your mind, read no further; hasten instead to the nearest video store, where it should be readily available. The essay can wait; first see the movie!

3. *Snow White and the Seven Dwarfs,* Disney's first animated feature, had been released in 1937, to be followed by *Fantasia* in 1940, *Dumbo* in 1941, and *Bambi* in 1942.

4. The myth of the unassailable ideological innocence of Disney's anthropomorphic zoology was shattered in 1971 with the publication of Ariel Dorfman and Armand Mattelart's pathbreaking *How to Read Donald Duck.* This intellectually ingenious and political explosive little paperback cut to the measure of a comic book applied

sophisticated interpretive methodologies derived from advanced literary and communications theory to examples of "low" or "popular" culture—in this case, Disney
comic strips. Writing in Chile in the first year of Salvador Allende's Popular Unity
coalition, Dorfman (a Chilean) and Mattelart (a Belgian) exposed the imperialist
subtext lurking behind the facade of innocuous and "childish" entertainment, revealing
all its underlying racist and chauvinist biases. One of their most intriguing arguments
highlights the asexuality of sex/gender relations in this Disneyan universe of cousins
and uncles, from which any acknowledgement of direct biological reproduction—
not just maternity but paternity as well—is mysteriously absent. Intriguingly, the
authors argue that rather than undermining unchallenged patriarchal authority, this
omission reinforces it. See *Para leer al Pato Donald* (Valparaiso: Ediciones Universitarias, 1971), translated into English by David Kunzle with the added subtitle *Imperialist Ideology in the Disney Comic* (New York: International General, 1975), Chapter
1, "Uncle, Buy me a Contraceptive," especially pp. 33–34. Other writers have also
noted the gender imbalance. Richard Schickel, in *The Disney Version: The Life,
Times, Art and Commerce of Walt Disney* (New York: Avon, 1968) notes "the
absence of the mother," "a theme that is implicit in almost all the Disney features,"
p. 225.

5. Cited in Schickel, *The Disney Version,* p. 223.

6. Allen Woll, *The Latin Image in American Film* (Los Angeles: UCLA Latin American
Center, 1980, revised edition), p. 55. The terms of the contract were generous.
According to Schickel in *The Disney Version,* p. 223, "The [State] Department would
underwrite each film he made up to fifty thousand dollars and . . . the traveling
expenses of Disney and his party [19 in all] up to the amount of seventy thousand
dollars."

7. Woll, *The Latin Image,* p. 55.

8. From Disney's point of view, the timing of these trips could hardly have been more
propitious. Disney Studios showed a one million dollar deficit in 1941, largely due
to the wartime collapse of foreign markets. To make matters worse, the union
combatted the consequent layoffs with a prolonged and bitter strike. Though the
strike was eventually successful, by its conclusion the staff was fifty percent smaller.
Conveniently, Disney happened to be "south of the border" when the strike was
concluded and the studio re-opened. See Richard Shale, *Donald Duck Joins Up: The
Walt Disney Studio During World War II* (Ann Arbor: UMI Research Press, 1987),
p. 20.

9. Robert Spencer Carr, "Ideas for More Walt Disney Films For South American
Release," January 1942. University of California at Santa Cruz student Larry Geller
found this studio report, submitted to the council on Inter-American Affairs and later
"leaked" to *Politics* magazine (July 1945, p. 212), among papers in the Walt Disney
Productions Archive, Burbank, California. I am grateful to him for photocopies of
selected pages from this forty-page document.

10. According to Shale, *Saludos Amigos* "became the first Hollywood film to premiere
in all Latin American countries before opening in the US" (*Donald Duck Joins Up,*
p. 47).

11. In his book *Animating Culture: Hollywood Cartoons From the Sound Era* (New
Brunswick: Rutgers University Press, 1993), p. 141, Eric Smoodin notes the chauvinism which underpins the entire enterprise, calling it the "flawless calculus of cultural
imperialism" according to which "Walt Disney, a representative of the United States,
could tour a foreign culture [*sic*—actually, *several* different cultures and subcultures],

come to understand it in just a short time, film it, and then bring it back home with him, all with the blessing and thanks of the culture he had visited."

12. The live-action footage suggests that in the mid-1940's, the beaches of Acapulco were inhabited by a remarkably homogeneous species: all female, all shapely and fair-skinned, all apparently between the ages of eighteen and twenty-two.

13. For Bazin's discussion of the photograph as fingerprint, see *What is Cinema?* Volume 1, translated by Hugh Gray (Berkeley; University of California Press, 1967), pp. 15–16.

14. See Shale, *Donald Duck Joins Up*, pp. 3, 98, 101–102.

15. Working primarily under the direction of Donna Haraway, Brett Kaplan wrote a fascinating undergraduate thesis on the kind of cross-species coupling (female homo sapiens to male of another order) that she first noted in *The Three Caballeros*. "The Animals and Their Women: A Sexy Species Story" (Literature, University of California at Santa Cruz, Spring 1990, 58 pp.) concentrates on *Who Framed Roger Rabbit?* and *Gorillas in the Mist*.

16. Barbara Deming, "Film Chronicle: The Artlessness of Walt Disney," *The Partisan Review*, Spring 1945, p. 226. This six-page essay is the most thoughtful and perceptive reading of the film that I have encountered. Shale's chapter on *The Three Caballeros* (Chapter 9 of *Donald Duck Joins Up*, pp. 96–108), which is the other major essay on this film, is interpretively indebted to Deming while supplementing her account with essential historical and technical information.

17. Jonathan Rosenbaum, "*Who Framed Roger Rabbit?*," *Film Quarterly*, 42, 1 (Fall 1988), p. 33.

18. Schickel, *The Disney Version*, pp. 234–235.

19. For the information in this paragraph I am indebted to Shale, *Donald Duck Joins Up*, pp. 20–24.

20. Fredric Jameson, "The Third World Novel as National Allegory," *Social Text*, 15 (Fall 1986), pp. 65–68, and Aijaz Ahmad, "Jameson's Rhetoric of Otherness and the 'National Allegory,'" *Social Text*, 17 (Fall 1987), pp. 3–25.

21. Shale, *Donald Duck Joins Up*, p. 107.

22. Among the scholars who have begun developing new lines of thinking on these issues, see Marvin Goldwert, *Psychic Conflict in Spanish America: Six Essays on the Psychohistory of the Region* (Washington, DC: University Press of America, 1982); Roger Bartra, *La jaula de la melancolía: Identidad y metamórfosis del mexicano* (Mexico City: Grijalbo, 1987), especially ch. 22, "A la chingada," pp. 205–44; and Charles Ramirez Berg, *The Cinema of Solitude: A Critical History of Mexican Film, 1967–1983*, University of Texas at Austin, 1992.

23. Anthony Wilden, *System and Structure: Essays in Communication and Exchange* (London: Tavistock, 1980), pp. xxxiii–xxxv.

24. Empirical data on how these films were received in Latin America is difficult to locate. Schickel writes that "about the only government-sponsored project that worked out profitably was *Saludos Amigos* . . . It returned almost $1.3 million in grosses" (*The Disney Version*, pp. 230–231).

10. Pato Donald's Gender Ducking

1. This article has a more "personal" companion piece, "Donald Duck Discovers the Americas," in Portuguese translation, *Lusitania*, no. 1, Spring 1993. I am grateful to Kate Bloodgood for her editorial and contextual comments on both articles.

2. George Black, *The Good Neighbor: How the United States Wrote the History of Central America and the Caribbean* (New York: Pantheon Books, 1988), p. 69. I am grateful to Ofelia Ferrán for bringing this book to my attention.

3. "Somoza" refers to Anastasio, the Nicaraguan dictator. See Black, *The Good Neighbor,* p. 71.

4. Ariel Dorfman and Armand Mattelart, *How to Read Donald Duck: Imperialist Ideology in the Disney Comic,* David Kunzle, trans. (New York: International General, 1975), p. 3.

5. Black, *The Good Neighbor,* p. 69.

6. As José Martí and other Latin American freedom fighters have called the United States.

7. For a film view of this sterilization campaign, consult Ana María Garcías' *La operación* (1980), which documents the position of Puerto Rican leaders, such as Rubén Berrio and Juan Marí Bras, before the United Nations' inquiry into US-sponsored Caribbean sterilization. I am grateful to Margarita Ostolaza Bey for this information.

8. The book *Conquest of the Tropics,* published by Doubleday in 1914, is a good documentary source to study the US commercial bananization/banalization of Latin America.

9. For Disney's own politics, first pro-Hitler and then anti-Nazi, including his wartime propaganda films such as *Victory Through Air Power,* see David Kunzle's introduction to *How to Read Donald Duck,* pp. 11–21. See note 2 for the publication information on *Good Neighbor.*

10. See notes 4 and 9 for publication information.

11. For a background on this subject consult the following texts: Cynthia Enloe, *Bananas, Beaches and Bases: Making Feminist Sense of International Politics* (Berkeley and Los Angeles: University of California Press, 1990); Julianne Burton-Carvajal, " 'Surprise Package': Looking Southward with Disney," in this volume; Julianne Burton, "Don (Juanito) Duck and the Imperial-Patriarchal Unconscious: Disney Studios, the Good Neighbor Policy, and the Packaging of Latin America," in *Nationalisms and Sexualities,* Andrew Parker, Mary Russo, and Patricia Yaeger, eds. (New York: Routledge, 1992), pp. 21–41. Ana M. López, "Are all Latins from Manhattan? Hollywood, Ethnography, and Cultural Colonialism," in *Unspeakable Images: Ethnicity and the American Cinema,* Lester D. Friedman, ed. (Urbana: University of Illinois Press, 1991), pp. 404–424.

12. When Kunzle quotes from the reaction to Disney's forties features by a contemporary as "gay dreams of holocaust," he gives the term "gay" its present-day homosexual overtones. See Dorfman and Mattelart, p. 19, and Richard Schickel's *The Disney Version: The Life, Times, Art and Commerce of Walt Disney* (New York: Simon and Schuster, 1968), p. 233. I would agree with his veiled suggestion of the connection between Disney's tongue-in-cheek view of international doom and a free-for-all Latin American wave of love, including homosexuality. Indeed homosexuality becomes attached to the notion of dubious entertainment and valid escape valve in times of a worldwide holocaust.

13. Dorfman and Mattelart argue Disney's subliminal pansexual masturbatory fantasy disguised as an asexual world policed by the Salvation Army in ch. 1 of *How to Read Donald Duck,* entitled "Uncle, Buy Me a Contraceptive," pp. 33–40; see particularly pp. 38–39.

14. There are records of national protests against such films. See Burton-Carvajal's reference to Allen L. Woll, *The Latin Image in American Film* (Los Angeles: UCLA Latin American Center, 1980).

15. Joe Carioca made brief appearances earlier on, in *South of the Border with Disney* (1941) and *Saludos Amigos* (1943).

16. Black, *The Good Neighbor,* p. 69.

17. Dorfman and Mattelart, *How to Read Donald Duck,* p. 19.

18. A book written by H. Marion Palmer and illustrated by the Walt Disney Studio (Boston: D.C. Heath and Company, 1945). I thank Amalia Gladhart for bringing this book to my attention.

19. Miami: Pretty Boy Publishing Co., 1991.

20. Burton-Carvajal finds a "Miranda-esque" quality in the araquan bird's "song."

21. I grew up addressing male genitalia as "Panchito"—no other same-age native informants from my hometown were available for comment.

22. See, as added evidence of the transgendering, Burton-Carvajal's comments on the dance of the phallic cacti, "Surprise Package," Fifth Proposition: "The *charra* sequence . . . makes Donald's phallic inadequacy most glaringly apparent. Dressed in a feminized version of a traditionally male costume and carrying a riding crop, the phallic woman (Carmen Molina) stomps her high boots in a self-confident *zapateo*. She is surrounded by a phalanx of dancing cacti which, as they deploy and metamorphose, alternately stomp, squash, obscure, fragment, and otherwise overpower Donald. At the end of the sequence, Donald runs through a forest of elongated cacti, each with a prominent lateral appendage dangling high above him, in futile pursuit of Carmen Molina, who has herself 'congealed' into a cactus before he can reach her."

23. *Ibid.,* Sixth Proposition: "After his ejection (ejaculation?) from the make-believe bull, which magically and terrifyingly continues to rampage unaided, Donald redirects his combative fury away from its original target (the 'friends' who have so persistently thwarted his amorous efforts) and toward this emblem of masculinity, charging the bull head-on as Panchito sings in ironic voice-over, 'like brother to brother / we're all for each other. . . .'"

24. *Ibid.*

25. The complete song precedes Burton-Carvajal's essay.

26. Palmer, *Donald Duck Sees South America,* p. 108.

11. Cultural Contagion: On Disney's Health Education Films for Latin America

1. Julianne Burton-Carvajal, " 'Surprise Package': Looking Southward with Disney," in this volume.

2. *Ibid.*

3. "A Survey Conducted for the CIAA by the Walt Disney Studio on the Subject of Literacy," Rockefeller Archives Center, Washington, D.C., Series, RG 4, Box 7, Motion Picture Division Folder.

4. Noted in Sergio Augusto, "Hollywood Looks at Brazil: From Carmen Miranda to *Moonraker,*" *Brazilian Cinema,* Randal Johnson and Robert Stam, eds., (Austin: University of Texas Press, 1982), p. 358.

5. For an interesting reading of Rockefeller's art collection, see Kwame Anthony Appiah, "Is the Post in Postcolonial the Post in Postmodern?" *Critical Inquiry* 17 (Winter 1991) pp. 336–357.

6. Citations taken from an anonymous biographical sketch, bound file, Rockefeller Archives Center.

7. Progress report on the office of the CIAA Motion Picture Section, Nelson A. Rockefeller, RAC Family Collection, Washington, D.C., Series, RG 4, Box 7, Motion Picture Folder, Alstock-Rockefeller letter and attached report, report p. 1.

8. Anonymous addendum to Alstock-Rockefeller letter and attached report.

9. Memo, FDR to vice president, RAC, Family Collection, Washington, D.C., Series, RG 4, Box 4, Communication Study 1942 Folder.

10. "Recommendations of Policy and Program of Action Adopted by the Inter-Departmental Committee," January 30, 1942, RAC, Family Collection, Washington, D.C. Series, RG 4, Box 4, Communications Study 1942 Folder.

11. English translation of Whitney/Alstock report on Mexican industry meeting, RAC, Family Collection, Washington, D.C. Series, RG 4, Box 7, Motion Picture Division Folder.

12. See Eric Smoodin, *Animating Culture: Hollywood Cartoons From the Sound Era* (New Brunswick, NJ: Rutgers University Press, 1993), p. 145.

13. See the Whitney/Alstock report.

14. Charles Higham, *The Films of Orson Welles* (Berkeley: University of California Press, 1970), p. 85, as cited in Augusto, p. 359.

15. On this point, see Smoodin, *Animating Culture,* p. 137.

16. Alstock-Rockefeller letter and report, letter page 1.

17. Augusto, "Hollywood Looks at Brazil," p. 358.

18. On animation's increasing mode of address to children during this period, see Smoodin, *Animating Culture,* pp. 178–183.

19. *Ibid.,* p. 137.

20. *Ibid.,* pp. 146–147.

21. These films also reassured potential managers, as well as consumers in the US, that an attempt was being made to institute in Latin American corporate locations the supposedly more sanitary conditions found in the workplace at home. The decontamination of hands, bodies, and homes of the individuals featured in Disney's health shorts assured US consumers that attempts were being made to keep the produce and products they consumed free of contamination. The irony of this fear is apparent when one considers the deplorable sanitation conditions during this period in, for example, the US meat-packing industry.

22. This view is supported by Burton-Carvajal's idea that the trilogy is, primarily, a document of Disney's journey, as well as an expression of Disney (and US) cultural imaginings and desires.

23. Alstock-Rockefeller letter, attached report, 1.

24. Carl J. Mora, *Mexican Cinema: Reflections of a Society, 1896–1988* (Berkeley: University of California Press, 1982), pp. 73–4.

25. See Alonso Alguilar, *Pan-Americanism From Monroe to the Present* (New York: Monthly Review Press, 1968), p. 70, as cited in Augusto, p. 358.

26. Didactic films which explain socially induced environmental hazards which accompany poverty as if resulting from individual ignorance were common within the US. Industrial safety shorts directed at factory workers frame carelessness and ignorance as the cause of industrial accidents.

12. Images of Empire: Tokyo Disneyland and Japanese Cultural Imperialism

I would like to thank my research assistant Laura Dowd, who compiled extremely useful bibliographies on Disneyland and the Disney corporation for me.

1. For how Japanese and German intellectuals come to terms with the issue of war responsibility and guilt, see Ernestine Schlant and J. Thomas Rimer, eds., *Legacies and Ambiguities: Postwar Fiction and Culture in West Germany and Japan* (Baltimore: The Johns Hopkins University Press, 1991).

2. Immanuel Wallerstein, *Geopolitics and Geoculture: Essays on the Changing World-System* (Cambridge: Cambridge University Press, 1991), p. 197.

3. Slavoj Zizek, *Looking Awry: An Introduction to Jacques Lacan through Popular Culture* (Cambridge: MIT Press, 1991), p. 156.

4. Zizek, *Looking Awry,* pp. 156–157.

5. Arjun Appadurai, "Disjuncture and Difference in the Global Cultural Economy," *Public Culture,* 2.2, pp. 4–5.

6. For a perceptive discussion of this book and the related issue of Japan-bashing in general, see Masao Miyoshi, *Off Center: Power and Culture Relations between Japan and the United States* (Cambridge: Harvard University Press, 1991).

7. Nemoto Yuji, *Tema paku jidai no torai: Miryoku aru chiiki sozo no nyu bijinesu* (Tokyo: Daiamondo sha, 1990), pp. 2–7.

8. David M. Johnson, "Disney World as Structure and Symbol: Re-Creation of the American Experience," *Journal of Popular Culture,* vol. 15, No. 1 (Summer 1981), p. 162.

9. Susan Willis, *A Primer for Daily Life* (London: Routledge, 1991), p. 57.

10. Theodor Adorno, *In Search of Wagner,* Rodney Livingstone, trans. (London: Verso, 1984).

11. Johnson, "Disney World as Structure and Symbol," p. 159.

12. Gavan McCormack, "Capitalism Triumphant? The Evidence from 'Number One' (Japan)," *Monthly Review,* vol. 42, No. 1 (May 1990), p. 6.

13. For instance, Japanese cinema in the 1970s was still obsessed with the dichotomy between country and city, and male protagonists typically escaping from a native, matriarchal community (cf. *Warming up for the Festival (Matsuri no jumbi),* Kuroki Kazuo, 1975, and *Bitter Sweet (Kaerazaru hibi),* Fujita Toshiya, 1978). In the 1980s, however, this opposition seemed to disappear from Japanese cinema. Even when a story takes place in a small provincial city, what is emphasized is not the contrast between Tokyo and the provinces but the permeation of Tokyo culture into almost every corner of the Japanese archepelago.

14. The Comprehensive Resort Region Provision Law of 1987 triggered a boom in the leisure industry (McCormack, p. 9), and Tokyo Disneyland has become a model for many resort projects. However, a simple imitation of Tokyo Disneyland—the idea

of the theme park, Disney management style, etc.—in other areas of Japan probably would not work because the success of Tokyo Disneyland is inseparable from the 1980s' transformation of Tokyo into a postmodern city.

15. Of course, it is questionable whether such notions as "original" and "authentic" have any meaning in relation to Disneyland. If we want to be more accurate, we have to say the "original simulacrum" and the "authentic simulation of America," which are, however, mere oxymora. See Mitsuhiro Yoshimoto, "The Postmodern and Mass Images in Japan," *Public Culture,* Vol. 1, No. 2, pp. 8–25.

16. In 1983, the opening year of Tokyo Disneyland, nine percent of the visitors were from neighboring Asian countries. Terry Trucco, "How Disneyland beat all the odds in Japan," *Advertising Age* (September 6, 1984), p. 16.

17. Stephen F. Mills, "Disney and the Promotions of Synthetic Worlds," *American Studies International,* vol. XXVIII, No. 2 (October 1990), p. 73.

18. Margaret Crawford, "The World in a Shopping Mall," in Michael Sorkin, ed., *Variations on a Theme Park: The New American City and the End of Public Space* (New York: Hill and Wang, 1992), pp. 3–4.

19. Michael Sorkin, "See You In Disneyland," in *Variations on a Theme Park,* p. 216.

20. Donna Haraway, *Primate Visions: Gender, Race, and Nature in the World of Modern Science* (New York: Routledge, 1989), p. 251.

21. Haraway, *Primate Visions,* p. 254.

22. Kato Shuichi, *Hybrid Culture: Japan's Small Hope (Zasshu bunka: Nihon no chiisana kibo),* (Tokyo: Kodansha bunko, 1974). In the essay titled "Hybridity of Japanese Culture," which was originally published in 1955, Kato convincingly shows not only that those purists who advocate a return to Japanese tradition are entrenched in Western material culture, but also that a conceptual framework in which the discourse on pure Japanese tradition is discussed is itself already a "translation culture" (*honyaku bunka*) borrowed from the West. However, he does not elaborate on the impossibility of the second form of purification, complete Westernization of Japan. Does this reluctance to explicate why absolute Westernization of Japan is impossible have something to do with Kato's attempt to create a new binary opposition between the absolute purity of Western—specifically, English and French—culture and the absolute hybridity of Japanese culture? By insisting on the existence of this binary opposition, doesn't Kato in the end reassert the uniqueness of Japanese culture which he tries to deconstruct?

23. Donna J. Haraway, *Simians, Cyborgs, and Women: The Reinvention of Nature* (New York: Routledge, 1991).

24. Maruyama Masao, *Nihon no shiso* (Tokyo: Iwanami shinsho, 1961).

13. The Mickey in Macy's Window: Childhood, Consumerism, and Disney Animation

1. Charles Eckert, "The Carole Lombard in Macy's Window," *Quarterly Review of Film Studies,* vol. 3, No. 1 (Winter 1978), pp. 1–22.

2. For an excellent bibliography of much of this work, see Lynn Spigel and Denise Mann, "Women and Consumer Culture: A Selective Bibliography," *Quarterly Review of Film and Video,* vol. 11, No. 1 (1989), pp. 85–105.

3. Cecil Muncie, *Disneyana: Walt Disney Collectibles* (New York: Hawthorne Books, 1974), pp. 85–105.

4. *Official Bulletin of the Mickey Mouse Club,* 1 January 1932, p. 4.

5. Letter from Roy Disney to Carl Sollmann, March 4, 1941. Unless otherwise noted, all letters are from the Borgfeldt Files, the Walt Disney Archives.

6. Letter from Carl Sollmann to Walt Disney, March 27, 1931.

7. Letter from Carl Sollmann to Roy O. Disney, August 27, 1931.

8. *Toys and Novelties* (December 1932), p. 42 (September 1931), p. 66 (October 1931), pp. 41–45; *Playthings* (October 1931), pp. 60, 90 (January 1932), pp. 117, 159 (December 1932), pp. 23, 43.

9. *Playthings* (December 1932), p. 33.

10. *Toys and Novelties* (January 1929), p. 290; *Playthings* (December 1932) p. 49. Of course, much could be said about the ways in which the aesthetics of window dressing borrowed from the aesthetics of the movies.

11. *Playthings* (July 1932), p. 47 (October 1932), p. 83.

12. *Film Daily* (April 12, 1931), unpaginated clipping, Disney Archives; Carl Sollmann to Walt Disney Productions, December 8, 1930; Carl Sollmann to Walt Disney Productions, May 13, 1931; Walt Disney Productions to Carl Sollmann, September 27, 1930.

13. "General Campaign Covering the Launching and Operation of the Mickey Mouse Club, An Organization for Boys and Girls," 1930.

14. Letter from George E. Morris to Carl Sollmann, September 2, 1930.

15. *Photoplay Magazine* (June 1932), p. 46.

16. "Official Bulletin of the Mickey Mouse Club," April 1, 1932, and *Greater Amusements* (April 21, 1931), unpaginated clipping, Disney Archives.

17. *Motion Picture Herald* (October 1, 1932), quoted in Cecil Muncie, *Disneyana,* p. 102.

18. "Theatres Form Matinee Clubs and Business Begins to Soar," *Exhibitor's Herald* (November 12, 1927), p. 41. The precedent of children's clubs based on predominantly noncinematic fictional characters should also be noted here. See the discussion of the Tribes of Tarzan in Eugene Provenzo, *Edgar Rice Burroughs: The Man Who Created Tarzan* (Provo: Brigham Young University Press, 1975). For an overview of commercial children's clubs in the 1930s, see E. Evalyn Grumbine, *Reaching Juvenile Markets* (New York: McGraw-Hill, 1938), pp. 176–195.

19. See the following clippings in the Disney Archives: *Motion Picture Daily* (January 16, 1931); *Variety* (November 5, 1930), p. 745; *Exhibitor's Herald World* (October 18, 1930), p. 63; *Motion Picture Herald* (January 3, 1931), pp. 121, 126.

20. Daniel Boorstin, *The Americans: The Democratic Experience* (New York: Random House, 1973).

21. For a more detailed account of the Mickey Mouse Clubs see my article, "Tracing the Child Audience: The Case of Disney, 1929–1933," in *Prima del codici 2: Alle porte de Hays* (La Biennale de Venezie, 1991), pp. 213–223.

22. Daniel Horowitz, *The Morality of Spending: Attitudes Toward the Consumer Society in America, 1875–1940* (Baltimore: Johns Hopkins University Press, 1985), pp. 134–166.

23. Roland Marchand, *Advertising the American Dream* (Berkeley: University of California Press, 1985), pp. 134–166.

24. See, for instance, Harold O. Berg, "One Week's Attendance of Children at Motion Picture Entertainments," *Playground* (June 1923), p. 165; Clarence Arthur Perry, "Frequency of Attendance of High-School Students at the Movies," *School Review* (October 1923), pp. 573–587; and Henry James Forman, *Our Movie-Made Children* (New York: Macmillan, 1933), pp. 12–27, 183–190.

25. There are obvious connections between the discourse around toys and the rhetoric of the play movement. Notable work on the play movement includes Dominick Cavallo, *Muscles and Morals: Organized Playgrounds and Urban Reform, 1880–1920* (Philadelphia: University of Pennsylvania Press, 1981); David Glassberg, "Restoring a 'Forgotten Childhood': American Play and the Progressive Era's Elizabethan Past," *American Quarterly,* vol. 32, No. 4 (1980), pp. 351–368; Stephen Hardy and Alan Ingham, "Games, Structures, and Agency: Historians on the American Play Movement," *Journal of Social History,* vol. 17, No. 2 (1983), pp. 285–301; and Alessandra Lorini, "The Progressives' Rhetoric on National Recreation: The Play Movement in New York City (1880–1917)," *Storia Nordamericana,* vol. 1, No. 1 (1984), pp. 334–371.

26. *Toys and Novelties* (February 1931), p. 223.

27. *New York American* (December 9, 1934), unpaginated clippings, Disney Archives.

28. Mary Ann Doane, *The Desire to Desire: The Woman's Film of the 1940's* (Bloomington: Indiana University Press, 1987), pp. 22–33.

29. T.J. Jackson Lears, *No Place of Grace: Antimodernism and the Transformation of American Culture, 1880–1920* (New York: Pantheon Books, 1981), pp. 144–149.

30. Little historical or theoretical work has been done on the representation of animals in the cinema. In the early 1980s, Raymond Bellour's Paris seminar focused attention on animality and the articulation of sexual difference in films such as *Bringing Up Baby,* though Bellour has not, to my knowledge, published any of his work in this area. Anne Friedberg organized an innovative panel, "The Other Species: Animals and Film," for the 1990 Society for Cinema Studies Conference, with papers by Friedberg, Kay Armatage, Marsha Kinder, and Holly Kruse. Finally, Ariel Dorfman's work on comic strips and animation offers a number of suggestive insights on this topic. See Ariel Dorfman, *The Empire's Old Clothes* (New York: Pantheon Press, 1983), and Dorfman and Armand Mattelart, *How to Read Donald Duck: Imperialist Ideology in the Disney Comic,* David Kunzle, trans. (New York: International General, 1975).

31. G. Stanley Hall, *Adolescence,* two volumes (New York: Arno Press, 1969). See also Lears, *No Place of Grace,* pp. 146–149.

32. Hall, *Adolescence,* vol. 2, p. 221.

33. *Ibid.,* p. 220.

34. *Ibid.,* pp. 227–228.

35. *Ibid.,* pp. 220–221.

36. Mary Douglas and Baron Isherwood, *The World of Goods* (New York: Basic Books, 1979), p. 59.

14. "Fantasia": Cultural Constructions of Disney's "Masterpiece"

1. Janet Staiger, *Interpreting Films: Studies in the Historical Reception of American Cinema* (Princeton, New Jersey: Princeton University Press, 1992). See especially pp. 45–48 for a discussion of the basic concepts of "Context-Activated Theories"

of reception, and ch. 4, "Towards a Historical Materialist Approach to Reception Studies."

2. *Ibid.*, p. 81.

3. "Music to Suit Audience Mood for *Fantasia*," *Variety* (February 19, 1941), p. 2.

4. Advertisement in *The Chicago Daily Tribune* (February 18, 1941), p. 13.

5. Review of *Fantasia* in *Photoplay*, vol. 18, No. 3 (February 1941), p. 15.

6. This essay does not offer as wide a range of reviews and critical responses as I would like. Given that *Fantasia* was only released to a handful of key cities during 1940–41, there are no responses from rural papers. Furthermore, Disney did not invest in publicity or exploitation for the 1953–1954 release, and I have found no reviews for the film from this time. However, as *Fantasia* tended to be released at times when it conformed to dominant production trends, its reception does have further implications for studies of the American film industry, audiences, and the cultural climate during these periods.

7. "Stoki-Disney *Fantasia* Roadshow Plan; Otherwise Stays With RKO," *Variety* (March 20, 1940), p. 5.

8. Leonard Maltin, *The Disney Films* (New York: Crown Publishers, Inc., 1973), p. 44.

9. Lee Mortimer, "The Movies: *Dictator* in 5th Week; Who Missed the Bus?" *New York Daily Mirror* (November 13, 1940), p. 33.

10. Tino Balio, "American Cinema of the 1930s," paper delivered at the University of Wisconsin-Madison, April 2, 1992.

11. "Goldwyn Advocates H'wood Cut from 600 to 150 Pix, All Quality Product and Get More at the B.O." *Variety* (August 21, 1940), p. 62.

12. "Why They Don't Go To Pix," *Variety* (August 21, 1940), p. 62.

13. "Public, not US Decree, Creating New National Exhibition Trend," *Variety* (May 7, 1941).

14. Advertisement for *The Ugly Duckling*, *Variety* (March 6, 1940), p. 19.

15. "Disney Again Tries Trailblazing," *New York Times Magazine* (November 3, 1940), p. 6.

16. "Screen News Here and in Hollywood: *Fantasia* Opens Tonight," *New York Times* (November 13, 1940), p. 29.

17. "Disney Again Tries Trailblazing," *New York Times Magazine*, p. 6.

18. Olin Downes, "*Fantasia* Discussed From the Musical Standpoint—Sound Reproduction Called Unprecedented," *New York Times* (November 14, 1940), p. 28; "Disney's Cinesymphony," *Time* (November 18, 1940), p. 55.

19. Thomas M. Pryor, "The Screen Grab-Bag," *New York Times* (November 10, 1940), Section 9, p. 5.

20. Mortimer, "The Movies: *Dictator* in 5th Week," *New York Daily Mirror*, p. 33.

21. "Disney Again Tries Trailblazing," *New York Times Magazine*, p. 6.

22. Edward Downes, "*Fantasia* Again: Second View of Disney-Stokowski Adventure—Can the Movies Interpret Masterpieces?" *Boston Evening Transcript* (February 8, 1941), part 3, p. 6.

23. Olin Downes, "Disney's Experiment: Second Thoughts on *Fantasia* and Its Visualization of Music," *New York Times* (November 17, 1940), Section 9, p. 7. Downes noted

that Disney had not intended the music to be "drowned" by the images, as evidenced by the care taken over the film's score and the successful innovation of Fantasound.

24. Edward Downes, *"Fantasia* Again," *Boston Evening Transcript,* p. 6.

25. Edward Barry, *"Fantasia:* Great Music Buried in Orgy of Color and Sound, Movie and Music Critics Find," *Chicago Daily Tribune* (February 20, 1941), p. 13.

26. Edward Downes, *"Fantasia* Again," *Boston Evening Transcript.*

27. Barry, *"Fantasia:* Great Music Buried in Orgy of Color and Sound," *Chicago Daily Tribune,* p. 13.

28. Mae Tinee, *"Fantasia:* Great Music Buried in Orgy of Color and Sound, Movie and Music Critics Find," *Chicago Daily Tribune,* p. 13. Tinee was the only film critic I found who did not like *Fantasia* on its initial release, and who broadly concurred with the music critics. This was sufficiently remarkable for the *Tribune* to provide an epigraph to Tinee's film review and Barry's music review, noting that "their respective views . . . were remarkably in agreement."

29. Olin Downes, *"Fantasia* Discussed From the Musical Standpoint," *New York Times.* Downes was not alone in voicing contempt for the "Pastoral Symphony" segment. After looking at fourteen reviews by both music and film critics, selected from the quality press, local papers, tabloids, newsmagazines, fan magazines, and the trade press, I only found four critics who approved of this segment: *Variety's* reviewer, Flin; Bosley Crowther for the *New York Times;* the *New York Daily Mirror's* Lee Mortimer; and Mae Tinee of the *Chicago Daily Tribune.*

30. Barry, *Fantasia:* Great Music Buried in Orgy of Color and Sound," *Chicago Daily Tribune,* p. 13.

31. Olin Downes, "Disney's Experiment: Second Thoughts on *Fantasia* and Its Visualization," *New York Times.*

32. Walter Benjamin, "The Task of the Translator: An Introduction to the Translation of Baudelaire's *Tableaux parisiens," Illuminations,* Hannah Arendt, ed., Harary Zohn, trans. (New York: Schocken Books, 1969), p. 71.

33. *Fantasia* Souvenir Program, 1940, p. 9. Wisconsin Center for Film and Theatre Research.

34. Tinee, *"Fantasia:* Great Music Buried in Orgy of Color and Sound," *Chicago Daily Tribune,* p. 13.

35. *Fantasia* Souvenir Program, 1940, p. 4.

36. Leonard Maltin, *The Disney Films* (New York: Crown Publishers, Inc., 1973), p. 40.

37. Review of *Fantasia* by "Flin," *Variety* (November 13, 1940), p. 16.

38. Walter Benjamin, "The Work of Art in the Age of Mechanical Reproduction," *Illuminations,* pp. 217–252.

39. Janice Radway, "Mail Order Culture and Its Critics: The Book-of-the-Month Club, Commodification and Consumption, and the Problem of Cultural Authority," in *Cultural Studies,* Lawrence Grossberg, Cary Nelson, and Paula Treichler, eds. (Routledge: New York and London, 1992), p. 513.

40. *Ibid.,* p. 514.

41. Theodor Adorno and Max Horkheimer, "The Culture Industry: Enlightenment as Mass Deception," in *Dialectic of Enlightenment,* John Cumming, trans. (Continuum Publishing Company: New York, 1989), pp. 120–167.

42. Radway, "Mail Order Culture and Its Critics," p. 520.

43. Barry, "Great Music Buried in Orgy of Color and Sound," *Chicago Daily Tribune,* p. 13.

44. "*Fantasia:* Completed and Continuing to Amaze," *Fantasia 50th Anniversary Commemorative Program,* p. 27 (this program was only included in the 1991 CAV laser disc rerelease of *Fantasia*).

45. "U.S. Defense Demands Stall RCA-Disney On *Fantasia* Equipment," *Variety* (November 20, 1940), p. 4.

46. "Disney Again Tries Trailblazing," p. 19.

47. *Chicago Daily Tribune* (February 3, 1941), p. 18.

48. *Ibid.* (February 10, 1941), p. 16.

49. *New York Times* (November 7, 1940), p. 33.

50. "Community Parties Hypo *Fantasia,* Hub," *Variety* (March 19, 1941), p. 8.

51. "N.Y. B.O. Upbeat Continues; *Woman* Weak $20,00, *Eve,* $87,00, *Yank,* 48G, Big H.O.s, *Fantasia* Ending Run," *Variety* (October 15, 1941), p. 9.

52. "B'way Down; *Wagons Roll*—Tucker Band—McLaglen Mild $30,000; *Kane* Stout; *Reaching Sun*—Rey OK 35G," *Variety* (May 14, 1941).

53. "*Fantasia, Dictator* Exit Eases Philly Jam; *Blondie—Heidi* 20G," *Variety* (April 30, 1941), p. 10.

54. "With Simplified 'Fantasound,' RKO Probably Will Distrib *Fantasia,*" *Variety* (April 16, 1941), p. 7: Leonard Maltin, *The Disney Films* (New York: Crown Publishers, Inc., 1973), p. 44.

55. *Fantasia* Souvenir Booklet, p. 7.

56. "Music to Suit Audience Mood for *Fantasia,*" *Variety* (February 19, 1941), p. 2.

57. "*Fantasia* in Its 11 Engagements has Grossed $1,300,00 to Date," *Variety* (April 30, 1941), p. 7.

58. See, for example, "Oldies To Get Another Whirl," *Variety* (April 8, 1953), p. 5; "Pic Prod'n Sights All-Time Low," *Variety* (April 29, 1953), pp. 7, 12; Exhibs Seek Re-Release of Classics To Offset Shortage; Distribs Shy Off," *Variety* (October 14, 1953), pp. 3, 18.

59. Staiger, *Interpreting Films,* p. 184; Susan Ohmer, "The Spectator in the System: Audience Research in Hollywood During the 1940s," paper presented at Society for Cinema Studies Conference, University of Southern California, May 24, 1991.

60. Staiger, *Interpreting Films,* p. 184.

61. "Disney Seem Emcee, Top Personality But Org's TV Entry Unlikely for Year," *Variety* (June 17, 1953), p. 18.

62. *Ibid.*

63. Stuart Miller, "Old Vids Are New Again With Special Packages," *Variety* (November 18, 1991), p. 16.

64. Michelle Hilmes, *Hollywood and Broadcasting: From Radio to Cable* (Urbana and Chicago: University of Illinois Press, 1990), p. 183.

65. See Bruce A. Austin, "Home Video: The Second-Run 'Theater' of the 1990s," in *Hollywood in the Age of Television,* Tino Balio, ed. (Boston: Unwin Hyman, 1990), especially pp. 336–337.

66. Miller, "Old Vids Are New Again," *Variety*, p. 16.

67. Marc Berman, "*Fantasia* reports animated vid sales," *Variety* (January 20, 1992), p. 25.

68. "Hot Numbers: *Fantasia* $113 Million," *Variety* (February 3, 1992), p. 1.

69. Kathleen O'Steen, "No Place Like Home Poll Says," *Variety* (March 30, 1992), p. 34.

70. "Sell-Through Revs Up," *Variety* (February 18, 1991), p. 30.

71. Bruce Ingram, "Home Theater Systems, CDI Turn Heads at Chi's CES" and "Gadget sales to grow in '91," *Variety* (June 10, 1991), p. 24.

72. Matt Rothman, "Mitsubishi buys 3.5% of Image laser disk biz," *Variety* (March 2, 1992), p. 32.

73. "Top Tapes: Double Fantasy," *Entertainment Weekly*, No. 94 (November 29, 1991), p. 103.

74. "Run on *Fantasia* outstrips supply," *Variety* (November 11, 1991), p. 24.

75. *Ibid.*

76. "Thoroughly Modern Midkey: *Fantasia* Poll," *Premiere* (February 1992), p. 97.

77. Tinee, "Great Music Buried in Orgy of Color and Sound," *Chicago Daily Tribune*, p. 13.

78. "Monitor Movie Guide," *Christian Science Monitor* (February 21, 1941), p. 17.

79. Richard deCordova's "Ethnography and Exhibition: The Child Audience, the Hays Office and Saturday Matinees," *Camera Obscura*, No. 23 (May 1990), pp. 91–106, is an excellent example of how one can study social and cultural changes through an examination of children's cultures and the pleasures that were deemed suitable for child audiences.

80. Downes, "*Fantasia* Again," p. 6.

81. Steve Daly, "New Rating for *Fantasia:* PC," *Entertainment Weekly* (November 29, 1991), p. 26.

82. *Ibid.*

Index

ABC television network, 75–76, 80, 83,
    189
About Bananas, 171
Abrahams, Jim, 94
Abreu, Zequinha de, 134
The Absent Minded Professor, 75
Adorno, Theodor, 188, 227
The African Lion, 57
Agee, James, 132
Airplane, 94
Algar, James, 57
Ali, Muhammad, 128
Alice in Cartoonland, 53
Alice in Wonderland, 11
American Federation of Labor, 73
American Graffiti, 95
Anderson, Benedict, 184
Anderson, Bill, 97
Animal House, 78
Animation, after Disney, 105; and art,
    218; and audio-animatronics, 65–67;
    and children, 210–211; and classical
    music, 224; and cultural difference,
    12; and the Depression, 17; and eco-
    nomics, 72, 77; and film scholar-
    ship, 4; and imperialism, 174, 178;
    and labor, 98; and live-action, 137–
    140; and multiplane camera, 54; pro-
    duction of, 24, 26–32; and propa-
ganda, 6, 132–133, 153; and public
    health, 176; reception of, 11, 17;
    self-reflexivity, 139; and sexuality,
    132, 140; and Technicolor, 106–
    111. See also Walt Disney, Donald
    Duck, Mickey Mouse, Technicolor,
    Inc., and specific cartoon titles.
Anthony, Susan B., 9, 127
The Apple Dumpling Gang, 98
Apple, Max, 3
Arachnophobia, 96
Armstrong, Louis, 128
Aronowitz, Stanley, 123–124
The Art of Walt Disney, 4
The Atlantic Monthly, 6, 11
Audubon Society, 49

Bach, Johann Sebastian, 26
Back to the Future, 192
Bambi, 47, 55–56, 59, 74, 81
Baldwin, Alec, 89
Balio, Tino, 217
Ball, Lucille, 128
The Banana Industry, 171
Banana Land, 171
Barroso, Ari, 134
Barry, Edward, 220–221, 224
Bass, Sid, 79, 101, 103–104
Batman, 96

List of Contributors

JULIANNE BURTON-CARVAJAL, Coordinator of the Latin American Studies Program at the University of California, Santa Cruz, is the editor of *Cinema and Social Change in Latin America: Conversations with Filmmakers* and *The Social Documentary in Latin America*.

LISA CARTWRIGHT is Assistant Professor of English and Visual and Cultural Studies at the University of Rochester. She is the author of *Physiological Modernity: Scientific Cinema and the Technologies of Life* (forthcoming).

RICHARD DECORDOVA is Associate Professor in the Department of Communication at DePaul University. He is the author of *Picture Personalities: The Emergence of the Star System in America*.

BRIAN GOLDFARB teaches computer art at the University of Rochester, where he is also a Ph.D. candidate in the Program in Visual and Cultural Studies.

DOUGLAS GOMERY teaches at the University of Maryland. His latest book is *Shared Pleasures: A History of Movie Presentation in the United States*.

JON LEWIS is Associate Professor of English at Oregon State University, and the author of *The Road to Romance & Ruin: Teen Films and Youth Culture*.

MOYA LUCKETT is completing her doctorate in the Department of Communication Arts at the University of Wisconsin-Madison.

RICHARD NEUPERT is Assistant Professor of Film Studies at Georgia Tech, and the translator of *Aesthetics of Film*.

JOSÉ PIEDRA is Associate Professor at Cornell and the Director of its Hispanic American Studies Program. Most recently, he is the co-author, with Chon Noriega, of *Revelaciones/Revelations: Hispanic Art of Evanescence*.

ERIC SMOODIN is Associate Professor of Literature at American University and the author of *Animating Culture: Hollywood Cartoons From the Sound Era*.

ALEXANDER WILSON has taught and written widely on popular culture, media, and the environment, and is the author of *The Culture of Nature: North American Landscape from Disney to the Exxon Valdez*.

MITSUHIRO YOSHIMOTO is Assistant Professor of Japanese and Comparative Literature at the University of Iowa.